Expect THE UNEXPECTED

EXPERIENCE HAITI WITH GRANDPA HAROLD

E. Harold Herr

ISBN 978-1-939084-05-7
Cover design: Teresa Sommers
Text layout design: Kristi Yoder
Artwork: Betsy Weber
Map of Alègue: Anna Etter
Printed in the USA
Printed October 2012
For more information about Christian Aid Ministries, see page 277.

Published by:
TGS International
P.O. Box 355
Berlin, Ohio 44610 USA
Phone: 330·893·4828
Fax: 330·893·2305
www.tgsinternational.com

TGS000553

Expect THE UNEXPECTED

EXPERIENCE HAITI WITH GRANDPA HAROLD

E. Harold Herr

La Gonâve
Island

Titanyen

Léogâne

Ti Goâve

Port-au-Prince

Alègue

Would You Go Back?

If you had been to heathen lands,
Where weary souls stretch out their hands
To plead, yet no one understands,
Would you go back? Would you?

If you had seen the women bear
Their heavy loads with none to share,
Had heard them weep, with none to care,
Would you go back? Would you?

If you had seen them in despair,
And beat their bodies, and pull their hair,
While demon powers filled the air,
Would you go back? Would you?

If you had climbed the Haitian hills,
Your hand within the Saviour's, still,
And knew He'd given a task to fill,
Would you go back? Would you?

If you had seen the glorious sight,
When heathen people in their night,
Were brought from darkness into light,
Would you go back? Would you?

If you had seen the Christians die,
With ne'er a fear tho' death was nigh,
Had seen them smile and say, "Goodbye,"
Would you go back? Would you?

Yet still they wait, a weary throng;
They've waited, some so very long.
When shall despair be turned to song?
I'm going back! Will you?

—*Author unknown*
Adapted by E. Harold Herr

Table of Contents

Alègue

Guardhouse
Medical Clinic
Bridge
Dry River Bed
Lea's House
← Shop
Nurse Apt.
Rick's House
Cholera Clinic /depot
Haitian Nurses' Key
School
Church
Mama Mlethew's Key
Harold's Key
Nette's Key

Drawn by
Anna Etter

Preface

I first went to Haiti in 1995 to help distribute Christian literature. That first trip to a Third World country was a shocking eye opener and a deeply heart-touching experience. It was a trip that altered my life. While there, I learned that Haiti had been dedicated to Satan. But despite the intense poverty and the dark bondage of voodooism and demonism I found there, the warmth of the people and the beauty of the rugged mountains at Alègue[1] immediately captivated my heart. I was in love with Haiti!

I continued to visit Alègue and helped to start a mission in this remote area in southern Haiti. Later I also spent six years serving as the director of the medicine program under Christian Aid Ministries.

From day one I had the most unusual experiences. The dangers, the difficulties, the demonic deliverances, the gunmen I faced, the hurricanes, and then the devastating earthquake of January 12, 2010, became the warp and woof of my life.

When I moved to Alègue in 1997, "expect the unexpected" became my Haitian motto. I began writing updates and sharing my heart. These letters soon went to many hundreds of friends and interested people. Their hearts became knit to the ministry in love, prayers, and giving. In all this I became known as "Grandpa Harold" to many.

"We serve God by serving others" became motto number two. Indeed, in a country filled with such dire needs, the opportunities to

---

[1]See pronunciation key for French and French Creole terms on page 273.

serve are numberless. Jesus specifically told us to share and bless "the least of these," a fitting description of many in Haiti.

I have used my past updates as the backbone of this book. Articles written by other mission staff help round out the story. The events are factual. In fact, one visitor who read earlier updates and then later spent some time at Alègue shared this, "The half has not been told."

Here are some purposes for sharing my experiences:

- To show the power, grace, and love of God in delivering and saving many souls in this land that was dedicated to Satan.
- To give insight into the everyday life of the Haitian culture.
- To help open our hearts and eyes to the spirit world, both the ministering spirits, our guardian angels who jealously watch over us, as well as the demonic forces which resolutely seek our downfall. In Haiti, these forces become much clearer and more real.
- To share the intimate struggles, soul searchings, difficulties, failures, victories, and blessings of missionary life on the field. I have chosen to bare my heart in this book.
- To challenge readers to develop a prayer burden for missionaries in Haiti and elsewhere.
- To bring glory to my heavenly Father. I am aware of the pride of my own heart, but God has His ways of dealing with me.

Grandpa Harold

Art Captions

Haitian peasant

Haitian poverty

Water boy—daily chore

Tarantula

Women's work

Machete—all-purpose tool

Bananas for sale

Voodoo drum

Mountain hauling

Lizard

Polaris Ranger

Palm tree

Braided for school

Demon altar

Grinding millet

Haitian fruit

Dinner for school children

Cockfight rooster

Off to market

Introduction:
A Knock at Our Back Door

"**L**ord, our skin is black, but our sins are blacker. You have delivered us from our sins and made us white," prayed an aged Haitian peasant. He, like so many, had been haunted and driven for years by fear, superstition, voodooism, extreme poverty, and illiteracy. But now he had freedom—glorious freedom! "But if our gospel be hid, it is hid to them that are lost: In whom the god of this world hath blinded the minds of them which believe not" (2 Corinthians 4:3-4a).

Tucked away in the Caribbean Sea southeast of Florida is a small country about the size of Maryland. This country was once a tropical paradise. Discovered in 1492 by Christopher Columbus, Haiti later became the cruel asylum for countless Negro slaves mercilessly shipped in from Africa by the French. After years of shameful and intense suffering, the African slaves declared themselves free in 1804. Haiti is truly Africa in our back yard.

After years of severe political, economic, and social turmoil, Haiti now lies in shambles and reels in despair and confusion. Its economy, weak and tottering for decades, was further crippled by a three-year trade embargo, which was finally lifted in October 1994. Devastated by savage outbursts of violence, the country, especially in urban areas, is a tinderbox where any tiny spark can ignite another flame of political violence.

This small country with a population of about nine million is teeming with poverty and has the lowest standard of living in the

Western Hemisphere. Eighty-five percent of the population lives below the poverty level, and the average annual income is $600 U.S. Many in rural areas have no access to any medical help. Eight percent of the babies die at birth and forty percent die before the age of two. The typical rural man lives in a thatched hut and has a few chickens and goats, and he might have a pig or a donkey. If he is well-to-do, he probably has a cow or a mule. Eighty percent of the Haitian people are subsistence farmers, struggling to draw a bare existence from steep, eroded hillsides and mountain slopes.

Illiteracy runs at about forty percent, and children make up about fifty percent of the population. Many children don't have the opportunity to attend school, and close to half of them are undernourished.

Catholicism is the state religion, but is deeply interspersed with voodooism. In 1791 Haiti was dedicated to Satan. In 1991, President Aristide rededicated the country to voodooism as its cultural heritage. Although they are no longer slaves to the French, the Haitians continue to be slaves to the trappings of voodooism brought with them from Africa. Fear, superstition, and fatalism are startlingly real to them, and are deeply ingrained into their being. Their sense of need to appease their gods is so intense that they will go without food rather than fail to give the gods some offering required by their witch doctors.

Since the earthquake of 2010, the desperate needs of Haiti have been compounded. Words are inadequate to describe the mass destruction of buildings and the infrastructure of the capital and other cities, and the loss of over 230,000 lives. Now, several years later, hundreds of thousands still live in crude tent cities with only the barest of necessities. But God's Spirit is at work. Many are opening their hearts to the Gospel.

"Whom shall I send, and who will go . . . To proclaim liberty to the captives, and the opening of the prison to them that are bound" (Isaiah 6:8; Isaiah 61:1b).

Yes, Haiti knocks at our back door!

Chapter 1

Experiencing Haiti

· December 1995

M y heart was full and running over. Coming face to face with the stark reality of unimaginable poverty, sickness, and pain, and seeing firsthand the despair of living under the power of evil and of dying without hope simply overwhelmed me. Yes, after seeing the immense needs in Haiti, the Spirit of God was speaking to my heart.

It was last July when I took my first trip to Haiti. I had volunteered to go along and help distribute tracts at a Gospel crusade in Port-au-Prince, Haiti's capital. While there, a number of us had the privilege of taking a trek to a Haitian church nestled deep in the scenic mountains in a remote place named Alègue. Here, we worshiped God with a group of openhearted black peasants in a small, roofless, stone structure. The roof had blown off in a storm some weeks earlier, and it was now crudely covered with palm branches and loose tin. But what did it matter? I found it a delight to share my heart with these dear black people.

As far as I know, only one white man had visited this mountainous area before. And small wonder. It lies fourteen miles from a good road—fourteen of the most rugged miles you can imagine. I'll never forget that first trip. It was the most grueling two-hour trip I ever experienced. With a four-wheel-drive truck—in low gear—we forded streams, chugged slowly up rugged mountains, and snaked around hairpin curves edged by breath-taking precipices. The road ended two miles from our destination, so we trudged up a rugged, slippery mountain footpath so steep in places that it snaked back and forth.

During this brief stay, my heart was touched by the genuine, gracious hospitality the Haitians afforded us. They treated us like royalty. I was humbled and felt almost guilty as I considered the roofless church building, the thatched huts, the poverty, and the destitution of these mountain peasants. I was amazed and challenged by their upbeat attitude toward life.

When I met the school teachers and we shared through an interpreter, they beamed with delight when I told them I had also been a teacher. As I talked with them, my heart burned within me. I knew that if it rained, the pupils got wet in the roofless building, or there was no school. I, on the other hand, wouldn't even think of not having a roof on my church house or on my home. As I pondered the unfairness of it all, a dream started welling up in my heart. Why couldn't I go down to Haiti next winter with some brothers and put a roof on that church building at Alègue and minister to these dear mountain peasants who had stolen my heart?

After praying about the idea and consulting with Lamar Nolt, who was serving in Haiti with Christian Aid Ministries (CAM), we estimated the probable costs of the necessary materials. In addition to the roof, the gable ends required stone work, and some loose stones in the walls needed to be mortared in.

After the plan was approved, Lamar soon received the funds to buy the needed materials. But how could we get everything to the construction site? No problem! Undaunted by what we would consider impossible, a group of Haitian men eagerly trudged the two miles to the place where the materials had been trucked and came back lugging ninety-four-pound bags of cement atop their heads. Altogether, ten Haitian men labored three days to cart everything up the narrow, steep mountain trails to the church building.

In early December, four other brethren and I arrived in Haiti to complete the roof project. Before starting out for Alègue, we loaded the four-wheel-drive Toyota pickup with two sewing machines, four tents, sleeping bags, suitcases, boxes of food and clothing, a generator, tools, containers of gasoline, six five-gallon Culligan water jugs, and thirteen people. With Lamar as our competent chauffeur, we spent hour after hour lurching, bumping, shifting, and dodging huge potholes. We ended up with burning eyes and parched throats—but I still loved it!

As we jostled through the towns, we saw people, people, and more people. Our nostrils were filled with the nauseating stench of human sewage trickling beside the street in the tropical heat and the putrid odor of rotting fruits, vegetables, and other garbage.

Again and again we saw beautifully uniformed children in shades of blue, brown, and green going to or from school. What would their future hold? Would they learn about Jesus? I knew someone must come to teach them, as many Haitians can't read. Even many pastors find reading a labor.

Finally it was time to park the Toyota and walk the rest of the way up the rugged mountain path. A group of Haitians soon hastened up the slippery path with the generator, sewing machines, water jugs, and suitcases atop their heads, going with incredible speed and agility. We *blans* (whites or foreigners) trudged on behind, and after about an hour we zigzagged up the last quarter mile to Pastor Matthew's house. We set up our tents in the stone courtyard between his house and the cookhouse. That night I delighted in the majestic beauty of the stars and the stillness of the black night as I lay on my bed, far from accustomed civilization. It was awesome and delightful.

The next day men, women, and children hiked from hidden mountain huts far and near. They gathered in scores on the hillside and watched with eagerness and wonder while we *blans* scrambled about constructing a roof, where for many months there had been none. Their appreciation was overwhelming.

The following morning we hiked the rugged mountain paths, going from hut to hut, inviting the peasants to a service that afternoon. I was stirred as I sensed the open hearts of these ignorant, needy people living in filth and poverty. Bruce, Pastor Matthew's nephew, spoke English fluently, so he interpreted for us and answered our countless questions about the ways of our Haitian friends.

Later that afternoon I had the unique privilege of preaching a simple Gospel message for my new friends in the dedication service held under the new roof. While I was preaching, a dashing rain suddenly beat and rattled on the new tin roof, nearly drowning out my shouts. It was like a baptizing benediction upon our work. Just as suddenly as it had started, it stopped, but the roof had done its job—everyone was dry! My dream had come true.

. . . .

Conquering Haiti

With the realization of this dream, another much larger one began to flood my being. I wanted to see many spirit-filled Christians lay their lives upon the altar of God and go to the mountains of Haiti. There, amidst those who are bound by superstition, voodooism, and ignorance, we could, with intercession and diligence, lead them to Jesus.

But we must not stop there. We must teach them and make disciples of them as Jesus commanded. We must pour our whole lives into teaching them the Word of God. The Word alone is able to transform them into people of integrity and moral purity—to become men and women of God in their homes and daily lives. We must teach them to read so they can study the Word of God themselves. We must live among them, learn to speak their language, and learn to understand their way of thinking. And in doing so, we must show them a better way to live—a godly way.

Chapter 2

Haiti in the Raw

· March 1996

Recently I again spent a week living in a rented house in the hills of Alègue, Haiti. This Haitian *kay* (house) is nestled on the steep slopes of our heavenly Father's scenic creation. I had looked forward to this visit with great anticipation. I wanted to personally experience Haitian mountain living in the raw. I wanted to tread their rugged stony paths and sit in their thatched huts. I wanted to eat their fried plantain, beans, rice, and goat meat and drink their water and their coconut milk. I wanted to hear their babies cry, sit with their children in school, be bitten by their ants, and sleep in their huts. I wanted to wake up with rain dripping on my bed sheet and live without a bathroom. I wanted to get soaked by an unexpected downpour while out on the mountain and slither and slide on the steep muddy paths after the rain. I wanted to hear their voodoo drums and listen to their chanting. In short, I wanted to learn to know the people's hearts, and in some small measure find out how they live and think and feel.

It was a bit daunting to be the only *blan* in this remote, inaccessible area, far removed from anything modern—no telephone, no electricity, no cars, no Walmart. But I was not alone; God was there. He was just as great, sovereign, loving, and faithful as anywhere else. Also, there were many of God's precious Haitian people there—black, openhearted, warm, and mostly destitute of what we call necessities. Sadly, many were also steeped in ignorance, fear, and superstition— blinded by "the god of this world." Although many of them knew

21

about our gracious Father, few were experiencing a walk with Him or living a holy life.

On my second day a mother brought to me her nine-year-old son who had fallen into an open charcoal cooking fire two days earlier. He had third-degree burns on his hand and arm. Ugly, raw, exposed flesh gaped at me. His bent fingers were tightly swollen, with gruesome, charred, loose skin dangling from his arm. It was obvious that the boy did not trust this strange new *blan*. Fear shone in his tear-filled eyes as he shrank back from meeting me. Dumbfounded with trepidation, I gazed at my first "patient."

Inwardly I drew back and muttered, "Lord, I can't treat this lad." But as always, God has ways to supply a needy, willing heart.

I scuttled up the mountain to my *kay* to grab my handbook, *Where There Is No Doctor,* and my first aid bag to which a few days earlier I had added penicillin and cocaine, a topical anesthetic. Then, on the dirty stone courtyard floor, with many curious onlookers staring at me with interest and wonder, I prepared a sterile saline solution. Next, while the little fellow writhed in pain and I inwardly empathized, I bathed his gruesome wound. Then I delicately trimmed the charred flesh with shears, all the while crying out to God for wisdom and coolness of spirit. I treated the wounds with ointment, covered them loosely to keep out insects and dirt, and with the aid of my doctor's manual prescribed the proper amounts of penicillin and cocaine. Whew! Yes, I guess I had wanted to experience Haiti!

There was no medical service in the area—no doctor, no nurse, not even an educated midwife. In my brief stay I treated facial wounds for a girl who had fallen from a tree, lanced and treated a man's swollen finger, and continued to treat the young burn victim.

It was obvious these people really needed medical help, and my vision was that someday there would be a clinic nearby, as well as a Christian midwife. But great as the need was for medical assistance, their need for the Great Physician was much, much greater.

Haiti's hold on me was like a magnet, and with each visit my heart became more and more fixed—this was the place for me.

Bruce's Vision

Another month-long stay during July helped me to really learn to know and appreciate Bruce. Not only was he Pastor Matthew's nephew, he was also one of the most influential leaders of the little church in Alègue.

Bruce had lived in the States for sixteen years and became fluent in English, but unfortunately he also got snared in the web of drug-selling and was caught and jailed. Through a prison ministry, Robert Martin and Galen Yoder of Dublin, Georgia, patiently discipled him and instructed him in the Scriptures. Slowly God started a work in his heart.

As a result of his crime, he was later deported to Haiti where he became an interpreter for Lamar Nolt, who was CAM's administrator in Haiti. Through Bruce, Lamar started visiting and ministering in this remote mountainous area where Bruce's uncle Matthew had been a pastor for thirty years.

Many of the children of this area had no opportunity to learn to read and write, so in 1993 Bruce started a school in a stone church building. During my visit I eagerly accepted the opportunity to visit this school. With well over a hundred students and seven teachers, it was a super-busy place. Although the classes were curtained off, the school still seemed too noisy for optimal learning.

The children and teachers each received a meal of beans and rice at noon, prepared at the pastor's cookhouse a few hundred feet away. It took five cooks most of the day to prepare and serve this meal. Water needed to be carried up from the valley in five-gallon buckets on their heads, the wood needed to be gathered and split, and the food had to be prepared and served in shifts because of insufficient dishes. Afterward, everything had to be washed and cleaned up. For many of the children, this was possibly their only substantial meal of the day.

Many of the older nationals can't read or write, and Bruce's deep burden is to help the younger ones be able to read and receive the

Word of God. Even Pastor Matthew is very halting in his reading.

Each Sunday morning, Pastor Matthew's son Levi or Bruce has a time of Bible memory recitation in which all ages are encouraged to participate. Bruce recognizes that the church is weak in its understanding of what it means to truly repent, be born of the Spirit, and walk in holiness, but he is trying his best to point the people to God.

. . . .

New Road

Bruce was very excited when I was able to secure funds from businesses in Pennsylvania to build a road in the last two-mile stretch to Alègue. Not one to sit around, he soon got everything organized. Sixty workers were divided into five groups, each with a supervisor. Their only tools were picks, shovels, hoes, wheelbarrows, and their hands. They needed to build many long and high stone retaining walls because of the steep hills. This road will give much-needed access to the area and greatly simplify the building of a mission house.

. . . .

My Vision

The local government asked the school to have a registered name, so Bruce, with Lamar's counsel, decided to name the entire Alègue work "Christ to Haiti Ministries." Bruce asked Lamar to come at least once a month to preach and help oversee the work. Bruce is hopeful that some church from America will establish a mission and eventually take over the church and school administration. This is also my vision for Alègue.

My goal is to complete the purchase of my small rented house and property and move to Haiti next spring. Afterward, I'd like to locate land to build a mission house for a pastor family. I'd also like to somehow have a small medical clinic, help Bruce oversee and improve the school, and have a weekly pre-service class, teaching the story of God and His people.

If the Lord continues to lead, I desire to give my closing years in the mission field. I know God is able to prepare a pastor, a midwife or nurse, and other workers.

"Ask of me, and I shall give thee the heathen for thine inheritance, and the uttermost parts of the earth for thy possession" (Psalm 2:8).

I have asked!

Chapter 3

Exciting First Days at Alègue

• March 1996

The long anticipated day finally arrived—moving day! After having our possessions shipped to CAM's headquarters in Haiti, my grandson Harold Weaver and I piled everything on a pickup and a small trailer. It was definitely overloaded, but in Haiti that's the normal way.

On Monday morning, April 20, we left CAM for our new home in Alègue. Laboriously we negotiated the pond-like potholes, which were punctuated occasionally with areas of blacktop. Because of our load, our trip to Petit Goâve, called Ti Goâve for short, took an hour and a half longer than usual. After a brief stop at Ti Goâve, we left the blacktop and traveled over two and a half hours in four-wheel drive to finally approach the church at the bottom of the hill of my Haitian home. The exhausting, stressful driving with my overloaded truck was nearly finished, or so I thought. But God had some lessons to teach me.

It was just past noon, and the place was teeming with school children. Previously I had been able to drive right up to a flat area in front of the church. Today, however, I saw to my consternation that the road had been altered, and at one place it was too narrow to continue. I soon realized I would have to put the truck in reverse and back down the steep hill with my truck and trailer. I was unable to see the narrow trailer with my truck mirror, so with much trepidation and caution I started to back up my rig. By the time I could see the trailer in my mirror, it was too late to get it straightened out. I had to turn the front wheels slightly downhill and attempt to drive forward. As I inched forward, my front wheel on the lower side spun and dug into the loose stones.

At the same time, Harold, who was trying to direct me, yelled, "Your front wheel is off the ground! You might upset!"

By now I had visions of my rig capsizing and rolling down the steep hillside. My Haitian friends, not realizing my precarious position, were swarming around and gawking with interest and amusement. "Quick!" I yelled desperately. "Hang onto the upper side of the truck so I won't flip over!" About ten men quickly grasped the truck, while others, now understanding my predicament, ran for ropes and straps. They hastily tied them to the truck cage and were able to keep my

truck from tumbling over.

Then, with extreme caution I climbed onto the truck and started to extract some items from the lower side to decrease the danger of a rollover. It was very difficult to extricate things from my tightly packed load. To the Haitians it was interesting and entertaining, but to me it was quite stressful and draining. After we unloaded, I asked a group of men to stand on the upper side of the truck bed. Then I tied a rope to the bumper and had another group pull the truck. Slowly I was able to inch forward to safety. Indeed, the laws of nature in these rugged mountains sometimes have overwhelming effects on me.

Next came the task of carting everything up the steep hill to my *kay*. The Haitian men—and women—were quick to hoist the sixty-pound suitcases, the filing cabinet, the huge storage batteries, and the small gas fridge and trek up the narrow, winding path to my simple Haitian *kay*.

Evening came after a grueling day. Though completely exhausted, I was happy when Bruce and Pastor Matthew, with his daughter Remòn and son Levi, and many others I did not know came to welcome me. It was a joyous time of visiting, singing, praying, and blessing.

The next day we assembled the forty-eight-foot radio tower we needed to communicate with the other missions. We secured the guy wires to the top and attempted to raise it. This time the steep mountains were to our advantage. Some men climbed the hill and lifted the tower while others below pulled on the guy wires. It started to go up as planned but then swayed treacherously from side to side.

"Hang on!" I yelled. Could we control the unstable apparatus? With a sigh of relief, we finally dropped it into the prepared hole and secured the antenna. By now, I had gained a great deal of respect for these mountains. When everything was hooked up, we were overjoyed to hear Lamar Nolt's voice from CAM's headquarters, loud and clear!

On Wednesday three groups of Haitians starting working for me— five men to build a courtyard entrance wall, eight to start building a mini road for an all-terrain vehicle (ATV) to be able to drive up to my house, and ten to dig the cistern at the right side of my house. The digging is hard work. Much of it is in solid rock—all of it by pick, sledge, and shovel. The work will take much longer than I had imagined.

The water in the riverbed has dried up, so all the water must now be carried over an additional mountain. Bruce hired a man to carry water every day with a five-gallon bucket on his head.

On Thursday the CAM truck came with the rest of our supplies, including my ATV. I was greatly concerned about whether the large truck could safely descend the extremely steep, curved section we called "Jackrabbit Hill." But after checking it out, the driver, stated simply, "It's a drink of water" —just as we would say, "It's a piece of cake."

The truck arrived safely. But how could we get my six-hundred- pound ATV off the forty-two-inch high truck bed? After a great deal of hilarious talking, discussing, and yelling, six Haitians simply grabbed the unwieldy beast and promptly set it on the road. Then a caravan of men started to carry the building supplies up the rugged trail to my house. I decided to go up to supervise.

Upon returning to the truck, I discovered the men had attempted to unload the half-ton cement mixer without my direction. This time it wasn't so easy. In the process they had dropped it, and its hitching tongue was now jabbed into the trail with the wheels still on the high truck bed. It was truly a dangerous situation. What if the monster slipped loose and fell on any of the hordes of men milling about? It was heavy enough to crush someone. I quickly got a set of ramps and placed them under the wheels. Then we pried the tongue loose and down came the mixer. Halfway down it slipped off the ramps, but no one was hurt. Again I thanked God for His protecting hand. I am so thankful for a sovereign God—and that He's my God!

On Friday I made the first use of my ATV—a 300 Polaris four-wheel drive. Bruce, Remòn, and Harold went with me. We pulled our new 40" × 60" trailer, custom built in Pennsylvania. I had high expectations about what this rig could do for me in hauling produce from the local markets, and I hoped that perhaps later, when the mini road was finished up to my house, I could haul a barrel of water all the way home.

Well, to my amazement and consternation, as we were going down the very first hill and around a sharp curve, the rig started to skid on the loose stones and almost jackknifed. From then on I was very cautious. Soon we came to Jackrabbit Hill with its multiple hairpin curves. For safety, I asked the trailer passengers to get off and walk. Even so, I barely made it to the top.

We then proceeded to the market, which consisted of hundreds of merchants lined up on both sides of the road heckling to sell their wares—beans, rice, ground corn, cabbage, tomatoes, yams, trinkets, bread rolls, matches, coffee, cloth, shoes, chickens, pigs, goats, and donkeys. There was lots of price bargaining, which I was not prepared for, so Bruce and Remòn bought what I needed.

On our return, Pastor Matthew wanted to come with us. I asked Harold to drive on the way back. When we were ready to descend Jackrabbit Hill, our super hill, we stopped and I asked our passengers to walk. In light of our earlier experiences of the day, I coached Harold to be extremely cautious and to keep as far away from the outer edge as possible.

I was very apprehensive as I sat on the ATV seat behind Harold. Less than a third of the way down the hill, we started a skid. The trailer immediately started jackknifing, and we headed for the edge of the steep bank. Harold wisely stopped braking and steered toward the inner curve where we finally came to a halt. The whole experience stressed me out completely, and I had to sit down on the road for a bit to regain my composure.

Cautiously Harold started down the hill again. This time Bruce and I held back on the load to help lessen the trailer's thrust. Another jackknife started, but since Harold was close to the base of the hill, he was able to accelerate and halt the jackknifing.

Right there a decision was made—we will not use the trailer to haul heavy loads on this steep, precarious, curvy hill. I also decided that the trail up to my house is simply too steep to build a mini-road for my ATV. I'll do as the Haitians do—use the legs God has given me! At the end of the day, I once again praised God for our guardian angels.

The next morning, however, I found out that all this stress was taking a toll on me. I woke up early and could not return to sleep. A fear seemed to be gripping me—a fear of using my vehicles on these steep mountains. And more than that. It was a nameless dread and fear of what could happen. It was haunting and distressing. As I lay in bed and meditated, God clearly gave this verse to me: "Return unto thy rest, O my soul; for the Lord hath dealt bountifully with thee" (Psalm 116:7).

That morning, Harold and I spent much time in praying and weeping before the Lord. It was a beautiful time of bonding and fellowship. Another verse also blessed me: "For God hath not given us the spirit of fear; but of power, and of love, and of a sound mind" (2 Timothy 1:7).

Then came the Lord's Day. How welcome and refreshing after such a strenuous week was our lovely time of worship and sharing as I sat on a backless, narrow bench with my Haitian friends. Even though I understood little, I could enter into the beautiful spirit of worship. How I needed this!

Chapter 4

My Mountain Goat

• May 1997

When another mission offered to pick up my mail at Port-au-Prince and bring it to Ti Goâve if I would meet them there, we decided to make the most of the trip—as we always do whenever we use a vehicle. We would again be using my ATV, which I dubbed the "Mountain Goat." I planned to bring back four bags of cement, five gallons of gasoline, and some other supplies. I learned by radio that my friends would not arrive with the mail until 6:30 p.m., but I decided to leave around 3:30 so that I could make all my purchases before then. If all went well, I could return home before dark. Just thinking of driving home in the dark was unsettling. Those rugged fourteen miles were bad enough in the daytime, let alone at night.

The ride to Ti Goâve was delightful. I made it in record time—one hour and twenty minutes instead of over two hours with the truck. By six o'clock I was done shopping and settled down to wait on the mail.

I had brought my Creole language materials and one of Andrew Murray's books to pass the time if I had to wait. Everywhere I went, several dozen children and young people surrounded me. I'm sure it was quite a sight, this white man with a white bicycle helmet, a blue backpack, and a green, overflowing ATV. I decided I had better be alert, especially since my wristwatch had been stolen right off my arm while driving through Port-au-Prince a short time earlier. After waiting about an hour and a half, I received a call on my handheld radio. It was bad news. The driver would not arrive till about eight o'clock. With a sinking heart I realized I wouldn't even get started for home before dark.

In the meantime, Pastor Matthew's son Malis found me and asked for a ride to Alègue. Good! At least now there would be someone with me on the return trip. God knew I needed someone. In the gathering darkness, I decided to strap a tarp over my bags of cement in case of rain, even though it was nice and clear. After all, we were in Haiti!

Finally a diesel Suburban rattled in with the mail. By now it was pitch dark. With a word of thanks, I grabbed my package of mail, which was secured with several rubber bands, and placed it in a backpack which Malis put on his back. "Okay," I told him. "You sit up front as far as you can. That'll keep us from tipping over when we go up the steep hills." Finally we were ready to go. With a prayer on our lips, we set off into the darkness.

As we traveled in the darkness, I was so thankful that my ATV had bright lights to show me the way. Steering was difficult with the heavy load, but I soon became accustomed to it. In fact, I started to find it enjoyable. We passed donkey after donkey and nearly hit a cow lying on the road. I was amazed at the many Haitians walking in the darkness, seemingly unaware that it was night. *Just like their lives,* I thought. *They're shrouded in darkness but pay no attention to it.*

Our thoughts were suddenly interrupted by several cold, wet drops on our faces. Rain! At least the cement was covered. As the rain became heavier, I stopped, asked for my backpack, and pulled out my new parka. I donned it, hood and all, then got my nice dry bundle of mail and shoved it into the empty parka bag to make sure no water could reach it. Then we sped on, slithering to and fro in the mud. For about a mile we traveled through ruts and oozing mud. We passed a group of Haitian women walking along with a faint little light and singing folk songs, as if the rain had no dampening effect on their spirits. As the rain intensified, so did the ruts and mud holes. Suddenly Malis yelled, "Brother Harold! Brother Harold! Book! Book!" Somehow my Andrew Murray book had fallen out of the pack and into the mud. I hastily retrieved it; then off we went again.

But almost immediately a disconcerting thought flashed into my mind. *How did that book get out of my pack?* I braked abruptly, asked for the pack, and thrust in my hand to pull out my precious bundle of mail. But to my dismay—no mail! This was the main purpose of the trip. How discouraging! Cautiously, I turned around in the mire and slowly started retracing my path in the oozy mud. All the time I was eagerly scanning the area between my recently implanted tracks. *Ah! That must be it! Hallelujah!* There, floating on a water puddle was my package of mail—hopefully with nothing missing. I flicked it vigorously several times, shoved it into the plastic parka bag, and put it back into my backpack, which I carefully placed on Malis' back again.

Meanwhile, drenching sheets of rain continued. I was dry except from my calves down. Malis, however, was drenched. Oh well, it's Haiti! Engine revving, off we went. We were almost halfway home when suddenly, without warning, all became darkness—pitch black darkness, the kind you can feel. Startled, I desperately braked to a sliding halt and flipped the high-low beam switch. Nothing, absolutely nothing. I dug around for my mini flashlight and tried driving by its feeble beam, but it was too dangerous. Besides, the batteries would soon be depleted anyway. I sat there pondering and praying about what to do. Here I was, stranded without lights out in the Haitian mountains, miles from Ti Goâve and my *kay*. "Lord, what shall I do?" I prayed. "Please give me wisdom." Slowly, praise God, a sense of peace returned to my spirit.

After some time the Haitian women who were singing folk songs caught up with us and passed us. *How ironic,* I thought. *Here I am, a man familiar with the modern world—stranded. But they have no such problems.* I decided to try my radio, even though I was sure I was not within range. I also voiced a general SOS to anyone who might hear me. All was grimly silent. After praying some more, I resigned myself to sit out the night. At least I had a dry parka to shelter me from the rain—but what about poor Malis?

After waiting for some time, I once more turned the key and flicked the switch several times. Darkness. I sat there for a while and tried again. Nothing. Then I cranked up the engine and tried the switch.

Yes, there was a very faint light! I turned off the switch and idled the engine a while. Again I flipped the switch. Light! Praise the Lord!

With a roar, off we raced. In a few miles the rain lessened and beautiful stars appeared. I was again lost in the wonder and beauty of the night. I rounded a curve and drove through a dip. No! Darkness again! This time it didn't seem so overwhelming. I decided by now that perhaps with the heavy load, the engine heated up and caused the fan to run. This overloaded the charger, making it unable to keep up with the current demand. After a brief wait, the lights worked again.

But soon the engine started sounding like a loud motorcycle—a muffler problem of some kind. At least we had only two miles to go. Then, on a steep hill a short distance from Pastor Matthew's house, the lights skipped out for the third time. Levi, however, was there with a flashlight, and I was able to keep on going.

I made it home safely, though it was 10:30 rather than 8:00 as I had hoped. What an experience! Where but in Haiti? My Haitian friends chided me for coming back in the dark, but I am learning that there are times when circumstances are beyond our control. I am also learning who is in control—our sovereign God!

Expect the Unexpected

Chapter 5

Life in the Mountains

• August 1997

We were so thankful that our supporting church had agreed to sponsor Christ to Haiti Ministries and had already found several families to serve in Alègue: Les and Kathy Reinford, Rick and Cherry Hess, and Ervin Martin. And now they were coming for a visit! Ervin planned to stay for a while, and the other two families were planning to move to Alègue in the near future. I was delighted to have them come, but I wondered where everyone would sleep, especially if it rained.

The evening before I was to go to Port-au-Prince to pick up my visitors, gale-force winds beat relentlessly. My temporary porch flapped and whined. The flimsy tin roof on my hut rattled, shook, and carried on so lustily that I thought it might take wings. I propped, nailed down, and weighted down whatever I could. The vibration and noise were so intense and disturbing that I could hardly sleep. Then came the rain—pounding, blowing, dashing—a real roar on my tin roof. *At least my water barrels are full,* I thought.

Driving to Port-au-Prince and back is no small undertaking, with around twelve hours of driving time. To allow for erratic flight schedules and to give us time to do some shopping, we were looking at a trip of about two and a half days. We would be leaving on Thursday morning, with plans to return late Saturday. Since the roads were muddy, slippery, and dangerous because of all the rain, I wanted to leave in plenty of time.

During a break in the rain the next morning, Bruce and I checked out the road and decided I should leave while I had the chance. "The way those clouds look," Bruce said, glancing toward the sky, "we're going to get more rain before the day's over. Maybe a lot." How true his words turned out to be.

We got about a dozen nationals to ride along to help push if needed. Then we loaded my things on the truck and hooked up the trailer. Bruce suggested that Levi tag along with the ATV and a rope until we get to the main road—just in case. He said a motorcycle had once pulled a truck out of the mud when it was stuck. I laughed at the idea.

Finally we were off. For about a mile all went well; then slither, slide, spin, and the truck stopped. Out jumped the Haitians and pushed us up the hill. Hurrah! Then we came to a steeper grade, but this time pushing wasn't successful. Quickly Levi pulled up with the ATV and a rope. We hooked up and off we went.

Next came our Jackrabbit Hill, the real test. This time the Mountain Goat failed; it simply spun its knobby tires. Bruce unhooked the trailer, and we backed it down to a level area with the ATV. As we hooked the ATV onto the truck again, we discovered that the "Goat" was not in four-wheel drive. After that it was a different story. With renewed determination, the frisky Goat, with a hop, skip, and a jump, easily pulled the truck up the steep, dangerous curves. Was I ever surprised! But the Haitians said, "It was a drink of water."

Next, with laughter and amusement, five nationals dragged the mud-laden trailer up the hill, where it was hooked up to the Goat and towed the rest of the way to the main road. By that time there were nearly three inches of mud heaped in the trailer bed, spun from the deep knobs of the Goat's tires. A trip that usually takes ten minutes had taken us nearly an hour—typical Haiti! After Levi and the ATV headed back home, we continued our trip to Port-au-Prince without incident.

Harold had stayed at home to tidy up, prepare beds for the visitors, oversee the work, and have a meal ready when we returned Saturday afternoon. He was feeling a bit sick when we left, but we thought it was because of the big meal of fried eggplant he had eaten the evening before. I was a bit concerned, however, when I wasn't able to contact him by radio that evening when I called from CAM's headquarters.

During my devotions early on Friday morning, God gave me a special concern for Harold. I sensed in my spirit that not all was well in the mountains. In my study I came to Psalm 46:1-3: "God is our refuge and strength, a very present help in trouble. Therefore will not we fear, though the earth be removed, and though the mountains be carried into the midst of the sea; though the waters thereof roar and be troubled, though the mountains shake with the swelling thereof."

At about seven o'clock we received a faint call from Harold on our radio. We tried to respond, but we got no further response from Harold. By God's grace I am slowly learning that in situations like this I must not fret and worry—I must simply trust my heavenly Father.

Later that morning I was in Port[1] shopping when I got a call from Harold. "There wasn't enough juice in the storage batteries due to all the cloudy weather," he told me. "So I couldn't use the radio until the sun shone on the solar panels for a while." Furthermore, he had been pretty sick and in bed much of the time. To add to that, there had been torrents of rain and the roof was leaking again—here, there, and everywhere. It had rained so hard that what we called our bridge (a built-up area through a normally dry ravine) was completely washed out. Now there was no way to use the truck to go the last mile. It sounded as if Rick and Cherry's introduction to Haitian life would be very real.

Typically, Haitians have no beards, or at most small beards, so Rick's large beard gathered much attention and produced much amusement everywhere we traveled. He immediately became known as *Gwo Bab* (big beard).

On Saturday morning we left early for Alègue, with Rick and Cherry riding on the back of the truck among the luggage. After traveling for over three hours, we turned off the main road onto the final rugged fourteen-mile stretch that leads to Alègue. About halfway there, as we passed a group of Haitians, one of them slyly jumped on the trailer and lay down. When I tried to make him get

---

[1]Common, shorter way of saying Port-au-Prince.

off, the others told me he was sick and we should take him with us. I tried my best to persuade him to get off, but he just lay there, eyes closed, limp as an unconscious man. I was pretty sure this was all faked, so I spoke more sternly and insisted that the others take him off. I had no success. Finally I removed the tailgate and, using all my energy—he probably weighed about 180 pounds—I grabbed him under his arms and lugged him off. But not for long! In a second he was back on and acting like a dead man again. At least this verified his "opossum playing."

Now what should I do? I repeated my bravado act but held on to him this time. I noticed his breath reeked with the sickening smell of brandy. He started to tussle with me, and I knew I had more than my match. I then yelled to Les to start driving. Meanwhile I jumped onto the trailer and held to the sides. The whole group started running after us and picked up large stones to throw at me. They ran a brief distance, and then I saw a smile appear on the "sick" man's face. He realized he had been outwitted, but he wasn't giving up yet. Dropping his rock, he simply ran after us as our speed increased. We splashed through a muddy stream, with water slopping over me, and bounced along wildly until we had gained enough distance that I could safely enter the truck again.

As we neared Alègue, I was able to contact Harold by radio. He felt somewhat better but was still pretty weak. He said the locals had taken it upon themselves to get twenty men to build a mini ATV path around the washed-out bridge. The path went down into the rocky riverbed and up a long, steep grade to the road again. I told Harold that when I got close to the area, I would call him and tell him to come to the bridge with the ATV. With the trailer hitched to the ATV, we could haul our suitcases and boxes to the church at the base of the path leading to my house.

Our plan worked and finally we reached my *kay*. Packing five people in my hut with all their additional luggage was no small feat. With mud everywhere outside and limited space inside, we had to play human checkers. But the spirit and enthusiasm of my guests made the cramped, muddy conditions much more bearable.

The pioneering spirit of my guests was outstanding. They proved that they were made of the material it takes to live with the rigors of mountain life. Our spirits blended, and we bonded in a lovely way during the short time they were here. It seemed we had known each other for a long time, and I anticipated the time when they would move here and Rick would be our pastor.

Bruce had asked Rick to preach on Sunday morning, but when Sunday morning came, no Bruce was in sight. He had not returned from a motorcycle trip to Ti Goâve. Disappointed, I resigned myself to this typical change in plans. At around 10:30 Bruce did return, in time to interpret for Rick. When I was asked to introduce the visitors, I used the native approach and introduced them as Pastor and Madame[2] Rick.

---

[2]In Haitian culture, a married lady is not usually addressed by her first name, but as "Madame," (Mrs.) in front of her husband's name.

Chapter 6
Adjusting to Alègue

• August 1997

Slowly but surely I am getting used to life in Haiti. Traveling the steep hills when they are wet and slippery is my greatest struggle. By now I have pretty well learned to master my Mountain Goat. It is certainly a most useful vehicle and delightful to operate. I feel much safer with it than I do with the truck. But I am surprised at how much gas it guzzles, especially when carrying a heavy load.

The foundation for the addition to my house is progressing slowly. It seems my house will definitely be "built upon the rock." Everywhere we dig it is rocky. Sometimes the rock is shale and fairly easy to break, but mostly it is quite hard. The cistern will soon be ready for the top to be poured. It is not under the house as I had planned, but in front of it because of the solid rock. This way the top will also serve as the porch floor. Everything seems to take more than twice as long as it should because of the rocks and the mountain. Just carting the sand here required twenty workers for over a week. Hopefully the task of building other mission houses in the future will be much easier down on the more level ground we were able to buy.

The arrival of Ervin Martin has been a godsend. He has a beautiful servant spirit and is doing well. He fits right into my simple lifestyle. Until additional families arrive, I suppose it will be a somewhat lonely life for short-term volunteers like him who come to help in these secluded mountains. It is also physically exhausting, but he is young and can take it.

A Typical Day

In the past I seldom had to use an alarm clock to wake me up in the morning. Not so in Haiti. Here, I work like a mule, eat like an elephant, and sleep like a baby. After the alarm clock rings at 4:30, I get washed and dressed and always make a mug or two of hot drink. I find I need lots of liquid with the strenuous work we do. My time for Bible study and prayer is from about 4:50 to 6:00. Without this I would not be able to cope with the extreme rigors of this lifestyle, either physically or spiritually. I often read the daily reading in Oswald Chamber's *My Utmost for His Highest*. This reading is often shared during our group devotions after supper.

Ervin and Harold get up between 5:30 and 5:45. Ervin enjoys going out on the bench below the cistern to meet with God while Harold uses the mini back room. We eat breakfast around 6:30 because workers come at 7:00, and I want to be prepared to greet them and give instructions for the day. The nationals are a warm, social people, and the morning greeting is very important.

Harold is our chief cook and usually prepares the meals. They are always sufficient and super. Ervin has the honor of washing the dishes—probably more dishes than he ever washed before in his whole life!

We have a crew of eight men to bag and carry sand to use in block making and also to make mortar to lay the blocks. Bruce brings the sand with the pickup as far as the washed-out bridge, where it is shoveled into bags, loaded onto the ATV, and hauled about three-quarters of a mile to the church. There it is parceled out into smaller lots and carried up to my house on people's heads.

Ervin is helping another man mix two types of sand with water and cement to make the concrete blocks. Often three women carry five-gallon buckets of water atop their heads all day long. It is hard work. I also have a group of four men gathering rocks to rebuild the washed-out bridge.

I regularly walk around to check the various work groups' progress, to give counsel, or to make changes. When it is almost time for lunch, Levi or I take Harold's place while he prepares lunch for us. The workers' day ends at 3:30, but by the time everything is cleaned, put away, and prepared for the next day, it is often four o'clock or later. After that we often spend some time in Creole study or just visiting and sharing with the neighbors. Soon it is time to prepare supper. We like to eat around six o'clock, but often that is not possible.

Right after supper, before dishes are done, we have group devotions with singing, meditation, sharing, and prayer. It is a time we all treasure. We usually sit out on what will be my future porch in the pleasant cool of the evening where we can look out over the lovely Haitian mountains and lift our hearts to our Creator. From then to bedtime the moments zip past. Before I know what has happened, it's nine o'clock or later and time for me to shoo the boys back to their nest, get my folded cot hanging from the rafters, stretch it out in my tiny family room, blow some missing air into my mattress, and settle down for another night. "The sleep of a laboring man is sweet, whether he eat little or much" (Ecclesiastes 5:12).

Chapter 7

This Is Haiti!

• September 1997

This morning Levi asked our permission to take the ATV to the main road to check on a big load of sand that had been delivered on Saturday. He has often used the ATV to haul sand, so we readily gave him the key. On his way back, with another passenger riding along, he failed to shift his body weight forward far enough as he climbed the steep bank beside the washed-out bridge. Being too light in the front, the ATV started to tip, but then dropped back down. When attempting to start off again, Levi accidentally did what amounted to popping a wheelie, and the ATV flipped over on the two riders. Both were badly bruised but had no severe injuries. Badly shaken, they righted the machine and drove on to Pastor Matthew's house, where they parked the rig. We thank God again and again for His guardian angels.

Recently while driving through this same spot, a bag of sand shifted for me. When I pushed the gear lever into neutral by mistake, the machine quickly started rolling back down the steep grade. Startled, I locked the brake and yelled, "Help! Help!" Several Haitians came running and pushed the heavy bag of sand back into place and strapped it down again.

We're all a bit scared of this dangerous spot by now, so we're hoping to get permission from the landowner to cut the grade down a bit before someone gets seriously hurt.

▪ ▪ ▪ ▪ ▪ ▪ ▪

Talk about "wearing down to the bone." That's the way I felt about my fingers last week. I am not a mason, but I was laying blocks much of the week. The combination of the rough, homemade blocks, the lime, and the other ingredients in the cement, wreaked havoc with my skin. Nearly all the fingers and the thumb of my left hand were worn down to the dermis, causing bleeding and sharp pain. Daily I covered them with first aid cream and gauze bandages, then wrapped them with masking tape. I discovered that the masking tape would stick better and last longer than Band-Aids. My Haitian workers laughed about it but felt very sympathetic toward me.

From a distance, our mason work looked fine, but a block layer from the States would be mortified at the very crooked blocks, which created joints up to one and a half inches thick. But everything will be plastered, so it doesn't matter too much.

. . . .

Recently Harold was hauling sand with the truck, and a sick man needed a ride back to his home near the church. He was extremely sick, vomiting, and probably dehydrated. Harold brought him as far as the washed-out bridge, and then loaded him onto the ATV to bring him the rest of the way.

When I heard about the sick man, I went down to the church where he was. I took his pulse and noticed his breathing was extremely fast. I told those standing by to give him water and a pad so he could lie down. He lay there, unresponsive and listless, but his eyes, the window of his soul, spoke so loudly they almost shouted. In them I could see despair, futility, pain, fright, bondage, and hopelessness. I told the people I would check my doctor books, and if I found any helpful information, Harold and I would return later.

I found nothing specific, but we decided to go down anyway and check his vital signs. When we got there, we discovered he was no longer there, as friends had carried him to his home. By then it was quite dark, so we decided to wait to find him until morning. Sad to say, we later got the message that he had died. It struck a chill to my heart. The man was gone—forever gone to a Christless eternity. I will never forget the look in those eyes.

■ ■ ■ ■ ■ ■ ■

A Traumatic Time

Harold, Ervin, and I had gone to Port-au-Prince to purchase supplies and to take a much-needed break from our busy schedule. As usual on such a trip, we stayed overnight at the CAM compound and enjoyed a refreshing and rejuvenating time with other missionaries.

On our return we needed to drive through an intersection dubbed as "robber's corner." Our truck was fully loaded, but the boys enjoyed riding on top of the supplies. As was often the case near this intersection, the road was jammed with traffic, causing vehicles to creep and many times simply sit for periods of time. The traffic had halted for a while when suddenly two legs appeared at my left mirror. Someone had jumped on the running board! Quickly the man reached up, grabbed Harold's backpack, and took off running. He disappeared behind a nearby wall and into a graveyard with many large tombs.

Traffic soon moved, and I turned to park nearby. Unknown to me, Harold had jumped off the truck and pursued the thief into the graveyard. When the thug saw that Harold had a watch and a Leatherman at his side, he roughly grabbed him and knocked his head against a tombstone, aiming to get the rest of his booty.

Thankfully a local worker saw the situation. He ran after the thug with his hammer and rescued Harold before he was further hurt or robbed.

A passing truck driver who witnessed the happening stopped and gave us some wise counsel. "Never pursue a thug," he said. "They will slit your throat for a dime."

Once again we thank and praise our kind heavenly Father for His guardian angels.

Chapter 8

Possessions or People?

• September 1997

We have finally moved into the addition to my house even though it is not completely finished. The 18' x 18' addition seems like a spacious mansion after living in a cramped, dark, musty hut for several months. But I realize that many of my dear friends and neighbors live in even filthier, cruder conditions with only a dirt floor. Just to have a place to be alone with God in my new little study is so healing. Simple as it is, the house seems almost like a miracle. Each step of progress was done painstakingly by hand.

The cistern for the first mission house, where the Les Reinford family is planning to live, has been dug, and the cistern walls are nearly half completed. A typical day has three men digging with picks and shovels, two hauling with wheelbarrows, three laying stone and mixing mud, three carrying water, and nine carrying rocks from the riverbed for the cistern walls. The next major project is making the hundreds of blocks to build the house. Being able to haul sand, cement, and other material directly to the building site is a blessed change from the way my house was built, where every item had to be carted up the steep, rugged mountain on someone's head or back.

■ ■ ■ ■ ■ ■ ■

As I sit at the desk in my little *kay* and look out the study window, the sun shines brightly on a distant mountain. The beauty is awe-inspiring. Outside it is 87 degrees, but at my desk it is quite comfortable, with a cool, pleasant breeze. I delight in this. How lovely! How restful! I can type with a laptop computer, listen to music and sermons on tape, flip a switch at night for a simple 12-volt light, and even turn a spigot and water comes from my cistern. You could imagine I am not living in a remote, isolated mountain area. But come with me outside my door, and let our hearts be moved with compassion like Jesus when He saw the people as sheep having no shepherd. Whether we live in the affluent United States or in poverty-stricken Haiti, it is so easy to focus on things, jobs, houses, and circumstances.

Jesus said of Himself, "The Son of man hath not where to lay his head. My meat is to do the will of him that sent me, and to finish his work. The Son of man is come to seek and to save that which was lost." What about me? What do I value most, possessions or people?

. . . .

The bells clanged and clanged; the doleful sirens shrieked and wailed. I edged to the ditch as two emergency vehicles bounced, jostled, and raced past me on the way to Ti Goâve. Where could they be headed at such reckless speed? About half an hour later I came upon a horrible scene. A large truck loaded with eighty to ninety people had been going down a long, steep hill when it lost its brakes and collided with two smaller trucks. The one lay in a large water ditch, crushed like a mere toy. The large truck lay on its side, with people, clothing, and merchandise strewn everywhere. People were screaming and blood was running. Later a policeman at a gas station told me twenty people had been killed. He shrugged it off so indifferently. Life seems to hold so little for the average Haitian. I pray that these experiences will give me a greater compassion and burden for the blinded, ignorant, and Christless lost. Yes, a love for people—not possessions.

. . . .

Imagine, if you can, the closest medical help being six walking hours away from you. Next ponder what it would be like to be unable to read or write, or to have little or no understanding of diseases, illnesses, infections, and the like. Having only the basic necessities such as food and clothing, you certainly would not have Band-Aids, first aid cream, antiseptics, or antibiotics. Many people living in such conditions come to us for medical help from miles around. It may be an abscessed tooth, a machete cut, pellagra, or an infected wound. It could be a tuberculosis patient whose doctor fourteen miles away gave him some medication and needles and told him to find someone to give him an injection daily.

I dream of a small clinic in the near future, but I have had my plans or expectations dashed so frequently that it has almost become a way of life. How much I need to "let patience have her perfect work" (James 1:4).

Once again I need to remind myself to focus on people, not possessions.

Chapter 9

Timely Surprise!

• September 1997

For weeks, Harold, Ervin, and I had looked forward to the visit of Myron and Roger, Harold's father and brother. I was disappointed that his mother Rachel (my daughter) wasn't planning to come along, because I knew it would mean so much for her to see Harold and get an insight of the work here in Haiti, but I understood. I will not soon forget the surprise I received when we picked up our visitors at the airport. Rachel had come along after all!

The two weeks they spent with us in Haiti were delightful and refreshing. I probed Myron's brain again and again about our generators, solar panels, and building needs. He was extremely helpful.

Another thing I really appreciated was the advice and concern Myron and Rachel shared with me about the intensity of my involvement with the work and the people here. "We're so glad you're enjoying yourself here," Rachel told me one day. "It's a worthwhile project. But be careful, Dad. We're afraid you might be overdoing yourself. We don't want you to ruin your health."

God so kindly showed me that I was like Martha—careful and troubled about many things. I have cried out to God, and it has been a help to me. But I still have much ground to gain. Right now I am in the midst of getting ready for Les Reinford and his family to move here. A work crew plans to come soon to finish the house for them. I eagerly anticipate their coming, but sometimes the preparations and duties seem almost overwhelming.

. . . .

Response and Openness

As time goes on, the hearts of the people seem increasingly open and receptive to spiritual help and direction. On Sunday Myron shared a simple message (with Bruce as interpreter) from the epistle of James about a fountain yielding both salt water and fresh. Apparently this message about the importance of living godly lives caused many to do some deep thinking. At the close of the meeting, many responded to the invitation to come forward for further counseling, prayer, or confession.

The first one, my closest neighbor, confessed to having gone to a witch doctor recently for help. Another stated that he hears the Word but then soon forgets it and it doesn't change his life. Another seemed to have the Catholic view of confessing sin without sensing any need for a change of life. These people's spiritual perception is very low, but their sincerity and openness is great. Bruce, Levi, and Remòn (the Moses, Aaron, and Miriam of the area) all share that they wish Rick would be here soon. They say they need a pastor to teach and guide them.

. . . .

Boils and Sores

For weeks I had been struggling with painful sores on my arm and elbow. They just would not heal. The problem started with a minor scratch or cut and then developed into a pus-filled center with a large, inflamed border. After a while it started to heal, but then erupted again. I thought it might be an abscess or a boil. Then some other pimples started on my arm and soon became like the first one. They were ugly and painful. I used a saline solution and triple antibiotic cream regularly, but the painful sores kept increasing in number. Ervin also had sores on his foot caused by a rubbing sandal. They, too, would not heal. They were gross, yucky, and pus-filled—and very painful. We were beginning to feel like Job with all his boils.

Rachel, bless her heart, decided to do some research in my *Village*

Medical Manual and discovered we both had a disease called yaws. In the first of its three stages, it usually causes an ulcer or lump at the site of a previous minor injury. In the second stage, it starts spreading out to other parts of the body. The sores look like a blob of dried pus and become very painful if on the palms or soles. This was our stage. The third stage develops horrible ulcers or thick, dry skin on the palms or soles, with painful cracks and ulcers. It may even eat away at the nose or mouth like cancer or leprosy. We were able to get an antibiotic at CAM that knocked it out before we reached the third stage, and healing is finally taking place.

Since we learned about yaws, we have had some nationals come with the same problem, and we are now able to help them.

▪ ▪ ▪ ▪ ▪ ▪ ▪

Ervin and Harold

Ervin will be leaving Haiti at the end of September and Harold in the middle of October. Their departure will produce a void that will be difficult to fill. First of all, they have been a tremendous help in the physical work that must be done—both in the construction and in the everyday household duties. Secondly, they are my close friends and I will miss them greatly. But thirdly, and most important, they have entered deeply into the hearts and lives of the people and have become their personal friends, thus opening their hearts to the Gospel. Harold has also become the doctor of this remote area, and I will not be able to take his place.

Chapter 10

Duped and Robbed

· October 1997

Yesterday was a day I will never forget. In my ignorance I traveled alone to downtown Port-au-Prince to buy two bunk beds for the Les Reinford family. I had just finished loading the beds when a Haitian pointed to my front right tire, but I ignored him because I had to pull out of the way of a big truck. I drove a bit farther up the crowded side street, jammed with merchants and buyers, before stopping.

I always carry my valuables in a soft case hanging from my neck by a strap, but whenever I climb into the truck, I remove the case from my neck and place it on the floor so that I can drive more easily. I had just slipped the case off my neck and onto the floor when a young man again urgently pointed to my right front tire and said, "Flat tire!" I quickly slipped from the truck, and indeed, the tire was flat. I immediately returned to my truck seat for my supplies.

To my consternation, I discovered that my soft case had disappeared! It was nowhere to be found. Dismay settled into my heart. *No!* I thought to myself. *This is not true! It can't be true.* But slowly the reality sank in—I had been duped and robbed.

Gone were the mission funds from the churches in the States. The Lord's money, several thousand dollars of it, gone just like that! Gone also were many important items: my international driver's license, my calculator, a first aid kit, my spare glasses, the mission checkbook, and my cash record book. But the biggest and most unsettling loss was the money. Money to buy another bed for the

Reinfords. Money for personal expenses. Money to pay for cement, sand, and steel for the house. Money to buy gasoline and to pay the many Haitian workers. All was gone. Now what would I do? Over and over I berated myself for being so careless. I felt angry, foolish, and humbled all at the same time.

I then proceeded to pump up the tire. It took so long that I finally stopped before the tire was quite full. While replacing the cap, I discovered two tiny pebbles inside and concluded that was how the culprits had let out the air. Starting off again, I had to drive slowly at first because of the crowds of people who continually bumped against my truck. By now I was very wary, very gun shy, and kept my eyes glued to the mirrors lest someone clamber up my truck cage and attempt to steal the mattresses. I was praying nonstop for safety and direction.

After driving a brief distance in heavy traffic, drivers kept pointing to my tire again. What? Was my tire flat again? Navigating through three lanes of heavy, honking traffic, I nosed my truck to the right and parked. But now I couldn't find the crank handle to release the spare and wind up the jack. As I continued my search, I was soon surrounded by a group of "helpful" Haitians, all offering advice and aid. And then, while trying to be extremely cautious, the unthinkable happened—I locked my keys in my truck. "Oh, no," I moaned in disbelief. Now I was really in a fix—a flat tire, no money, no key, and a weary mind and body.

Nearby a policeman was trying to direct the complex traffic jam. I got his attention, and he said he would stop another Toyota vehicle and perchance its key would work. Before long he did stop a vehicle, but the key did not work. By now a big crowd had gathered. I'm sure they thought this rich *blan* would pay handsomely for any help they could give.

Everybody was trying to help with wires, radio aerials, keys, and hooks—you name it. In the attempt to unlock the door, several big fellows broke the window. And then, to top it off, it began to rain. A young man ran across the street and soon returned with a heavy wire which he twisted to form a handle for the jack. Finally they were able to change my tire. Then, of course, they wanted payment. Since I had no money, I gave them a box of cereal. Enough excitement for one day!

As I headed on up the road, I came upon a roadblock. There were about seven police vehicles and twenty policemen, each brandishing a rifle or pistol. Scores of people were standing around, gawking at something. Finally I saw the object of all the attention—a bloody, dead man lying on the road. I was only about thirty feet away.

I asked a policeman how to get around the blockade, and he told me to wait and I could soon go. While waiting, the policemen suddenly ran toward the crowd, flashing their guns and yelling. The people rapidly dispersed. In seconds, police everywhere were ducking behind cars and trucks, with guns poised, ready to shoot. I was in a possible crossfire!

An officer ran over to me and told me to follow him. Getting into his car, he sped back the other way, while I willingly followed in hot pursuit. He led me to another street and motioned for me to go on. No sooner had I breathed a sigh of relief when I became embroiled in a horrendous traffic jam and a truck nearly hit me. To make matters worse, I now had no horn, not even a feeble one. I had enough of the city. I was ready to be in the mountains with my dear, needy friends.

I learned later that shortly after I was escorted away by the police car, there was a major shoot-out, and a robber and a policeman were shot to death. Once more I thanked God for safety.

After I sheepishly admitted to the mission board in the States what had happened, they graciously scraped together some replacement funds and sent them my way. The whole experience was a lesson well learned: be very careful in the city, never drive alone, and when carrying money, by all means hide it.

Chapter 11

Les Reinford Family Arrives

• October 1997

Harold Weaver and I were overjoyed when the long-awaited day finally arrived for the Les Reinford family to join us in Alègue. They temporarily moved into a rented house with four small rooms. The house is nice by Haitian standards, but it's pretty tight for a family of nine.

They are adjusting exceptionally well in spite of the fact that people are coming to them daily for medical and physical help. With Harold's help, they pretty well have a mini clinic on their porch. They do lots of sutures with Krazy Glue, set broken bones, and give other minor medical help. One mother walked for two hours and brought a malnourished five-year-old girl who was extremely emaciated, her skin flaking and peeling off. Madame Les (Kathy) and Harold prepared a rehydration mix. At first the child could not even keep water down, but as they fed the girl a spoonful at a time, she was able to keep it down. Kathy has a compassionate heart for the physical and spiritual needs which surround us.

Les has taken over the automotive responsibilities and is in charge of maintaining the trucks and our two ATVs. His son Leslie has an interest in the radios, which is also very valuable. He has already done some important reprogramming.

Having a family here to help share the responsibilities is a special blessing. The weight on my heart and shoulders does not seem quite so great, and I am able to enjoy life more fully. Harold and I often

55

eat with the Reinfords at noon. This saves us a trek up the mountain to our own house to prepare lunch. Sometimes we even get rolls or a dessert such as cake with cherries and whipped cream. Imagine that!

Les will head to Port to pick up the work crew at the airport on Monday. It is almost like a dream that a work crew of ambitious, skilled workmen are coming down to work on Les's new house. They plan to pour the concrete pad, lay the blocks, and put on the roof. I look forward to a time of sharing with them.

The men will sleep and eat breakfast in my *kay* on the mountain. It will be quite a chore for Harold to cook breakfast for eight hungry working men, but he will do well. Kathy and the girls will supply the other two meals.

· · · · · · ·

I recently learned that Les's neighbors are witch doctors. They told others they are afraid of us because their powers do not work against the *blans*. Another man, Alfred, whom we treated for pellagra, is also a witch doctor.

In the past, these neighboring witch doctors had their witchcraft meetings on the land purchased by the mission where we are building Les's house. So after the roof was completed Friday morning, we had a worship service to reclaim the land for Jesus and consecrate the new house to God. We also prayed that Les's family could be used for the glory of God and the salvation of the neighboring heathen.

Bit by bit I am beginning to understand a little more of the culture and customs of these deceived people. How great is the need for the redeeming, liberating Gospel of Jesus! Indeed He came to set the captives free. I sense a continual need for the covering of the blood of Jesus. Eternity is drawing nearer. The time is short. I must be more diligent to learn the language and spend more time with the people.

· · · · · · ·

It is quiet in my little *kay* today. I am alone with God. All the *blans* left. Even my grandson Harold, who was with me from the beginning—nearly seven months—has flown home for Bible school. The work crew that was here for twelve days to finish Les's house has left for home. Even Les and Kathy and their family are gone, as they took the workers to Port to fly home. With everyone gone, it is super quiet at my house. It is a quietness I enjoy and need—a time of solitude with God.

Alone with God, the world forbidden,
Alone with God, O blest retreat!
Alone with God, and in Him hidden,
To hold with Him communion sweet.
                                    —Johnson Oatman, Jr.

Chapter 12

Deep Conflicts

• November 1997

When I first came here, I thought voodooism and demonism were not very evident. But now we seem to find these forces of evil on every side as we continue to work with these needy people. As we counter the work of Satan, he raises his ire against us. This "accuser of our brethren," the world's greatest liar and deceiver, is at work against us. But praise God, we can overcome him by the blood of the Lamb.

I understand the words of Jesus to the Apostle Paul in a way I never have before. "I send thee, to open their eyes, and to turn them from darkness to light, and from the power of Satan unto God, that they may receive forgiveness of sins, and inheritance among them which are sanctified by faith that is in me" (Acts 26:17b, 18).

* * * * * * *

Eddy and Eslèn

On Sunday after the service, we were told about Eslèn, who had been in labor for nine days and was now in critical condition. We walked to her house not far away, where several dozen Haitians were gathered. Here we found an agonizing, moaning girl. Her father was deep into voodoo and had already tried his powers on the suffering woman, but to no avail.

Kathy examined the woman after shooing the curious onlookers away. There seemed to be no heartbeat from the unborn, but Kathy was not sure. What should be done? Since the visiting Lamar Nolt family would be returning to Port soon, we finally decided they would drop off Eslèn and some locals accompanying her at the Ti Goâve hospital. After she was admitted to the hospital, she had a C-section and delivered a stillborn child. The doctor told them later that Eslèn would have died within an hour or two without the operation.

After she returned to Alègue, Eslèn stopped periodically for help from Kathy and seemed to own her as her mother. Several times after she returned home, she had fits where she became "unglued" and would not keep her clothing on. Levi and Bruce dealt with her using the Scriptures and prayer, and now she seems to be in her right mind. She and the baby's father, Eddy, want to become Christians and get married. We long for wisdom as we attempt to disciple these poor souls who are illiterate spiritually and physically. May God give us grace to teach them His will.

Again and again our medical contacts are opening doors for the Gospel of Jesus. Again and again I see the urgency of helping people learn to read so that the Gospel, which is "the power of God unto salvation," can more readily enter into their hearts.

■ ■ ■ ■ ■ ■ ■

Yvette and Itanya

Yvette and Itanya are two young girls who are attending school. Although they are seventeen and eighteen years old, they only learned to read two years ago. They have an intense eagerness to learn. They are gracious, intelligent young girls who desire to be free from the clutches of voodooism and want to serve the Lord.

Their older sister Edline had been an excellent teacher at school, but Remòn learned of some deceit in her life and dismissed her. Instead of repenting, she turned from the Lord. To take revenge on her sisters who were on good terms with Remòn, she persuaded her mother to insist that Yvette and Itanya should become mistresses to certain well-to-do men so that money would be available for the family. The two girls wisely said they couldn't do that, but Edline severely abused them and made life so miserable that Yvette considered going to Port to escape.

We prayed earnestly for Yvette's spiritual and physical safety, and after some visits by Remòn and Levi, she decided to stay. The two girls live with their grandfather, who is very poor. They have decided to give their birth certificates to Remòn and claim her as their spiritual mother. After school, they work for Remòn whenever they can. Remòn is teaching them to cook and sew. We see tremendous potential in these girls, but so does Satan.

. . . .

Jochèn and His Children

I just learned his name last evening—Jochèn. I hope I never forget him, although he has been buried for some months now. He was the man in whose eyes I saw death, hopelessness, despair, bondage, and extreme fear. He was the man I had wanted to help with what I hoped to learn from our medical books, but the next morning he was dead.

About a year before his death, Jochèn had come to Bruce and Remòn and said, "I want to give my children into your care. I have made a pact with Satan and am bound to the devil. I can't be freed, but I don't want my children to go this way."

Those children are coming to school now. They are learning to read and write and are receiving teaching from God's Word. They come to church every Sunday. Just last Sunday Bruce read a letter they had written, asking for prayer because of persecution and oppression.

Because of their schooling, they are open to the Gospel and can read and write. To me this is exciting—very exciting!

. . . .

Voluntary Workers

My grandson Harold returned after attending Bible School. Our Haitian friends were so delighted and excited that they prepared a royal, full-blown feast. Kent Martin also came to serve for several months. He had learned to weld and repair vehicles in his father's welding shop, and it seems God sent him to us at the exact time needed. He was barely here when one day we were driving up a steep incline a tenth mile from Les's house. Our truck frame suddenly broke in two and the bumper started dragging on the ground. By all appearances, the truck became a dump truck.

It was dark, and Kent, who was riding on the back, thought, *Wow! These hills must be terribly steep!*

Upon closer inspection the next day, we discovered that one side of the frame had apparently been severed for some time already. The other side could have snapped at any time, but thankfully it happened when we were close to home. And even more amazing, we have an experienced welder and vehicle repairman to weld the broken truck frame. Yes, God truly supplies all our needs.

· · · · · · ·

Mr. Bean Man · December 1997

We plan to build Rick Hess's house on the last parcel of land that we purchased. This land had been leased to a local Haitian before we bought it, so we let him plant beans, telling him we would need it later to build. To protect us, Bruce got him to sign an agreement saying the beans must be off by December, meaning December 1, but failed to write the day. We discovered that Towo, or "Mr. Bean Man," as I have dubbed him, was just eagerly waiting for me to set foot in his bean field and start digging so that he could tramp off to Ti Goâve and sue me for big money.

Finally Bruce and Levi talked to the local judge, a good friend of mine, who in turn talked to all the other area judges and explained the situation. Jointly, they issued a statement to Towo telling him the beans must be pulled by Friday evening, December 6, or on Saturday the beans would be pulled by others. In addition, he was told not to bother the missionaries.

· · · · · · ·

Rick Hess Family

The Rick Hess family is now at CAM, where they are enrolled in the Missionary Orientation Program. For two months they will study Creole and start experiencing the Haitian culture, with many hands-on experiences. After that they will come to the mountains, and Rick will be our pastor and spiritual administrator.

We pray and long for the salvation of these blinded people. Although their medical and educational needs are great, their spiritual needs are much greater. The fiery darts of the deceiver fly fast in voodoo-infested Haiti. The frontline is dangerous, and we are on the offensive.

Chapter 13
Trip on Horseback

▪ December 1997

I'm at Bainet, a small outpost school and church about six hours from Alègue. It's six o'clock Sunday evening and very dark. I have no light switch for my 12-volt lamps and no computer to type my letter, but my pen works well and the wax candle stuck to my water jug lid makes decent light. I'm sitting on the Haitian-made bed that I slept in last night and will use again tonight. It consists of slats every four inches and is covered with a banana leaf mat—where I heard the insects chewing last night. I slept very well last night, considering everything.

Bruce and I had planned to travel to Bainet early Thursday and return Monday afternoon. Four mules were supposed to arrive from the Bainet district to carry Bruce, Remòn, the deacon, and myself. But no mules appeared Thursday or Friday. We were beginning to think everything was off, but then we got word early Saturday that Bruce and I would leave around seven o'clock on two horses. Before we left, I was warned to be ready for extremely steep mountains—too steep to stay on your mount—and for the possibility of an extremely sore seat from the arduous trip.

My mount was Pastor Matthew's small horse, while Bruce's was Judge Alsiyis's larger horse. We loaded our duffel bags and started off, but my horse wanted to stay home. She kept turning back, and I was too much of a "green horn" to control her. Finally Pastor Matthew led her to the thick wooded path and we were off. I sat stiff and tense and could feel my legs getting sore. Bruce instructed me to hold on to the horse's mane when going up the steep mountains and to grasp the tail strap when descending. In other words, hang on for dear life!

It took me about fifteen minutes to learn a beautiful lesson: sit back, relax, and trust your mount. When I realized that, I started enjoying the trip. There was no need for any mane grasping or tail-strap holding. I just held onto the front of the saddle, and what a memorable trip it became. I loved every bit of it. U.S. tourists pay big money to descend into the Grand Canyon on horseback. This was just as good. I actually discovered a mini "Grand Canyon" of Haiti, complete with falls, gorges, huge boulders, streams, and large trees. Indeed, it was a hidden tropical paradise. There were places where my trusty mount had to descend rocky paths with multiple rocks having up to two-foot drops. She did it with the greatest of ease and poise.

Bruce's mount wasn't as trusty. Several times she just flopped down on the trail with Bruce astride the saddle. The first time I supposed she was hurt or sick, but Bruce said she was just not trained properly and whipped her to her feet.

Many of the trails were so treacherous that we had to pick our way. Occasionally my horse trotted on the few flat trails we traversed. The ride was much quieter than with my normal ATV Mountain Goat, and there was much more time to observe and explore and visit with others. For several miles we traveled in and out of rocky rivers, with water splashing on our shoes and legs.

After two hours we made our first stop at the home of a family who regularly attends our services. They served us coffee and bread shaped like a fish. The house was immaculate for Haiti.

Our next stop was at a Saturday morning market along the riverbed. Here we met the deacon's wife from a local church. From her we learned why the four mules had not been brought for us to use. Two young men who had been at Alègue brought back the report that Bruce was at a funeral and therefore we would not be coming this weekend. I think there was another reason—I had been sick and wasn't sure about the wisdom of going. The night before the planned departure I woke up aching all over. God knew I needed a few days to get better.

As we traveled, Bruce pointed out a small red flag on the hillside. That flag marked the home of a local *bòkò* (witch doctor). A short time later we heard drums beating, and Bruce said, "Look ahead! There's a voodoo worship group!"

Our mountain trail led us right through the center of the group of chanters and worshipers. In the middle of the group was a cement altar with a cross, a candle, and a bottle of incense. In their demon worship a *lwa,* or voodoo spirit, leaves the candle and enters someone who is then under its control. "Look!" said Bruce, pointing at a young woman who was dancing crazily. "She is probably the one whom the evil spirit has entered." How thankful we were to have the blood and power of our dear Jesus to cover and protect us, especially here, hours from any village, in the middle of nowhere.

As the hours stacked up, my sitter bones and muscles kept getting sorer, but the fascination of the unique trip outweighed the pain. We finally reached our destination, the home of the deacon of the small Bainet church.

Immediately upon our arrival they gave us each a glass of water, which I thought was to drink, but soon discovered was for a mouthwash or gargle, a custom of the area. They also brought out a huge basin of water and a cloth for washing and drying. Then, in a few minutes, they served us a cup of hot cinnamon drink and a piece of bread.

Meanwhile, they "killed the fatted kid." They had not been expecting us, but that did not matter. They just got to work and served a scrumptious meal—goat meat, rice and beans, onion sauce, pan-fried cabbage, plantain, and citron juice. It was truly a royal feast, even if the rain dripped on the table as we ate.

Later in the evening our host climbed a twenty-five-foot coconut tree and threw down some huge coconuts. Using a machete, he prepared them, and we drank fresh coconut milk on the spot. It was delicious!

The deacon and his wife gave us their bedroom. It was a lovely room even though it had no windows. The walls were about seven feet high and beautifully white-washed. The room looked huge to me, much bigger and nicer than my own. It turned out to be completely free of spiders, lizards, tarantulas, and ants—how different from my own bedroom. We could see this area was more well-to-do than some.

On Sunday we had a simple service in a crowded mud and stone building. I shared a simple message from the Beatitudes. The Haitians listened with rapt attention. They are a hungry, seeking people, wide open for the Gospel. There are so many open doors to enter.

I discovered that Bruce and Remòn have three other small schools they support financially. They have a vision to help these people hear the Word of God and learn to read it themselves.

How we take for granted our knowledge of the Scriptures and our ability to read. "And that from a child thou hast known the holy scriptures, which are able to make thee wise unto salvation through faith which is in Christ Jesus" (2 Timothy 3:15).

Chapter 14

From Horseback to Ambulance Driver

• December 1997

We had just gotten back from our three-day horseback trip to Bainet when Les shared that Pastor Matthew did not feel well and had stopped at their back-porch clinic for a blood pressure check. When Kathy checked him, she found it dangerously high. After giving him medication, she told him to see a doctor without delay.

Later that day I was helping Les at his house when Bruce came hurrying up. "Pastor Matthew is worse!" he blurted out, concern showing on his face. "He doesn't talk, and we think he may have fainted. I think Kathy should come and check on him again."

"That doesn't sound too good," Les replied. "I'll get Kathy and we'll head up right away."

A short time later they radioed me to say Pastor Matthew was paralyzed on his right side, so I hurried up with my ATV. After singing and praying for him, we decided it was best to take him to a hospital for help.

We had a recent 1.6-inch rain and were not sure if we could get to his house with the truck, but thankfully we made it and backed right up to his front door. I rushed on up the path to my *kay* to get ready while he was being loaded. After he was loaded, Remòn and Bruce sat on either side of him on the back seat, while I got in the driver's seat.

Roles change so rapidly in Haiti. A day ago I was an itinerant horseback rider sharing the Gospel. Now I had abruptly become an ambulance driver, transporting a critical patient to a hospital five hours away with a four-wheel-drive truck over the most rugged roads you can imagine.

It was a trip we won't soon forget. The poor man started gagging and throwing up almost immediately and continued till we arrived. He seemed so sick that we decided to stop at the Ti Goâve hospital, where Bruce searched in vain for even one doctor or nurse on duty. Then we stopped at a house in Ti Goâve where some of Pastor Matthew's children lived. When we told them about their father, they were devastated, and the one daughter started weeping and wailing.

Several of them decided to go with us, and we soon continued on our way. Around 4 p.m. we reached the hospital in Port. We were thankful to have some of Pastor Matthew's children along, since in Haiti the family supplies almost everything in the hospitals—food, clothing, medicine, and water. They do everything a nurse's aide would do. I decided to go to the CAM guest house for the night and come back the next noon.

When I returned to the clinic the next day, the doctor informed me that Pastor Matthew had been transferred by the Red Cross to General Hospital. I knew this hospital was located somewhere downtown—the place where I had been robbed and had been advised not to travel alone. But duty demanded it, so off I went in search of Pastor Matthew. As I neared the downtown area, I wondered and prayed about how I was going to find this elusive hospital. Suddenly I saw a policeman and knew what I would do. Generally I shrank from them because of past experiences, but resolutely I pulled over and asked him where the hospital was located. I had poor Creole and he had no English, so he finally crawled into my truck and said he would show me. What a relief! I was escorted through the bad section of Port with a policeman at my side!

We finally found the hospital, where the policeman rounded up an attendant to help me. Before he left, I showed my appreciation with some cookies and a small tip.

I attempted to tell the attendant that I was looking for a very sick man by the name of Matthew, but he didn't seem to understand. He took me here and there with no success. The hospital was a large place, with a section for the military, for internal medicine patients, and for the very poor. There was also a large morgue.

Finally the man seemed to understand. We got into my truck and drove through the shabby-looking complex all the way to the other end. He told me to back up to a building. To my amazement he had taken me to the morgue! In desperation, I asked him to take me to the admissions office. Here I found a lady who understood English, and I was assured I would soon see Pastor Matthew and Remòn.

I was escorted into a huge emergency examining room with no curtains. The room had about thirty tables and mini beds, all filled with an assortment of men, women, children, and babies. It was so full that some were lying on the floor.

What I saw on the first table as I entered still haunts me. It was a gruesome sight, too terrible to look at closely but also too terrible not to notice. On the table lay a hulk of a man that looked much like a swollen, roasted pig, with blistered pink and black skin peeling all over his nude body. He reeked with the odor of burnt flesh and medicine. He died an hour later while I was there, and his body was rolled outside the rear iron gate and left there for the time being. I was told he had poured gasoline on himself and ignited it. Oh, what terrible demonism, what horrible futility!

On the beds all around Pastor Matthew were people of the most pathetic appearance. Children screamed in agony, and babies cried for their mamas. There were gory, bloody, mangled arms, a head cracked open, blood being mopped—or rather smeared—off the floor, and the stench was nauseating. I was with Remòn for several hours until Bruce returned. Often I went outside to try to get some fresh air, but walk where you would, the ground reeked with aged urine. Three times policemen came in with wounded criminals. One time six policemen escorted a man inside with a wrapped-up head.

I later learned that this hospital is where interns get their training, and the very poorest are brought here when they are almost dead.

Lamar once took an injured man he found on the road to this emergency room and later found out he lay there for two full days before they did anything for him! Unbelievable! When I saw how ruthlessly nurses applied catheters and how crudely they cared for the suffering patients, I thought, *God spare me from ever being in such a place as a patient.*

Bruce asked me to come back the next morning and transport Pastor Matthew to another hospital, but when I arrived in the morning they were gone. They had learned about a better hospital and hired a taxi to transport Matthew there. I discovered that this actually was a good hospital. I found Matthew in a clean, private room, resting well and on oxygen—a striking contrast to the former hospital. Tests showed that he'd had a severe stroke and was paralyzed on his right side. "Thanks so much for everything you've done," his family told me over and over.

Chapter 15

Pastor Matthew's Death

· December 1997

B ruce and Levi were at my house Friday evening sharing possible
plans to bring Pastor Matthew back to Ti Goâve where the children
would take turns caring for him and giving him therapy. Bruce planned
to come to my house the next day to update me about the situation. It
was not to be. About 6:30 the next morning Bruce's brother Mèjil came
with a note from Bruce. Opening it quickly, I was shocked as I read:

> *SAD NEWS.*
> *Thank God, He still is on the main line, so He is in control.*
> *To my dear friend, Papa Harold,*
> *May God bless you. We received bad news last night. Pastor
> Matthew died. I chose not to wake you up. I decided to go. I'll
> talk to you when I get back. My friend, brother, and papa,
> pray for me, for I feel weak.*
> *See, I don't want to wake you from your sleep.*
> *Thank you.*
> *Bruce*

Even though I had known death was possible, I was not prepared
for this. It struck me deeply and brought pain to my heart and tears
to my eyes. I was reminded of the truth in Psalm 31:15: "My times
are in thy hand."

Pastor Matthew had died Friday morning already, apparently from
a heart attack. Remòn and one of her sisters were with him. By the

time details were taken care of and they got to Ti Goâve, it was late Friday, and they were not able to get the news here to the family at Alègue until after midnight.

After getting the news, Bruce, Levi, and Mama Matthew, as Matthew's wife was commonly called, left for Ti Goâve in the middle of the night. I left around 8 a.m. with my ATV. Pastor Matthew had been widely known as a kind, gracious man and was highly respected, so I stopped at numerous places and reported his death.

In Ti Goâve I found a grieving, hurting family. Remòn had faithfully stayed with her dear papa ever since I had taken him to Port last week. I found her with a barely audible voice and bloodshot eyes because of sleepless nights and much crying. It was a heart-rending time as we wept together. Various friends came to share their condolences throughout the day. The women, in true Haitian custom, gave each one of the family, including me, a gentle peck on the cheek. Sometimes the daughters and Mama Matthew attempted to sing and weep and say, "Papa, Papa, Papa," all at the same time.

I was quite concerned with Remòn's lack of sleep and weakened condition, so Levi and I went to a pharmacy and bought some medication for her. It was Valium, which is pretty rank, but I felt she needed the medication so that she could relax and regain some strength of body and mind.

Bruce hired an ambulance to go to Port and transport the body to Ti Goâve, but before they could leave, he had to find someone who would loan him some money to pay the hospital; otherwise, the hospital would not release the body.

Levi showed me the cemetery in Ti Goâve where some workers were digging to prepare a burial site.

They plan to rent a church building for the funeral. The folks from Alègue will come by foot, by mule, or by vehicle if they have the money.

A funeral director in Ti Goâve is caring for the body. There is very little embalming in Haiti. They just place the body in ice until burial.

The cost of the coffin and funeral will be quite high. I hope our influence and teaching can change these procedures in the future. For both weddings and funerals, Haitian customs bind people financially.

Chapter 16

Pastor Matthew's Funeral

· December 1997

It is with deep longing that I open my heart to understand the inner thinking, the feelings, and the customs of the dear Haitian people, as well as their bondage, fears, and needs. The longing of my heart is to truly see the power and glory of God in this dry and thirsty land. It is so barren and thirsty, and so steeped in darkness that even those who have some truth need much more enlightenment. I was made more deeply aware of this as I was intermingling with my friends in their homes during the week between Pastor Matthew's passing and his burial.

For a whole week the community of Alègue came to an abrupt halt of almost all activities—work, school, and church—until after Pastor Matthew's funeral on Saturday. Even the clinic patients dropped from about twenty a day to five or six, in deference to the one who had been a counselor, pastor, or friend for well over thirty years. Yes, there were those who were glad he was dead; he would no longer lay hands on and pray for those who had been cursed by the *bòkò*, setting them free by the power of Christ. Others accused Bruce and Levi of causing his death and aspiring to his office. But I knew this was not true. Again and again they have told me they can hardly wait till Pastor Rick comes and gives them counsel and instruction.

I made three trips to Ti Goâve with my Mountain Goat to be with the family, to help them and to attend the funeral on Saturday. I found the hour and fifteen minutes spent on my four-wheeler a special time of relaxation and meditation, a time of healing.

Lamar's family and Rick's family, still taking language classes, came from CAM to attend the funeral. Bruce asked all the *blans* to sing a Creole song together with the family at the funeral. The morning of the funeral he met me and asked if Rick could preach a funeral message. I said I wouldn't see him until noon, so he told me a Haitian pastor would preach. The service included group singing, prayers, several Scripture readings, a rundown of circumstances relating to Pastor Matthew's death, a reading by one daughter, our singing, a message, a selection by a local band, and a closing benediction.

Midway in the service, Bruce came to me at the rear of the packed auditorium and asked again if Rick would preach a message for them. I found Rick and he agreed, proving himself "instant in season, out of season" (2 Timothy 4:2).

It is difficult for me to sort out my various observations and thoughts during the viewing and the funeral: the finery—each of the family dressed in black and white—the formality, the overt display of emotion, the wailing by friends, the fainting of the children, the band procession, and the march from the funeral home to the church and from the church to the burial vault.

"I'm glad the really poor people from Alègue aren't here to see this," I told Bruce.

"Oh, they wouldn't have expected anything else," he replied. "That's just the way it's done in Haiti."

Sure enough, some of my poor Haitian friends from Alègue who could hardly scrape together enough money to feed their children appeared at the funeral dressed like the mayor and his children.

. . . .

Pastor Matthew's death produced ripples that will continue for a long time. I was amazed at the deep respect the community had for him. He had developed many personal friendships and was revered as a counselor, mediator, pastor, friend, and a father—way beyond the confines of his own family. The grieving for his loss flowed deeper than that of any other death I have ever witnessed before. There is no doubt that they were and still are a very influential family in this area.

Though highly respected, members of Pastor Matthew's family are constantly under attack because of their commitment to the truth, especially Levi, Remòn, and Bruce. There is jealousy because the *blans* help Bruce's school and church but not theirs. Therefore they attempt to plant fear and hostility in people's hearts. They even tell the children that the *blans* capture children and eat them!

Yes, there is increasing confrontation with the enemy, and the battle is intensifying. The witch doctors and voodoo worshipers don't want the Gospel here. They have discovered that their powers and curses are not effective against the missionaries. Now their strategy is to attempt to kill the people we are closest to—Bruce, Remòn, and Levi. The witch doctors openly say they are using their voodoo against the family. They predict that the family will all die, and then the *blans* will leave. Truly they are ignorant of the power of the resurrected Jesus, at whose name every knee shall bow. I say with Paul, "None of these things move me."

Chapter 17

In the Darkness of Night

• January 1998

It started late Friday night. On Saturday the raucous group went drumming, prancing, singing, shouting, and dancing off into the neighboring areas, proclaiming their demonic message. A voodoo ball was in full swing.

That night at 11:30 I awoke to the powerful, resonating *tom-tom* of the voodoo drums shattering the dark night. The wail-like chanting and moaning of many voices pulsed up from the valley below my *kay*. For several days I had been pondering, praying, and seeking to better understand the unique culture of my dear Haitian friends. My earnest prayer had been for a deeper insight into the hearts and lives of these voodoo-entrenched people.

Finally wide awake, almost on impulse I dressed and walked out into the night. I wanted to see what takes place in the deep of night. There was no moon to light my path, but in the intense darkness the magnificent canopy of stars overhead shone out as bright points of light, like a blessing and a watch of my great God over me. I thought of God's promise to Abraham, "I will multiply thy seed as the stars of the heaven" (Genesis 22:17).

Cautiously I slithered down the gravelly, slippery mountain path. I used my flashlight sparingly on the meandering, snaking trail. Then I came to the road. I didn't want to advertise my *blan* face, so I gingerly began walking in the semi-wooded area in total darkness. It was the kind of darkness you can feel. Suddenly a man appeared, and we side-swiped—a Haitian and a *blan*. We were both startled, but nothing was said by either. Thoroughly on edge now, I decided to proceed more carefully.

As I neared the clamorous gathering, I hid behind a shrub about twenty yards from the ball. Flickering flames from a dwindling wood fire cast eerie shadows over the milling crowd, and mini tin-can torches bobbed about in the hands of the floating throng. The *bong-bong, tom-tom, klank-klank* intensified, and I wished for earplugs. Red-turbaned women danced to the music, and the entire milling mob swayed to the beat of the key item, the *lwa* drum used to call up the evil spirits.

As if planned, two people started a united dance and plummeted down the bank to the road. Apparently one had been mounted[1] by a *lwa*, or demon. Just as rapidly, a group of about twenty persons congregated amidst much high-pitched conversing and shouting. With their mini torches they seemed to float down the road away from me—chanting, dancing, and yelling. Older men and women sat about the fire joking and laughing. Some stood for long periods of time as if transfixed. Music, dancing, and drumming seemed to come and go in spurts.

As I asked God to help me understand the sadness, bondage, and deep control of demonism, a man suddenly gyrated toward the road, lunging forward, spinning rapidly, and shrieking as he went. He passed me at a high rate of speed. No one seemed to pay any attention to him. Apparently it was only normal.

By now it was well past midnight. I decided to return to my bed. As I slowly climbed the mountain to my *kay*, I was overwhelmed by what I had experienced and began praying for a deeper love and burden for these poor lost souls. Once again I looked up to the canopy of brilliant stars and remembered the promise of God to Abraham. Yes, the promise was for the mission here at Alègue also.

---

[1] Haitians say a demon or evil spirit "mounts" a person, giving the picture of a rider who takes control of the horse he has mounted.

Chapter 18

Pall of Darkness

• February 1998

A few days ago I was told not to go outside on the afternoon of Thursday, February 26, as there would be a major eclipse of the sun. The press apparently publicized the eclipse as an episode that would produce cancer, blindness, and other ills. The nationals believed the event would be the power of Satan at work, and they were extremely fearful. I called Lamar at CAM, and he told me that indeed most people would not work, but would house themselves in seclusion the whole afternoon.

This morning, the day of the eclipse, there was no normal activity except the roosters' crowing. There seemed to be a pall over the place. Only one young Haitian, Nèli, decided to take his chances and work beside the *blans*. Twelve-thirty came, then one o'clock, yet there was no complete darkness as feared. Meanwhile, a work crew from the States cheerfully worked on Rick's house.

The unusual silence continued till about 1:30, when a youth who saw one of the *blans* looking at the sun through a welding helmet got enough courage to take a look for himself. After seeing the wondrous sight, he ran to each house in the area, coaxing them to come and take a look. Suddenly the silence was broken as people poured out of their houses. Even the witch doctor marveled at the sight of the moon crossing the sun.

Nèli ran over to the witch doctor and said, "I worked all day and didn't die." He also scolded another professing Christian for hiding in his house.

After a recent Sunday service, Levi invited me to walk with the school children to the home of two pupils to sing for them. The mother of these children had died the day before after having been sick for a week. She also left behind a four-week-old baby. To add to the sadness, the father had also died recently. As we approached the house, we could hear heart-wrenching shrieking, moaning, singing, and wailing. It seemed like the wailing of people without hope, a sound difficult to describe.

As we met and shook hands with the two orphans, I kept gazing into the eyes of all these hurting, spiritually destitute people, people whom the "god of this world" has blinded. The experience tugged at my heart and brought tears to my eyes.

In a few brief moments God gave me a tremendous confirmation. Yes! This mission was deeply needed. The Gospel must be lived and preached for these lost Haitians. Yes! It was worth all the suffering and financial sacrifice.

Sacrifice? No, it was just our reasonable service.

Chapter 19

Klomàn, Itanya, and Yvette

The church at Alègue is excited that Rick and Cherry and their family have finally arrived here to live. Since Pastor Matthew's death, the local church has been struggling and the door has been opened in a unique way. Only God could have planned it thus.

Pastor Rick, as he is called, began teaching and preaching immediately because of the vacuum created by Matthew's death. Bruce became the official interpreter. There was an immediate hunger and receptivity, but resistance was also evident. It seemed that God was brooding over this remote area.

Although we had observed demonic manifestation and control at voodoo balls, so far we had not had any direct experience with such situations. This was about to change, however, as God gave us powerful lessons and experiences in the lives of Klomàn, Itanya, and Yvette.

■ ■ ■ ■ ■ ■ ■

When Klomàn was a baby, she was dedicated to Satan and was destined to become a *manbo*, or lady witch doctor. When she became a teenager, the House of Matthew (Pastor Matthew's extended family who lived in or near his house), especially Remòn, took a real interest in her and invited her to live with them. Longing for a better life, she agreed. But Klomàn's family feared retaliation from Satan and tried desperately to make her come back.

A demon persistently tried to take her back, often tearing her with torturous pain and causing uncontrollable hiccups, belching, and serpent-type hissing. After one of these severe demonic attacks, Pastor Rick counseled her and shared the plan of salvation, only to have her respond that she had never sinned. Rick then described what sin was and finally ended their time together in prayer.

Yvette and her sister Itanya had been part of a financial arrangement between their mother and a wealthy, much older voodoo practitioner. They were, in essence, sold to be his mistresses even though polygamy is illegal in the country of Haiti. Wisely, the girls did not agree to this arrangement and in desperation fled to Pastor Matthew's house for refuge.

During this time, a heated battle raged over these girls. The alleged "owner" went to a *bòkò* and paid him to send demons after the girls to bring them back. Often when Pastor Rick got up to preach, the demons would rise up in these girls with great intensity. When this happened, the girls would fall to the ground and hiss or writhe like a snake. Sometimes they would shriek out in pain as though being stabbed. Other times they would fall to the floor, unconscious and stiff as a board. We would carry them out, pray for them, and command the spirits to leave. When the girls became conscious, we sat down and counseled them, yet these experiences kept recurring.

Later, Brother Mose came down from Pennsylvania for a series of meetings. He too acknowledged that this was a different demonic possession than he had ever dealt with. As we all prayed to the Lord for wisdom, several things became clear. First, we needed to address the spirit in Creole; the spirit did not appear to respond to English. Second, we needed to command the spirit to leave in the name of Jesus, using the demon's personal name. Also, we needed to persist until the demon fled.

At least one of the girls had a demonic attack in church for three Sundays in a row, with violent hiccups, severe chest pains, and even unconsciousness. When this happened, we would gather and pray, sing praise songs and songs about the power of Christ, and read the Word to them. After a time the girls would appear normal again.

We sensed a need to counsel them privately and decided to have a meeting with them during the week. After picking them up at the appointed time, we headed for the church. Before we even got there, Itanya started having the hiccups. We began the meeting with prayer and singing, and as we continued, the hiccups and pain got worse. Brother Rick then read from Colossians 2, explaining that when Christ was nailed to the cross, He blotted out the handwriting of ordinances that was against us. As he was explaining this, Klomàn also started with the hiccups. We decided to focus our attention on her before she got too bad to talk. "Did the Lord convict you of something while I read this Scripture?" Rick asked her.

With eyes downcast she finally nodded her head and whispered, "Yes."

"Tell us about it. Then you can be free," Rick encouraged.

Finally she started to talk. She explained that her parents practiced voodoo and had dedicated her to Satan at an early age. After she started coming to church, her uncle Towo became angry and put a curse on her to stop her. Recently her family told her how to pass this curse on to a goat, which she agreed to do. By doing this she had opened herself up to another foothold of Satan.

We counseled her about the serious effects of this move. Bruce then questioned her, and she started hiccupping so violently that she could not talk. We started singing "There Is Power in the Blood," and before we were done, she had fallen to her knees. As we were singing, Kathy encouraged her to cry out to God. By the time we finished singing, she had calmed down. She was then led in a prayer in which she confessed her wrong actions, renounced her involvement in voodoo, and begged God to fill her with His Spirit and help her walk by faith. She was encouraged to keep an open heart before God because He might reveal other sins that she needed to repent of.

After more than two hours, we once again turned to Itanya and found a similar situation. She had also been dedicated to Satan by her parents as a child and taken to voodoo services where an evil spirit, or *lwa,* spoke through her. The demon told her what clothes to wear and other things to do. If she did what he told her to do, he would reveal his name to her. We proceeded with more questions and more reading from the book of Deuteronomy. We read about God's judgment on witches and those involved in witchcraft in the Old Testament.

During this time Klomàn again started with mild hiccups, but she immediately bowed her head and cried out to God in prayer. Thankfully, the hiccups left her and soon she was "sitting, clothed, and in her right mind" (Mark 5:15).

As we continued to probe into Itanya's life to get an idea where she was in her spiritual understanding, we learned some things about her past that clearly indicated there was a great deal of work to be done yet. We realized that all of these girls would need more counseling to bring them to the Lord Jesus Christ, who could truly set them free.

A few days later Brother Mose, Rick, Bruce, Les, and I were counseling with the girls again. As we talked, Brother Mose spoke about the need to confess with the mouth the Lord Jesus Christ and to believe in the heart that God has raised Him from the dead. Suddenly Klomàn dropped to her knees and began to pray, pleading for the power and blood of Jesus to help her. We laid hands on her and prayed for her as well.

That night this shy fifteen-year-old stood before a packed church and publicly renounced her former sin and voodoo involvement, as well as Satan himself. She gave a bold confession of Jesus Christ's deliverance and went on to ask her mother, who was in the congregation, to stand up so that all could pray that she, too, would become a Christian. Those who knew her said this was not Klomàn speaking, but the Spirit of God. Hallelujah!

The following Sunday Klomàn sealed her faith with Christian baptism as her voodoo family and many others observed. The next Sunday both her father and mother were in church. That was unusual, but they wanted to speak to us. We talked with them till nearly four o'clock in the afternoon. Klomàn's mother, Madame Banav, had an intense fear about what her family would think. She also feared the voodoo curses her angry relatives would undoubtedly try to place upon her.

We listened with rapt interest as she went on to tell us what made her begin to consider the ways of Jesus Christ. As we listened, we saw the power of God at work. She told us that the goat which had been marked for sacrifice to the devil had suddenly started trembling and bleating loudly, and had finally dropped dead. As we pieced it together, the timing appeared to coincide with the day Klomàn first renounced her sin and the devil. Indeed, God holds both life and death in His hand. He is in control. We praise God that Satan's bondage can be broken.

■ ■ ■ ■ ■ ■ ■

Pagan Pains

Easter weekend is usually the culmination of the *rara*—the Haitian version of the Catholic Mardi Gras. These marches weave folklore, voodoo, rum, songs, and sensuality together wildly. While waiting for Bruce at Ti Goâve one day, *rara* group after *rara* group forged their way up the street past me. I continually heard what sounded like the crack of a pistol as the leader of each group wildly gyrated in front of the swaying, dancing, surging mass of men, women, and children. He would take his bullwhip and unleash it with all his muscles, with a resulting *crack* like the shot of a gun. This was a means of calling up the demons, which are an integral part of the *rara*. The endless repetitious show of parade and costume, dance and song, beating of drums, blaring of trumpets, and sensuous sway of bodies dragged on and on. It continued all night long.

Drunkenness, debauchery, and immorality run rampant at these *rara* groups. Countless are the *rara* babies born to unwed mothers. It all seems so hopeless, but the Gospel is the power of God unto salvation. We will be so glad when the *rara* season is over. This noisome pestilence continually keeps us from our sleep. Since the *rara* groups frequent the witch doctors' homes, their path takes them right past Rick's house. During the weekend meetings with Brother Mose, Lamar and his family were sleeping in Rick's house, or trying to sleep, when they heard the *rara* marchers stop and say, "Let's kill the *blans* now." But praise God, our lives are in His hands.

Chapter 20
Sit Where They Sit

• April 1998

The gale winds shriek and my wind generator whines like a jet impatient to meet the clouds. As the rain dashes against the windows and sneaks in at every visible and invisible crack, I need to mop up the water on the floor. Even with the doors and windows closed, papers blow off my shelf. I now live in the cement block addition to my native hut, and right now it is cold and damp. I need a warm jacket. Yes, even here in Haiti. There have been two days of sixty-degree weather with extreme dampness and high winds, bringing the chill factor much lower.

But then my heart turns to some of the locals in their reed huts with thatch roofs. I can only imagine the gale-force winds whipping through sizable openings and the water coursing over mud floors where babies are trying to sleep. There is no stove, no heat, no comfortable chairs, very little food, no medicine, and no bathroom. Is it any wonder these people are continually sick? In my *kay* there is plenty of nourishing food, a small gas stove, a commode, running water, and a mostly dry floor. I have an abundance of clothing, shoes, books, Bibles, a computer, and other things. Yes, I have enough—way more than enough!

As we visit these homes and sit where they sit, pray with them, and sing with them, my heart is broken again and again with shame at my own thanklessness, prayerlessness, lack of love, and lack of burden for their souls. There is such a depth of poverty in this nation and an intense spiritual darkness and bondage.

The work here is demanding. It calls for much discipline, determination, dying to self, and sacrifice. But isn't that what the Word of God calls us to?

. . . .

As I climbed the mountain to my *kay* last night, my heart was filled with thanksgiving and praise. The *blans* meet together each Sunday evening for a time of worship in singing, Bible study, sharing, prayer, and praise. How needful and refreshing are our times of corporate worship! Pastor Rick pointed us to Christ in Proverbs 8, and we recounted the exciting events of the day.

In the regular Sunday morning service, from the beginning of the memory verse period shortly after 9:00 to the dismissal at 2:00, and on to the end of counseling at 3:30, a pageant of events unfolded, including demonic deliverances and testimonies of seekers.

I am always amazed at the willingness and fearlessness of these people in giving testimonies. Take Brother Obès, for example. He's eighty years old and loves to sing. The only problem is he can't carry a tune. But does that keep him from giving his testimony at church? No way! He just loves to give his testimony, and he always includes a song!

Bruce was not here to interpret, so the school principal shared a challenging message on true values and eternity. Afterward, Levi gave an invitation and people started responding.

Leda is a fifteen-year-old girl whose father burned her birth certificate in a drunken spree and disowned her. Even when sober, her father and mother chased her from home. She is now with her grandmother, but must leave. How our hearts bleed for this hurting, homeless girl seeking physical and spiritual help. So far she hasn't fully grasped her true spiritual need, so we are encouraging her to continue seeking the Lord.

Jakline, an eighteen-year-old girl deeply involved in voodoo, spirit mounting, and everything that goes with it, found deliverance. Mary

Rose, a single parent, also sensed her lost state. As she confessed her sins of the past and renounced Satan, she found new life in Christ.

Many were awaiting their turn. Suddenly Selès, Brother Obès' son, started running through the church, thrashing his arms violently and screaming incoherently. As he leaped out the door, people moved to get out of his path. A demon had mounted him. He continued to shriek as he somersaulted down the trail and into the mountains beyond. The accounts in the Gospels certainly become alive in new ways as we experience such happenings. How these people need Jesus!

> *Rescue the perishing, care for the dying;*
> *Jesus is merciful, Jesus can save.*
> —Fannie Crosby

Chapter 21

Snatched From the Enemy

· May 1998, written by Rick Hess

Madame Jil, the seventy-five-year-old wife of a local farmer, came to the clinic for medical help. She told Kathy she wanted to be converted, so I went and talked with her for a while. We suspected she may be suffering from brucellosis and started her on a course of treatment. We also scheduled a time to visit her in her home.

We found her lying on a mat on the floor in deep agony and pain. We spoke to her husband, who decidedly said he will not be converted till he sees what happens if his wife is converted. They had been Catholic but did not seem to find any hope or consolation in their religion. We explained to Jil that if God is speaking to his heart, he should take advantage of it right away rather than wait.

We continued talking about the issue of sin. Madame Jil could not think of any sins she was guilty of, so we named some sins and told her she should think about them and ask God to reveal her sins to her.

Later we returned, and her younger sister was there to help her. The sister told us her own story, and I was astonished to tears. She was the mother of fifteen children, of whom nine had died. Voodoo curses were strongly suspected, as the children had died one after the other. In desperation, she had fled to a Christian church where they encouraged her to fast and pray, and the deaths were stayed.

She also shared more about Madame Jil. Although Catholic, she and her husband were steeped in witchcraft. "The reason Jil refuses to get converted is because he owes the devil a cow," she said. "If I owed the devil a cow," this bold little widow then said, "I'd eat it and tell the devil to go to heaven and ask God for one if he wants one."

When we first visited Jil, he said he wanted us to convert his wife, but said he wasn't ready yet. Several visits later, however, his heart had changed and he answered the call of God's Spirit. He publicly prayed, renouncing the devil and all his works, as well as the Catholic Church and its deceptions, including bowing down to statues, praying to dead saints, and calling on Mary as a mediator. Then, after recognizing his sins, he asked God to reveal any other sins in his life. At this point he asked Christ to come into his heart, making Jesus the King of his life.

This all happened while he was kneeling on the front porch of his house. When we were finished praying, Jil invited us to come inside. He threw open the door to reveal a voodoo altar built of stone and mud. While we sang "What Can Wash Away My Sins" and "There Is Power in the Blood," Jil took a digging iron and with vigor broke down the altar, stone by stone. Afterward we prayed again and dedicated the house to the honor and glory of God, asking that Satan would have no more dominion over it.

Madame Jil was very ill and had been sleeping when her husband prayed. When she heard what had happened, she too was ready to pray. Willingly she renounced her sin and the works of the devil. Then she confessed her faith in Jesus Christ. It was a blessing to see this seventy-five-year-old woman and her husband wipe away tears and radiate joy on their faces because of their new life in Jesus Christ. They are among the brands plucked from the fire. Indeed, Jesus came to seek and to save that which was lost.

We are greatly encouraged. Although there are hindrances, God is working a mighty work here. Jesus' words to the Apostle Paul, I believe, were not meant for him only but for all of us. "I send thee, to open their eyes, and to turn them from darkness to light, and from the power of Satan unto God, that they may receive forgiveness of sins, and inheritance among them which are sanctified by faith that is in me" (Acts 26:17b, 18).

Chapter 22

Joy and Pain

- May 1998

Klomàn's mother, Madame Banav, was not home when we went to share with her on Saturday. The next day, however, both she and her husband were at our service. Afterward, she waited till Pastor Rick, Bruce, and I were free to talk with her. She told us she had been warned strongly by Madame Moyiz, a friend of hers, to stay clear of the missionaries. She had been told that Klomàn would die just like Pastor Matthew had died. Nevertheless, Madame Banav acknowledged that God had spoken to her. She was very open to the way of salvation, and we planned to meet with her again soon.

■ ■ ■ ■ ■ ■ ■

Christian Joys

On Sunday morning Jil gave an inspiring public testimony at church. He shared his new-found hope in Christ and his resolution to follow Him the whole way. "When I say yes, I mean yes," he said. "I will not turn back! I renounce the devil and all my past involvement with him. I spent much money and gave many sacrifices to the devil in the past, but got no help. No more! All my money and energies will go to the Lord. Whether I live or whether I die, I will serve the Lord!"

It was a pleasure to have the three girls, Itanya, Yvette, and Klomàn, come to visit Rhonda and Regina, Les's girls, the other day. They sang, shared photos, read Scriptures, and visited. We need to support them with prayer, counseling, and encouragement.

Rick and I visited an older couple last week. Their house was bare except for a little crude bed on which we sat, a chair, and a bucket. The man, Klesiyis, has suffered stomach problems for years and had been taken advantage of by the witch doctor, who demanded more and more—his goat, his chickens, and ultimately, his cow. In other words, the witch doctor stripped the couple of their money but helped not a whit. In the past, Madame Klesiyis had been a low-key herb doctor.

Pastor Rick shared the beauty of the Gospel of Christ. He read about sin and led them to repentance and renunciation of Satan and his works. To continue victoriously, both will need to make a public renunciation of Satan and demonic involvement.

Continued conversions have put a special spark of enthusiasm and revival in the church. It was touching as a group of about fifteen traipsed to Jil's house to sing and pray for him and Madame Jil. How exciting it was to hear them enthusiastically singing about Jesus as they walked the trails among their heathen neighbors. God is truly working here in the darkness of Alègue.

■ ■ ■ ■ ■ ■ ■

Madame Banav

Madame Banav has been seeking God and regularly attending services ever since Brother Mose was here and her daughter Klomàn found deliverance from her demonic holds. I am concerned for her and have placed her high on my prayer list.

On Sunday she shared that she was so torn by the spirits and demons that her head felt hot. Rick, Bruce, and I again talked with her and her husband and presented the Gospel in its power and simplicity. They heard, they pondered, and they knew we were telling them the truth, but they weren't quite ready to take the final step. Banav said, however, that he wants to have his house clean and free from all voodoo involvement. We asked them to pray and ponder deeply the truths we had given them, and asked to meet with them again. They are not far from the kingdom.

Madame Moyiz

An annual voodoo convention is held at Madame Moyiz's property. It is normally a big event for the voodoo *lwa* worshipers. Three times it has been scheduled and come to naught. This, we believe, is because of the prayers of God's people. The first time, Madame Moyiz was robbed in Port-au-Prince, so she had no money to fund it. The second time she was beat up in Port and had to recuperate. The third time she was sick.

Sister Kathy recently had the privilege of going into Madame Moyiz's home and singing and praying with her. Madame Moyiz seemed somewhat softened and open to the Gospel. She even said she was "coming," meaning she wants to become converted. But we found out that her "controlling spirit" then appeared and spoke to her, asking why she had rented out her house. She claimed she had not, but was told she had allowed the *blans* to come into her house and pray for her. After that when she saw the *blans* coming, she sometimes crawled under the bed or sneaked out the back door into a banana grove and hid herself.

Regrettably, her last voodoo convention did take place, but it was low-key and dampened by heavy rains Saturday night and Sunday. What was to be a three-day party lasted only about a day and a half, with about a hundred participants. But it did stir fear in the hearts of new believers, as well as the seekers. How thankful we are for the promise of 1 John 4:18: "There is no fear in love; but perfect love casteth out fear."

Chapter 23

Serving God by Serving Others

▪ June 1998

Ambulance Trip

God has His ways of zeroing in on a needy heart. It was two o'clock on a Saturday afternoon. I had my desk full of bills and paperwork and was scrambling to finish my monthly report for the mission board. Although I was running a bit behind schedule, I still hoped to finish in time to spend several hours working in my flower beds. Full of native Haitian flowers, these flower beds are not only a source of personal satisfaction, but also a place to unwind and be refreshed—physically, mentally, and spiritually. Today I was especially excited—I planned to begin work on a set of steps I had been dreaming about for months.

Earlier that afternoon I had heard Les talk to Rick on our two-way radio about a patient who had come in for emergency medical help, but I hadn't paid much attention. It wasn't long, however, before the radio crackled to life again, and this time it was for me.

"We need help!" Les said desperately. "We have an elderly man down here who is critically injured. He hit himself with a pick, lost his balance, and went crashing down the mountainside for over a hundred feet. He has a deep, horrible gash in his head, and we have to take him to the hospital. Could you come down?"

Leaving my paperwork, I rushed down to the clinic to help. Upon arrival I found Levi trying to comfort a weak, battered old man with blood dripping from his mouth and a huge, ugly gash on his forehead. I wondered how he could ever be transported on the back of a four-wheeler. His daughter, desperate to be with him at the hospital, had already left on foot to run the fourteen miles to Ti Goâve. She knew there would be no room for her on the ATV.

Although Les soon appeared with the ATV, our doubts whether we could safely transport such a critically injured man on a four-wheeler increased. Making a quick decision, we rushed to prepare the mission truck. The next question was, Who will drive it? Les said he felt he should be with his family since his wife had flown to Pennsylvania, and Rick needed to be at a meeting. That left me to take him—and I had my plans. I did not want to go and resented the interruption, so it was with some reluctance that I finally consented. With Levi and another man on board to help support Lewo, the injured man, our ambulance was off.

As we traveled over the rough, rugged terrain, I drove very carefully so as not to further distress the wounded man. In the meantime my heart smote me for my selfishness, and I had plenty of time to repent for my unwillingness. I thought of Jesus in Philippians 2 and of how God so lovingly and willingly came to earth in the form of a man. I thought of my own calling to be a servant as Jesus was. As God broke my heart, tears of repentance and compassion flowed. Talking to God as I drove, I promised to be a willing servant. God took me at my word and tested me again later that night.

Lewo was admitted to the hospital and immediately placed on IV. In the meantime, Levi was given a list of medications to buy. We soon got all the meds except the tetanus medication. Then began a ludicrous hunt as we went from pharmacy to pharmacy—little bitsy shops stuck at the strangest places—to hopefully buy the anti-tetanus serum. The number of stops finally reached eight, but with no success.

Time was rapidly fleeting, and I stressed to Levi that we must leave soon so that I could get back before dark. I greatly disliked driving these treacherous mountain roads after dark. The head nurse, however, informed me that Lewo had to stay till another doctor came from Port later that evening to check him further and administer the anti-tetanus serum. When the doctor finally arrived, he found that Lewo had suffered deep shock and required many stitches, but had no broken bones. When we finally left the hospital, dusk was settling in.

As I drove up toward Les's house, I was surprised to see a large crowd of Haitians. *What are all these people doing here?* I wondered. I soon found out.

On the floor of Les's porch lay an unconscious five-year-old girl who attends our school. Little Darla had lost her footing and tumbled several hundred feet down the rugged mountain. *Wow! Are accidents contagious?*

At first there was talk of making a litter and having four nationals carry her to the hospital because of our concern about a broken neck and the rough ride on a truck, but six hours by foot carrying a stretcher seemed too long for this critical case. Bruce could have possibly taken her in, but the next day we were having a special baptismal service, and in Haiti you never knew how long a trip like this might take. It didn't take me long to figure out what I should do. God had already dealt with my heart, so I offered to take her in, knowing full well that it would get very late and I would have to sleep in Ti Goâve.

With a board as a litter, little Darla was placed into the waiting truck onto the laps of her father and Bruce's brother. Although Darla's father was not a Christian, tears came to his eyes as Pastor Rick prayed for the serious situation. After the prayer, we set off into the dark. My body was exhausted, but praise God, my spirit was refreshed and willing.

Driving in Haiti is always a challenge, especially in the dark, so it was with a sigh of relief and a prayer of thanksgiving that we finally arrived at the hospital around 11 p.m. We went to awake a doctor at his house. *Knock, knock! Bang, bang! Toot, toot!* No success, so back to the hospital we went. Little Darla, who was finally starting to regain consciousness, was carried carefully into the hospital.

Soon Remòn returned to the truck with a medication prescription list the nurses had given her, and we started our rounds trying to locate a pharmacy that would open its doors to us. It was now nearly midnight. Remòn had already roused her brother-in-law, a young policeman in Ti Goâve, to help her in this process. Again we used the knock-bang-toot approach at two places with no success. We then went to a friend's place at midnight and roused him from his sleep, and he fortunately knew a pharmacist who might have the meds. Once more we tried the knock-bang-toot process loudly and repeatedly. This time we were successful.

We finally delivered the meds and headed for some of Pastor Matthew's relatives in town. Once again we banged and banged to rouse the sleepers to let us in. It was now after one o'clock. I slowly relaxed and fell asleep, but soon noises started that continued off and on till morning. It was like a carnival—a Haitian-shouting, dog-barking, rooster-crowing contest all combined with the rasping, blaring horns on many large trucks. I tried to block out all the noises, but without ear plugs it was impossible. It was a fitful night.

By 5 a.m. everyone was stirring and by 6:00 we returned to the hospital, where I was able to see both patients. Little Darla seemed to be stable and was resting well. No one was available to give any report about her condition, but there were no broken bones. Poor Lewo looked quite pathetic and worn out. After giving him some encouragement, we left for home. We reached Alègue around 8:30 a.m. Even though I was tired, I did experience special grace, for which I praise the Lord.

Chapter 24

Beautiful Baptism

• June 1998

Sweet the moments, rich in blessing,
Which before the cross I spend;
Life and health and peace possessing
From the sinner's dying friend.
                    —Walter Shirley

On the same day of my ambulance trip, seventy-five-year-old Jil was baptized. In his public testimony at church he told how God had saved him and his wife, and how he wants to serve Jesus till his dying day. "I have already been baptized in my heart," he said.

Then Madame Jil gave her testimony. She thanked and praised God for her salvation and told how for a long time she could not even support her head from falling to the side, and her body was racked with pain. With joy she shared how God, through the missionaries' help, had touched her body. She also desired baptism but was not able to climb the high, treacherous mountain behind Pastor Rick's house and descend to the river on the other side. She would be baptized at her own house or the church building later.

How inspiring and rewarding it was to hear the Gospel ring out through the valley as the simple, sincere Christians sang heartily from the bottom of their hearts. What a testimony to the voodoo-worshiping neighbors!

My body was exhausted from the previous long night, but God gave me special strength as I hiked up the mountain. At the top, we had a choice of two paths to descend to the river. I followed the left one, which descended abruptly. We climbed down a sheer cliff with only protruding pieces of small rocks as miniature steps here and there.

As much as I enjoy hiking, this was a test for me. It helped me to understand how five-year-old Darla could tumble several hundred feet down a mountain cornfield, and how the aged Lewo could lose his balance while raising his pick in his own field and then tumble down the mountain.

As I stood in the shade of the cliff to protect my head from the sun, I noticed some secret observers on top of the next range—curious children and adults who came from upstream where they had been washing their clothing.

Close beside me were my special friends, Banav and his wife, who had finally committed their hearts to the Lord. With joy I observed their rapt attention and sometimes verbal response to Pastor Rick's teaching on baptism. On a huge boulder stood Bruce as interpreter. In the water with Pastor Rick was Levi, who assisted Rick in the baptism. Nearby was Sister Remòn, who received Madame Edgar after her baptism.

What jubilation was expressed afterward as we sang "I Have Decided to Follow Jesus"—except for the tears of Madame Rene, who had hoped to be baptized but whose testimony of salvation was not clear. She and a few others who requested baptism will receive further instruction and counsel to help ascertain their relationship with Jesus. We in no way want to discourage true believers, but we do not want to give an uncertain hope through baptism. Oh, for the wisdom of the Holy Spirit in all these matters.

On the homeward trek I again chose the rugged path. Ever since I was a child, I've delighted in climbing rugged rocks. For me, climbing up was always easier than descending. Ahead of me was eighty-year-old Brother Obès. Despite his age, he scrambled up the rugged terrain and cliff with the alacrity of a nimble goat. I followed, but not as nimbly.

In the evening we had a small fellowship meal with the missionaries and Bruce, Remòn, and Levi at Pastor Rick's house. Having had but three and a half hours of interrupted sleep the night before, I retired to my *kay* fairly early and was soon lost in sleep. I had turned off the handheld radio to prevent interruption, but that did not prevent Bruce and Levi from coming to talk with me. They discovered a groggy-eyed dreamer and soon left. I was off to dreamland again.

Next I heard, "Papa Harold, Papa Harold!"

Yvette and a friend had come for some water from my cistern. I mumbled out my window, giving permission, and sank back into oblivion—or so I thought. A short time later I awoke to the sounds of raucous drums and music similar to rock and roll, accompanied by the demonized shouting and conversation of the voodoo party on the knoll overlooking my house. They had carted in a generator and were using a type of boom box. I groped for the earplugs I keep close to my bed for such intrusions, stuffed them into my anxious ears, and dropped off to a fitful doze.

Chapter 25

Adventures of the Gospel Team

• June 1998, written by Andrew Weaver

Spending a week in Haiti with a Gospel team was a dream come true for me. How well I remember that first Sunday morning in Alègue, our first introduction to a Haitian church meeting.

A typical meeting is supposed to begin at about 9 a.m. In reality, people straggle in over a two-or three-hour period. After some songs and prayer, a seemingly interminable memorization period begins. The leader announces a reference and the congregation repeats it. He chants through the verse phrase by phrase, with the congregation repeating after him. There are frequent corrections and reprimands from the leader, as well as constant exhortations to increase the volume. With the high rate of illiteracy, this memorizing is very important since it is almost the only way to get God's Word into the people's hearts.

At seemingly random intervals, there is more singing or prayer. The prayer is sometimes led by an individual, but is more often corporate. It begins slowly and softly, but quickly builds to a deafening babble. For someone unaccustomed to praying in this way, the noise is badly distracting. Add to this the fact that we're packed shoulder to sweating shoulder, with more people arriving all the time, and prayer becomes a real exercise in discipline. It is a comfort to know that this apparent bedlam is no confusion to God, and that He hears the cry of each sincere heart.

The pastor or moderator often leads the congregation in deafening chants of "Praise the Lord! Praise the Lord!" It always takes several tries before he's satisfied that they're shouting loudly enough.

Testimonies make up a major part of the service. In fact, if someone wants to share a testimony, they need to hand in a paper to the moderator, requesting a turn. At some time during the service, the opportunity is given to share, and how they share! Most testimonies end with a song, often a solo. Some of the ones who sing have no talent for it, but that's no deterrent. They still make a joyful noise and are heartily applauded for their efforts when they finish. It appears that stage fright is a uniquely American concept, because it seems to be unheard of in Haitian culture.

All this time the packed bodies are radiating more and more heat, the sweat begins to run, and still more people keep arriving. Benches that are apparently full somehow find room for one more person, and then one more . . . .

The patient endurance of the people is almost incredible. Hour after hour they sit on those narrow, hard benches, looking satisfied and cheerful. Even the men who are fully decked out in suits somehow manage to appear comfortable. Meanwhile, the visitors are stealthily sneaking sips of water from their bottles, fanning themselves, and trying not to look miserable.

Cultural tradition calls for women to cover their heads while in church. Apparently they utilize anything that happens to be available: doilies, scarves, washcloths, kerchiefs, straw hats, or even baseball caps. Although few people understand the principle behind the covering, they consider it very important. During one testimony period we attended, a woman began to sing her solo without having covered her head. A man in the front row solemnly rose from his seat and draped his white handkerchief over her hair. She calmly accepted it without missing a word of her song.

Most of the people are very attentive to the preaching in spite of occasional distractions by dogs, chickens, lizards, or tarantulas. It is not unusual for the audience to applaud the pastor when he finishes his sermon and takes his seat. The service was dismissed at 2:30 p.m., which gave just enough time for those who had walked from six hours away to return home by dark.

. . . .

Off to the Mountains

Our trek into the mountains was to have begun at 5 a.m. on Monday morning. In truest Haitian style, we finally set off at 7:30 in a noisy confusion of people, horses, and mules. Besides our team, there were Rick Hess and his son Nick, Grandpa Harold, our interpreter Bruce, his cousin Remòn, Yvette, Klomàn, and Itanya, along with some boys and men to help with the pack animals.

Barely thirty minutes after starting, we were caught by a sudden rain. We took shelter in a cockfight shack where they hold weekly cockfights, but not before we had been thoroughly drenched. We sang and tried to keep up our spirits until the rain stopped and we could continue. The trails were much more slippery and treacherous after their soaking, and we had to pick our way carefully among the rocks and mud. It was with a rather drippy, soggy sense of relief that we arrived at our destination a few hours later.

We were just beginning to realize what Haitian hospitality meant. Within a short time of our arrival, we were being served bread and coffee, and then had a full meal shortly afterward. We were shown to a room and left to ourselves while everyone else ate outside. Although our hosts would not have considered eating with us, they would have willingly given us anything we asked for. It took some time to get used to the idea that we should feel honored at being left alone to eat. It was especially hard when we saw that we were being served better food than the others, but it was a cultural tradition we were forced to accept.

Our first time at setting up tents drew quite an audience. The people seemed dumbfounded that it was possible for a "house" to come out of those tiny bags we were carrying. We tried to imagine how they felt and finally decided it would be comparable to having a tribe of desert Bedouins camp in our back yard.

There was a service that evening in spite of intermittent rain. The team sang, and a few of us shared our testimonies. Before Pastor Rick began preaching, a savage dogfight broke out right among the seats. The dogs were so fierce and determined to continue fighting that we wondered if they weren't diabolically inspired. At least it gave us something new to pray for. Before each meeting, we would ask God to prevent any distractions that the devil could use to hinder the truth from being heard.

Our first night in the tents was memorable, to say the least. The courtyard was so narrow that the tents rubbed walls on each side. Worse yet, a low stone wall ran along the front of the tent, so we had to climb over it while at the same time ducking to enter the door. We boys were packed in shoulder to shoulder, dirty, sweaty, and uncomfortable, but we wouldn't have traded places with anyone in the world. Someone mentioned the fact that we could be at home, warm and dry and comfortable, while someone else could be in our place. We agreed that it would have been a tragedy.

. . . .

School Visit

Tuesday's hike was much more pleasant than the previous day's. The trails had dried and were much less treacherous, although still difficult because they were mostly uphill. It was a pleasure upon arriving at Kadèt to find a relatively large flat area for our tents, as opposed to the previous night's alley.

That afternoon we climbed farther up the mountain and visited a school that Bruce supports. It was hard for me, a former teacher, to imagine successfully teaching with so few resources and such a primitive building. Very few of the students even had books, so most of the work was done on the blackboard. With the holes in the roof and the gaps in the walls, we could only imagine what it was like when it rained. The students were very respectful, standing as we entered the building and singing a song of welcome for us. We reciprocated with a few songs of our own.

. . . .

Home Visitation

On Wednesday we got to try our skills at creek-side laundry. The results were far from impressive. There was green scum and slime in the water that seemed to make the clothes only dirtier. We finally managed to replace the dirt on the clothes with scum, then took the clothes up to the house and hung them over the bushes to dry. One of the Haitian girls was so dismayed at seeing the condition of Nick's formerly white trousers that she washed them again, with much more professional results.

The rest of the day was spent in visitation—on the run! The pastor who led us and set the pace wanted to visit every member of his church so no one would feel slighted, so he kept us busy. We would begin singing as we neared a house, then squeeze inside while the song continued. Next came prayer, which always concluded with everyone quoting the Lord's Prayer in French. After a testimony or exhortation and more prayer or singing, we scurried to the next place to repeat the process.

That was the day we were introduced to nature's great healer and refresher: coconut water. Pastor Rick had told us how delicious and refreshing it was, so we tried to be enthused about it for his sake. We didn't all succeed. After all, Pastor Rick had told us he liked every food he had ever tried, so his conviction that something tasted good was not too reassuring.

We had a service that evening at the schoolhouse, where the team again shared some songs and Pastor Rick preached. The little building was packed, as usual. The students who attend the school are expected to attend the church services also, so there is always a large group of children present. It was exciting to realize the potential they represented. If they continue to receive godly instruction in their school and church, they will be the next generation of missionaries to their own people.

When we began our hike the next morning, our hosts, as usual, accompanied us for almost half the trip before saying goodbye and returning to their homes. It was humbling to realize to what lengths they go to show hospitality, especially when I compared it to what we do for most of our guests. If those people find out in heaven that they occasionally entertained angels unawares, they will have nothing to be ashamed of.

One evening we wanted to take a "shower," but there was no water available right then. We naively volunteered to go get some. The old lady who showed us the way was highly amused at the idea of three white men going to carry water, and we could see her shoulders silently shaking with laughter most of the way down the trail to the water source. Judging by her expression, she probably had some doubts as to our ability to handle a full bucket of water too. It was at least a mile, and although it was downhill and our buckets were empty, we were sweating by the time we arrived. The real test came as we staggered back up the hill carrying full buckets. The Haitians who saw us were amazed that we were so ignorant as to carry our buckets by the handles. Everyone knows you carry water on your head!

Saturday's hike brought us to our final stop, where we went through the routine of setting up camp one last time. Most of the Haitian girls traveling with us became suddenly ill that evening as a result of something they ate. Thankfully, it was a short-lived attack, and some of them even recovered quickly enough to attend prayer meeting that evening.

Several of the team members seemed to sense an oppressive power of darkness in that place, so we spent extra time in prayer together until we received an assurance of God's protection. Seeing the power and victory that come through the name of Jesus Christ gave us a totally new sense of awe and reverence for our almighty Lord. His presence was very real and comforting for the rest of our stay there.

After such an eventful week, it was almost a letdown to think of returning home. However, we were deeply thankful to have been blessed with the opportunity to experience the things we did. I believe each team member would agree that our lives will never be quite the same. The same Lord who brought us together accompanied us each moment, and He is the One who must receive all the honor and glory.

Chapter 26

Mango Tree Meeting

▪ June 1998

It was four o'clock Thursday afternoon when we started gathering under the mango tree. At first it seemed only children were coming to the meeting which we had planned for the local families to come and hear about God. Mose was here to preach for us. He was accompanied by a Gospel team. People started trickling in as we sang, but the spirit of the singing seemed low-key and weak. Mose told us later that at that point he had no inspiration to preach. Bruce also seemed quiet and somewhat discouraged. We saw people standing off in the shadows, simply watching and waiting. The Gospel team sensed the spirit and went off to pray.

Suddenly people started coming. I was trying to find seats for them as they meandered in toward the mango tree. I soon saw Madame Moyiz, the main *manbo*, coming. As is custom, I took her by the hand and led her to a seat. I noticed she did not wear her normal red head kerchief but a white one.

Levi went to the cockfight building nearby and started bringing the men in. There was no cockfight that night. I led a red-turbaned woman to a seat near Madame Moyiz. I discovered later she was also a *manbo*. Soon we were packed out and more were coming. All around I observed people gazing and listening with interest or curiosity. By now Mose had become inspired and spoke earnestly about Jesus and His many miracles, showing His love, interest, and ability to help in every need. Bruce interpreted in a powerful way.

Suddenly Klomàn's uncle Towo came walking along the trail with his

105

pick. I walked up to him, took him by the hand, and asked him to sit with me on the ground for the service. He is also involved in witchcraft.

Later Alfred, Madame Moyiz's brother who is a *bòkò*, stood out on the road. I went and led him into the gathering. It was amazing! Four witch doctors were hearing the powerful Gospel of Christ through the preaching of Brother Mose!

Next came the testimonies and some singing. Klomàn shared a fearless, powerful testimony of her deliverance and sang with a few other young Haitian sisters. Yvette, Itanya, and others also gave their testimonies.

Now the climax! Sister Kathy shared a simple testimony in Creole, telling of her salvation through Jesus, and how precious and loving He is to her. She went on to tell how God had given her a great love for the locals. The Spirit moved her to tell of her special love and burden for Madame Moyiz. Then she asked this despised *manbo* to come stand beside her. Madame Moyiz came, and Kathy embraced her, telling her how much she loved her.

Next this *manbo*, feared by all the heathen locals, spoke. "This is a wonderful meeting. I think this is the first time in my life that I have really felt love and acceptance. Everyone else hates me. When anything bad happens, like when people get sick or when their crops fail, they blame me! I feel so sad and lonely sometimes. But tonight I can feel the love of God. It is so wonderful! I am not a Christian yet, but I would like to learn more and become one."

How we all rejoiced and praised God as she was seated again. Bruce told us he has a burning in his bones like the prophet Jeremiah. Brother Mose asked to speak once more, and with beauty and power he wielded the sword of the Spirit once more. Oh, the power of the simple Gospel and the true love of God!

Brother Mose told Kathy to tell Madame Moyiz that should the demons cause her problems tonight, she should come to Les's house for prayer. As the group was dispersing, many of the Christians went to Madame Moyiz and hugged and blessed her.

While speaking to Pastor Rick, Madame Moyiz asked if Kathy

would pray with her. We decided to meet with her on Les's porch. Kathy and Bruce talked with her while a few of us prayed in the living room. Kathy asked if it was okay for Brother Mose to pray for her. "No problem," she said.

Then this feared witch doctor fell on her knees while Brother Mose laid hands on her and prayed to the God of heaven. Many of us knelt and joined in prayer, asking that all her wickedness, her demons, and her selfishness would be dumped out of her like water from an upside-down barrel, and that she would repent of her sins, give her life to Jesus, and be filled with God's Spirit.

"Thank you so much for everything you've done for me tonight," she said when we arose from our knees. "I want to know more about God, about Jesus. I will keep coming to your meetings. Please keep praying for me."

We rejoice for this breakthrough, but realize that we need humility, brokenness, and wisdom as we try to teach Madame Moyiz the way to salvation.

■ ■ ■ ■ ■ ■ ■

Mariklòd, an applicant for baptism the next Sunday, shared her story with us. My heart was wrenched with pain for this tenderhearted youth, and at the same time I was intensely indignant as she shared her plight. Her parents lived in Port and on occasion visited Alègue. Mariklòd had to care for three younger children and an older brother while her parents were in town. Often there was no food. She shared how she has given her heart to the Lord, renounced the devil, and has chosen to live for Jesus. My heart bled as she told how she must go into hiding at night among the trees to be kept from "lewd fellows of the baser sort" if her older brother is not at home. She now spends much time at the House of Matthew with some of the other young sisters.

Another girl shared how she struggles with guilt and inferiority because she is not the daughter of the father in her home. Brother Mose gently helped her to realize she was free from the sin of her parents.

Our prayer is that these young girls might truly find victory and comfort as they set out in their life of faith.

Chapter 27

Manbo Under Conviction

• August 1998

Today Madame Moyiz came to the clinic and said she can't eat well. Kathy took her aside and suggested that maybe the reason she can't eat is because God is calling her.

She said, "Yes, I know He's calling me. When I lie down to sleep, He calls me." She had such an open face as she spoke.

"You know how other people have repented of their sins and said they are finished with the devil and all his works," Kathy reminded her. "You saw how Madame Banav burned the voodoo things in her house. Are you ready to do that?"

"Yes, I am ready," she replied.

"Good!" Kathy replied. "I'll tell Rick and he'll want to meet with you soon. We'll keep praying for you."

The next day Rick and Cherry, Les and Kathy, and Bruce went to see Madame Moyiz. Even though Rick had made arrangements with her, she was not there when they got there, but came after a short while. She had been hiding at her brother's place and had told someone she was scared. They prayed together when she arrived, and then talked with her for a while. She seemed very open and again confessed her desire to be a Christian. "I have some voodoo items that are partly owned by others and I can't burn them. I'm planning to give them back on Tuesday. Then I am going to get right with God. I'm not going to wait," she declared.

This is exciting! Oh, that she would become a beautiful, powerful handmaiden of God, a testimony of the delivering and keeping power of our Lord Jesus Christ!

· · · · · · ·

The Girls

Klomàn, Yvette, Itanya, Mariklòd, and some of the other young girls who have been delivered from voodoo are staying at the House of Matthew. They are being nurtured and guided by Remòn, Bruce, and Levi. This is causing some conflict with Mama Matthew. She feels threatened and does not comprehend all the changes taking place. Furthermore, there are too many people at her house even though it is much larger than the average dwelling. Wisdom says they cannot all continue to live there. But for many of them, going back to their homes seems like placing lambs in the midst of wolves.

· · · · · · ·

New Home

I finally found a house to rent for Yvette, Itanya, and a newcomer, Benedit. Yvette and Itanya continue to grow and be faithful to Jesus, though they are still being abused and persecuted by their family. Benedit is a woman who is being mentored by Kathy. Her husband left her three years ago. Her heart was opened through a clinic contact. She has also been persecuted and abused by her voodoo family. She will serve as mother for her own two children and Yvette and Itanya.

There is a disturbing lawsuit against Remòn, Bruce, and the girls which will go to the courts. Yvette and Itanya's wicked, jealous sister is the instigator. Among other things Bruce is being charged with having the girls as his mistresses. It is unsettling, but God is in control. Bruce has many strikes against him currently—the loss of Pastor Matthew, the huge funeral debt, and now the lawsuit.

Chapter 28

Furlough

· September 1998

Ineeded new eyeglasses and had some other business to do, so I took a much-needed furlough to Pennsylvania. What a stark contrast the affluent States are to Haiti, the poorest country in the Western Hemisphere. I got some dental work done and updated my glasses. I spent more money for each than my dear friends in Haiti make in a whole year.

I had the special privilege of fellowshipping with precious friends whom I had not seen for fifteen months. What joy! What an inspiration! I was humbled, grateful, and inspired as I heard how God's people were deeply involved in praying for the work in the dark hills of Haiti.

Anna Joy Kauffman from Bedford, Pennsylvania, traveled back to Haiti with me. She will be Kathy's right-hand helper in the clinic. We're really excited to expand our medical services now that we were able to rent two rooms in a large house in which to have our clinic. It will be so much better than using Les's back porch.

On the trip down I told Anna Joy, "I am going home."

"I am going home too," she responded.

Indeed, that is her spirit, and she has already proven to be a great contribution to our work.

We arrived at Alègue much later than we had hoped. Bruce, Remòn, and Levi received me with warmth and love. I got a quick briefing from Pastor Rick to bring me up to date with the happenings while

I was gone. I rejoiced for the new conversions and the continuing growth of our people.

What a lovely, inspiring welcome awaited me when I arrived at Mama Matthew's house. As I approached, I heard lovely singing. Madame Matthew, Yvette, Itanya, and some others were there to bless and receive me. In my weariness, great joy flooded my spirit. Soon Klomàn also came running to greet me.

My dear friends eagerly hoisted my luggage on their heads and willingly carried it up to my *kay*. I slowly followed them up the rugged path. It was pitch dark, but over my head, gleaming with an intensity that can be seen only in a remote place like this, were the stars of heaven. They seemed to say, "Welcome home and God bless you."

Arriving home, I found a freshly scrubbed porch with pots of native flowers sitting and hanging here and there. My Haitian spiritual daughters had done what they knew would please and bless their "papa!" How lovely, yet humbling! The same was true of my white "grandchildren"—Les's children. Leslie had started my mini fridge and filled my water container with drinking water, while Rhonda, Regina, and others had cleaned my house, fed my roaches (with deadly roach cookies), washed sheets, and prepared a welcome poster.

■　■　■　■　■　■　■

The responsibilities of day-by-day family life and chores, the intense spiritual and natural demands on us, the increasing involvements of the clinic, the living in continual public view, and the requests of the nationals are extremely time-consuming and depleting to the spiritual and emotional lives of the workers here. There are countless decisions to be made. How to find time to be alone with God and be refreshed in spirit, body, and emotions is an age-old problem for missionaries. Many missionaries burn out in Haiti. Indeed, I understand why. I have heard many reports of inner conflict and turmoil among workers of various groups in the country. How we need to guard our hearts lest the enemy take advantage.

Chapter 29

Madame Te

• October 1998

Idistinctly remember the first time I met Madame Te. She was crippled and it appeared that only her skin held her emaciated body together. From the time she was a baby, she had scooted about on her knees, as she had no strength in her puny, malformed legs. She lived in a dilapidated hut, her scant food and clothing provided by those who took pity on her. Her clothing was always tattered and filthy, and the air reeked with her body odor. Outwardly I was repulsed, but inwardly compassion welled up in my heart. She often talked about God.

One day during a severe rain and windstorm, the rotted supports of her hut collapsed, and she had to crawl under the debris for shelter from the dashing torrents of wind and rain. When I learned of her disaster, I went to visit her. Vivid is the memory of her emerging from under the debris and filth of her collapsed shack. We immediately provided an old tent for temporary shelter. No one else wanted to help her because whoever helped with her house and survival would be responsible for her burial when she died. Sometime later, compassionate visitors and local workers who saw her plight provided means to erect a simple new hut for her.

Last Sunday afternoon we got word that she had died. Her closest relatives lived in Port, except for a deranged son in Ti Goâve, so people thought we should be responsible for the funeral since she had sometimes come to our church services. It was urgent that we bury her promptly, so we decided to make a coffin and planned a service for one o'clock Monday afternoon. On Monday morning Rick and I scurried to rip, plane, and sand boards to assemble the coffin. We soon got word that the service would be at eleven o'clock. We scrambled and finally finished assembling and lining the crude yet comely coffin.

As I approached the little hut that housed the dead body, the stench of death blasted my nostrils. The Haitians who placed the corpse in the box had draped their faces with heavy cloths. Some people standing nearby stuffed green leaves into their nostrils. We had the service at the home of Judge Alsiyis, a relative, where the coffin was later placed in a family vault. The assembled group was not large. Pastor Rick had no interpreter and preached a simple message in Creole, telling about the call of God to all men. It was a simple, subdued service with some group singing and also a selection by the missionaries.

While Pastor Rick was preaching, I observed his son Nick sidle up to him and share a few words. Then Pastor Rick asked me and a few sisters to pray with and encourage Yvette, who appeared to be having a spiritual and physical attack from the enemy. We have learned that there are times when fear, anger, or unforgiveness seem to open the minds of these young Christians to Satan and his demons, who then seek to take advantage.

It was a faith builder as we again saw the power of Satan lose its grip on this dear young sister as we earnestly prayed for her and encouraged her to cry out to God for deliverance. Oh, for a simple childlike faith for all our needs!

Yes, Madame Te's body was returned again to the earth. To many, she was a nobody. But she was definitely one of those Jesus was talking about in Matthew 25:40: "Inasmuch as ye have done it unto the least of these, ye have done it unto me." Yes, Madame Te was the epitome of the "least of these."

Chapter 30

"Brake Their Bands in Sunder"

• October 1998

The Lord's Day dawned clear, lovely, and beaming. While preparing for the day, I listened to the Gospel of Mark on tape and was struck with Christ's interest and power over evil spirits, as in the case of the possessed Gaderene. This was especially vivid to me in light of our experiences here. The worship service was inspiring and uplifting as the believers poured out their hearts in worship to God, all the while packed on the benches like sardines. Pastor Rick then preached a message about Peter walking on the water. At the close of the service, Brother Levi gave an invitation and four came forward.

Suddenly pandemonium broke loose with hideous snake-like hissing, hooting, growling, and shouting. Demons had once again mounted Brother Obès' only son, Selès. He began to thrash violently. Brother Banav jumped over his bench to try to restrain him. Soon several others jumped to his aid, as Selès had supernatural strength. After getting control of him, they carried him to the front of the church, where they restrained him on the floor. As he continued to growl, hiss, and chant, the church surrounded him. We cried out in prayer and rebuked the evil spirits in the name of the Lord.

"Isn't that the man who ran out of the church a while back?" a sister asked.

"Yes," a man replied, "but we got him this time!"

Probably the most outstanding thing about this satanic attack was the church's response. Only six months ago these same people would have cringed in fear when confronted with something like this. They would have stood back, waiting for the missionaries to do something. But today they were boldly battling in the name of the Lord Jesus Christ. Praise God! Some seemed almost indignant that Satan would dare try to dominate the service.

Pastor Rick and I soon joined the group that had seized Selès. Like the Gaderene demoniac, he had superhuman strength. We took him into the little back room and laid him down on the floor. Several Haitian brothers helped hold him as we demanded the spirit to give his name. The first demon left reluctantly, only to have another one manifest itself. This one argued at length, demanding that we had no right to tell him to leave his house.

The national brothers responded, "That's a lie!"

By the time Selès calmed down, several demons had given their names and left.

Finally we were down to Selès, drenched with sweat and covered with dirt, but sitting up and truly in his right mind. With the demons gone, he was now able to call out to Jesus for deliverance from his sins and to renounce the devil and all his works.

It was a glorious time in the Lord. Of special beauty and encouragement were the bright faces of Yvette, Itanya, and Klomàn standing right beside the unfolding drama, praying to God. They were singing and lifting their hands heavenward in trust, prayer, and praise. They knew what Selès was going through!

I shall not soon forget Selès's face. It was no longer tense and cruel-looking, but relaxed and pleasant as he renounced the devil and his works and committed himself to the Lord Jesus Christ.

Papa Obès's joy knew no bounds as he embraced his "new" son.

■ ■ ■ ■ ■ ■ ■

Benedette Delivered

A week later we rejoiced to see Selès in our worship service "in his right mind." We also rejoiced to see how packed the church house was. Truly God was working in people's hearts.

About mid-service, the peaceful atmosphere was shattered by another demonic episode. A lady named Benedette was near the front and suddenly began struggling and thrashing about while Anna Joy and some others tried to support her. Her face was cruelly contorted, and her eyes were gruesomely rolling back into her head. She was quickly taken to another room.

In the whole ensuing deliverance, Anna Joy was by her side, pleading to God for her, often wiping from the woman's face the perspiration which literally poured from her body. We prayed in the name of Jesus and commanded the demons to reveal their names and leave. Several exposed themselves and left.

At one point Benedette came to her senses and wanted to speak, but a dumb spirit seemed to possess her. While this was going on, her little child cried disconsolately and refused to leave her mother. Several times I placed her on my lap, wiped her eyes and runny nose, and tried to comfort her.

Because of the planned baptisms, Pastor Rick, Levi, and some others had to leave for the river with the congregation, so some visiting deacons and leaders from outlying churches helped in the deliverance. Finally the demons revealed that they were twenty-one in number. By the authority of Jesus they were cast out.

Immediately the air was filled with testifying, praising God, and praying by Benedette. She renounced Satan, confessed that Jesus Christ came to this earth in the flesh, and committed herself to the Lordship of Jesus. By now the dear woman was completely exhausted. But her face was clear, no longer contorted, and her eyes showed rest and peace. Afterward she went to the House of Matthew for food and rest.

Once again the great Lord Jesus vanquished Satan! How beautifully He set the captive free! Benedette is now a handmaiden of the Lord Jesus! "He brought them out of darkness and the shadow of death, and brake their bands in sunder. Oh, that men would praise the Lord for his goodness, and for his wonderful works to the children of men!" (Psalm 107:14-15).

Chapter 31

Hurricane Georges

• October 1998

T he news was everywhere. "Prepare! Hurricane Georges is coming!" High winds were the first evidence of the approaching storm. My wind generator whined and roared. The edges of my aluminum roof flapped, groaned, rattled, and creaked. By 7 p.m. the rains started. It pelted my aluminum roof with a deafening din, and the winds roared to gale-force proportions. I wondered if the house and porch would stay intact. I had lost a porch to a storm before and wondered if something worse might happen this time. I finally stuffed foam plugs into my ears, committed my circumstances to the heavenly Father, and went to sleep.

Later I awakened to dripping water and was relieved to find that it was only the intense winds driving the water under the overlapping tin. By four o'clock in the morning, my flashlight revealed that the rain gauge was overflowing. My cistern, which had been half empty, was also overflowing. By then, water was seeping through the walls, so I used some heavy towels to soak it up. The winds also forced water through the window edges onto my desk and computer. Another towel! By then, the cold, wet conditions were seeping into my body.

Daylight came slowly. I was startled when water started flowing in through my ground-level study window. I quickly donned a rain jacket and boots and with a shovel soon corrected the problem.

By 3:30 that afternoon it was so dark that I lighted a kerosene lamp. It was still pouring, and over twelve inches of rain had fallen.

The next day it was still raining, but I put on my rain gear and headed down the mountain. I was told that our bridge had washed out again, so I headed down to take a look.

I was startled at what I discovered. The bridge was totally gone, with a torrent of rushing water where it had been. There was no way we could go anywhere, even on foot, until the turbulent flood waters subsided. I found deep washouts all over the place.

I wondered how all my Haitian friends were faring. They lived in such crowded, unsanitary, muddy huts. I struggled as I attempted to imagine myself in such conditions. I am sure there will be much sickness in the wake of this hurricane.

The hurricane was in no hurry to leave. Rain and high winds continued for several more days until it gradually subsided. With the bridge washed out, we obviously couldn't use the road until it got fixed. Bruce got permission from Alfred the *bòkò* to make a temporary ATV trail through his land, down into the riverbed, and up the steep cliff to the road again. Thankfully, Alfred's heart has become soft toward our mission, another evidence of God's work here.

Chapter 32

Pressing On

▪ October 1998

Rhode, one of Madame Moyiz's daughters, is a police officer in Port. One evening, bedecked with earrings, red fingernails and toenails, and a hat to match, she came to visit Kathy with several of her younger siblings. Her hardened face matched her attire, but she came, nonetheless, and on her own accord. She said she would be happy if the rest of the family got converted, but she wasn't ready to take the step herself. Besides, her three-year term as police officer did not expire till February. She seemed a bit aloof and uncertain at first, but shared that she had gone to a local church out here some years ago and was now a Catholic.

Kathy shared some verses with her and brought out a bottle of clean water, which, she explained, represented a newborn baby. She added some iodine, telling her the iodine represents the sins that cloud our lives. She then added some bleach to represent the blood of Christ. The bleach chemically reacted with the iodine and made the water clear again. "That is what Jesus does for us," Kathy told her.

Later Rhode joined Les's children in singing some songs. Apparently God is working in her heart. We pray for a genuine conversion; not just a conversion to a different religion, but to Jesus.

▪ ▪ ▪ ▪ ▪ ▪ ▪

Lamatinye

At the entrance to the mission drive there are weekly cockfights with demonic overtones. These weekly gatherings include much gossiping, ribald talking, and general works of darkness. Although it makes the poor even poorer, it is "blessed" by the local witch doctors. My dream is that someday the cockfights will stop and the place will become a place to share Gospel literature.

Down the road just a few hundred yards from the cockfight shelter lives a heathen man named Krismàn. Steeped in voodoo worship and ungodliness, this man is very poor and unversed in Bible truth.

In Krismàn's home lives Lamatinye, the daughter of Krismàn's live-in companion. Lamatinye is a single parent and is expecting another child. At one time she lived with an aunt in Port and gained some knowledge of the Bible. A few days ago she let us know she wanted spiritual help, so Pastor Rick, Cherry, Anna Joy, and Bruce stopped by to talk to her. They soon saw that she was serious about changing her life. When asked if she was ready to turn her life over to God, she understood her personal need of deliverance and repented of her past immorality. She fell on her knees, confessed her sins, and wept and cried out to God for forgiveness and salvation. Then she was led in a prayer of consecration. Praise the Lord!

During this time, Lamatinye's heathen mother listened with rapt attention in the adjoining room. Also, unknown to us at the time, Madame Moyiz came past and secretly observed everything. She still has not made a complete surrender. It is clear that a battle is raging in her heart.

· · · · · · ·

Wedding in the Water

It was truly an inspiration to see around 150 Haitians down by the river to observe the baptism of fourteen converts who had committed their lives to Jesus. We were at a new location where the service could also be a testimony to a new group of neighborhood observers. As I scanned the banks and hillsides, I saw many groups of curious observers gazing from their little huts, peeping through the weeds, and standing on nearby banks.

Banav and Madame Banav were the first to enter the water. They had also requested a marriage ceremony by Pastor Rick, since they had only had a civil marriage previously. So, without any special wedding apparel, they stood there in the water as Pastor Rick married them. Then he proceeded to baptize them. Madame Banav's baptism was of special beauty and inspiration to me as I remembered the time she had been seeking the Lord and had said her head was hot because of the intense struggle with the demons. Now she had power and grace to serve Jesus.

■　■　■　■　■　■　■

Slow Learner

The tables are turned. I am taking classes at CAM to learn Creole. I used to teach school, but now I am a pupil. I have worked with many slow learners, but now, ironically, I find myself in that very same position. Perhaps I can now better identify with the struggles of a slow learner. We are using the equivalent of a beginner's primer as part of our work in reading and translating. Although the rigors of learning a foreign language are tough, I do thoroughly enjoy it. I am making slow but persistent progress.

Each afternoon I spend several hours doing hard physical labor under the direction of Pastor Enèl, a Haitian who is foreman over the grounds crew at CAM. This gives my mind an opportunity to rest from the intense work of studying. It is also provides an opportunity to practice the intricacies of the language I am seeking to master.

I am a slow learner spiritually too. Missionaries are continually on the cutting edge and are daily giving of themselves. They must daily commune with the Eternal One and die to their selfish impulses or they will stagnate and simply work in their own strength. The work then becomes their own work, and their program becomes more important than the people they serve. The enemy then has ground to work havoc with interpersonal relationships.

Oswald Chambers in his book *My Utmost for His Highest* states, "God is at work, bending, breaking, molding, doing just as He chooses. Why He is doing it, we do not know; He is doing it for one purpose only—that He may be able to say, 'This is my man, my woman . . .' Let Him have His way."

Chapter 33

The Worth of a Soul

· November 1998

As I was driving from the CAM base to Port, my thoughts were rudely interrupted when ahead of me I saw a clamoring mob hovering over what I thought might be a dead animal. I had noticed a bloody, zigzagging path stretching down the road ahead of me for over half a mile. *What's up?* I wondered. *Why are they dragging this animal?* I came to a halt and ran up to the boisterous mob.

My eyes popped, and my heart nearly stopped because of what I saw and heard. Waves of shock, pain, anger, disgust, and sympathy, all mingled together, coursed through my body. I gazed but a few moments before recoiling abruptly. A rope was fastened around a man's neck, and I found myself staring at a gory, mutilated body with intestines dangling. He was dying, being butchered like a cow!

My shocked, angered face elicited their response, "He stole a cow! He stole a cow!" They spoke as if I should readily and easily understand their horrible, self-styled justice.

I was dazed. I started driving away but had to pull to the side of the road to recuperate. My mind was in a turmoil. Did these people not realize the worth of a soul? Seven hours later I returned. The bloated, ghastly-looking corpse still lay there, unattended. A little branch lightly covered him.

It was a sobering time. The man, one of God's creation but marred by sin, was in eternity—likely unprepared. *Are we doing everything we can to help these people?* I wondered. *Do we truly realize the awesome worth of a soul?*

Madame Ogitè Assaulted

Another recent happening was along a similar vein. After an exhausting trek up the mountain for a funeral service, Pastor Rick was heading home to his family. He was nearly home, and his feet fairly flew down the rugged, steep ravine. He had only one small mountain to go.

As Rick crested the top of the mountain, he saw a crowd beginning to form. Crowding in to see what was going on, he gasped in surprise. There on the ground lay Madame Ogitè. A recent convert, she had been baptized only two weeks earlier. Now her almost lifeless form was lying there.

What had happened? It appeared her own godchild whom she had raised was filled with bitterness and hatred toward her and had tried to choke her. He would have killed her if it hadn't been for others who had come upon the scene. Anna Joy was sitting beside her now, checking her out. As the crowd got larger and family members began to arrive, the account was retold. As the crowd listened, they got visibly angry.

Suddenly the crowd saw the man who had done the deed standing down in the riverbed. "Let's get him!" someone cried, and two women dressed in their traditional red, white, and blue voodoo garb went charging down the mountain. Anger and revenge burned on their faces. Rick quickly called out to Les, farther down the valley, "Hurry! Get down to the riverbed! There's someone down there who's going to get killed if we don't do something!"

As fast as possible, Les and a national brother raced down over the hill toward the man, only to find out that anger and hatred had outrun them. Rick watched helplessly from the mountain and screamed at the top of his voice, "Don't do that! Don't do that! Don't do that!" But hatred only obeys itself. The man was down, being beaten mercilessly with rocks when Les and the national brother got there and broke up the melee. Getting a four-wheeler, they loaded the man, with blood running down his face, and hurriedly took him to the House of Matthew before the crowd could gather and take him back by force.

The crowd was gathering beside our mango tree, where a meeting was scheduled to take place soon, arguing loudly about what had happened. Some of the believers and Rick took songbooks and went out into the crowd. Rick stepped up on one of the benches, and after shouting to get their attention, told them firmly, "You will never settle anything by fighting. Anyone who wants to fight must leave the mission property, because a service is about to start." As the songs started, some left and others came. The brethren prayed fervently for peace in the community.

A local brother stood up and said, "This is why we need the missionaries—to teach us how to live together." After a few minutes it began to rain, so the meeting was postponed until the next night.

Madame Ogitè regained consciousness the next morning and was able to talk again. She even asked to see the man who had done this to her, because she wanted to forgive him like Jesus had forgiven her.

■　■　■　■　■　■　■

Trash Pile People

Between CAM's headquarters and Port-au-Prince, right along the oceanfront, is an area which seems to be a "no man's land." Here the refuse of modern man is hauled and dumped among the scrub bushes and thorns. There are numerous Haitian squatter families who have built their huts and shacks with whatever they could find in the trash piles. A few chickens, dogs, and turkeys roam among the nondescript hovels—and hovels they are.

Miriam, Lamar Nolt's wife, had invited everyone in her Creole class to accompany her to the weekly Thursday afternoon worship service in this poor area. It was held in an 18' × 18' shelter supported by sticks cut from scrub wood. The flat roof was partly covered with woven banana leaves, and a small part of the sides had a skimpy covering. It was the crudest place of worship I have ever entered, yet it was beautiful. About fifteen adults and eighteen children were gathered there. Their welcome was warm and inviting. They sang lustily with joyful expressions and listened with rapt attention and many amens as a young pastor shared from 1 Timothy 1:3. He shared as though he were preaching to a large group of important people. And they were important people! My heart was touched as tears welled up in my eyes. Jesus died for these people. I listened raptly as the pastor told them of God's great love.

Yes, I had left my business and much of my "stuff" in the States, but what did I really leave? I left nothing in comparison to what Jesus left and did for these people. I still live "high on the hog." As I sat on a crude bench beside these lovely, contented Haitian people, my heart smote me. Their hearts were so open, so trusting in God, so hungry for His Word. We have so much, we are so able, we are so refined, so complacent. I needed this convicting "shot" in my heart.

After the service I asked if we could visit a few of the homes. Homes? You call these filthy tin, cardboard, thatch, or plastic hovels homes? Yes, these were their homes. It was all they had. No, we don't want to live like them, but it is good to have our hearts searched often. Where is our treasure? The Apostle Paul said so plainly, "And having food and raiment let us be therewith content."

As we returned to the CAM base, I saw a most gorgeous sunset over the ocean. Yes, "the heavens declare the glory of God; and the firmament sheweth his handiwork." What a contrast between the grand handiwork of our great, holy God and the filth of man's handiwork—plastic, tin, junk, string, cloth, buckets, and other ugly trash. Yet, in the midst of that ugly refuse were beautiful people—the trash pile people.

It's 5:30 now and time to eat supper, but I'm not hungry. I'm still thinking about the trash pile people. Where do I put such needy people in my thinking? On the trash pile? I remember that I, too, was on a "trash pile" when God found me. If it weren't for God's redeeming grace, I would still be there.

Chapter 34

Another Mango Tree Meeting

• November 1998

With Brother Mose here again, another outdoor service was held late Saturday afternoon. First there was a time of singing and testimonies. Madame Banav was one who testified of her deliverance and new-found life in Jesus. Then Mose talked about the many happenings of the past days, the wicked hearts we all have, and the freedom that can be found in Jesus. Afterward Pastor Rick gave an invitation. The first person to respond was Benedette, who had continued to struggle with demons. Others also responded.

Remòn and I talked with Selina, a young girl who has been coming to the services recently. Selina did not yet understand her true need, but her heart was soft and open. As we talked, she began to sense her need of cleansing and forgiveness. Then, on her knees, she confessed her sins and committed her heart to the Lord Jesus.

Bruce and Mose dealt with Benedette. Another demon had manifested itself and threatened to kill her. Benedette lives in a common-law relationship with a man who does not want to get married. She felt she was a Christian, but Mose explained her need to find deliverance from sin and her fears and to allow the Lord Jesus to enter her life with the power for victory. She then knelt and Brother Mose laid hands on her, praying for her understanding, complete deliverance, and readiness to pay whatever the cost to follow Jesus. She rose with a relaxed face and was told to ponder and pray and come back later in the day.

Brother Mose and Bruce also spent some time talking with Madame Moyiz and her husband. They still say they want to become

Christians sometime but have not displayed a broken spirit and a sense of genuine personal need. Rather, they hold grievances against others. One grievance is toward Mama Matthew, whom Madame Moyiz blames for causing others to turn against her.

· · · · · · ·

Madame Ogitè

After Madame Ogitè was nearly choked to death, she recuperated, forgave her assaulter, and showed a lovely testimony that was so encouraging.

But then things started to change. Her voodoo sister kept trying to convince her that justice had not been meted out. Before long, bitterness started rising in Madame Ogitè's heart. We were deeply burdened for her, so recently a group of Haitian Christians went to counsel with her and pray for her. By the time they left, she was again ready to forgive and lay down her resentment.

She was present at our regular Friday morning prayer service, where a Haitian believer updated us about her situation. He told us that a demon had again manifested itself and spoken through her. He had also found out that her family owned another house that still had a stone altar dedicated to Satan worship. This had not been disclosed earlier. This altar and all other satanic strongholds need to be renounced and destroyed.

At the close of the meeting, Pastor Rick, Levi, and a few others laid hands on her and prayed against the demons and for her complete restoration. Everyone rejoiced as she opened her heart and resubmitted her life to God.

· · · · · · ·

We still have a huge chasm created by Hurricane Georges where the bridge had been. At this point no vehicles except ATVs can go in and out. After much discussion, we have decided to construct a real bridge with metal truss beams and three-inch wooden planks. Tentative plans are for Lawrence Martin from Pennsylvania, a skilled welder, to come to Haiti and construct the steel trusses to span the chasm. We are all looking forward to the day when we won't be so penned in.

Chapter 35

From Darkness to Light

• December 1998, written by Rick Hess

As the Spirit of God continues to move in these remote mountains, many are suddenly showing up at church wanting to be saved. There are so many that I don't even recognize all the new converts, much less try to visit them all myself. But God is doing a beautiful thing. He is raising up men in many areas who love the Lord Jesus Christ and their own people. Although they're not officially church leaders, they go home to their own communities, witnessing, praying, counseling, and visiting the sick as Jesus taught.

Several of these men come from a mountain area northeast of us called Larifi and farther east in Dibonno. Norès, a brother of Pastor Matthew, is doing the same here in Alègue. Norès is truly a man of wisdom and is highly respected. Although he is still illiterate, he is starting to take reading lessons. Sometimes these men accompany me to visit homes in their districts that I'd never find without them. And sometimes they bring people from their districts to my house. What a blessing to see these men growing in grace and in the knowledge of the Lord and Saviour Jesus Christ! What a challenge to see their zeal and faith! Although they are poor, they willingly sacrifice their time for the kingdom's sake.

On Wednesday, a group of us made the grueling climb to Dibonno. We counseled with a couple concerning their fornication and their need to repent. We could see the Spirit working deeply. We also visited two other homes in the same area and enjoyed good fellowship with other Christians. Then we headed on up the mountain.

As we passed an old homestead, a gray-haired man came running out after us. "Stop! Don't pass by! I want to get saved!" While we preached the Gospel in his courtyard, many others stood by to hear and observe. Both the old man and his wife knelt and called out to God to receive forgiveness of sins and to renounce their former darkness in voodoo and Catholicism.

When they were finished, an old man who had been working for them said, "I want to be saved too!" As we talked with him, we learned that this seventy-year-old man was the father of ten children but wasn't married to their mother, so we scheduled some time to counsel with both of them.

The next home we visited was that of a man who had attended church for the first time on Sunday. At the service he had introduced himself as a Catholic, but he seemed to have little knowledge of the saving grace of Jesus Christ. When Brother Levi boldly took the opportunity to ask him if he wanted to be converted, he replied that he had promised his wife he was only coming to visit and wouldn't make any decisions. Well, by the time the service was finished, God's Spirit had spoken more loudly than his wife, and he called out in faith to God, repenting and renouncing his past.

Soon after the service, we arrived at his neat, well-kept home. His wife, quiet and meek, a pattern of modesty to her own people, sat beside her newly converted husband. When we asked her if she was upset that her husband had not kept his promise to her, she said, "No, I rejoice because he made the decision I know I want to make now." After some more teaching, both of them knelt down and the tears flowed freely as both husband and wife cried out to God. After this the husband shared what had led them to this decision.

When his best friend had died in a far-away area, he and three others were called upon to bring back his body. The four started carrying this dear friend's remains and were caught in a terrible rainstorm. After struggling through mud and water for hours, they finally arrived home about sundown.

With no embalming, the burial had to continue. After the empty Catholic rites and the hopeless shrieks and wails of the unbelieving mourners, someone needed to crawl inside the massive concrete tomb to arrange the coffin when it was handed inside. It was a ghastly job.

The tombs are shaped like a large old-time bake oven, with an opening at one end just big enough for a coffin to pass through. Inside the dark, damp tomb is a pit about four feet deep. These tombs are used repeatedly, as the coffin and the remains don't last long with all the termites and the tropical heat. A year or two after someone is buried in the tomb, someone else is buried on top of what remains. This man was chosen to climb into this nest of death and arrange the coffin, then climb out the little opening again.

All of these experiences were too much. When he got out of the tomb in the pitch darkness, he threw his hands up over his head and screamed, "Oh, my God!" and passed out. When he woke up, he found his hands and feet tied so that he wouldn't hurt himself or anyone else. It was then he determined to seek something better till he found it.

After listening to his story and sharing tears of grief with him, we asked if he had any voodoo fetishes, idols, crucifixes, or beads. We were going to encourage him to burn them, but he informed us that he and his wife had cleaned out their house before he even visited our church. Praise the God of heaven! Their minds were made up; their course was set. So sure were they that they weren't turning back that they had happily burned their bridges!

The church house is bursting at the seams. If people don't get there early, they won't find a seat. God is raising up workers in our midst, and Satan's stronghold of fear is losing its power. People are seeing that they don't need to believe the devil's lies. We pray that God will continue to help the church be rooted and grounded in love, so that we can grow not only in numbers but also in grace.

Chapter 36

Open Doors, Open Hearts

• January 1999

They came, nearly sixty of them, some an hour's trek away, some six, but it mattered little to them. They were hungry for instruction. A dream was coming true: a leadership seminar for the school teachers and church overseers from remote areas with no roads or access.

My heart was blessed to see Brother Denny, on a visit from Pennsylvania, and Brother Mose give of their hearts to this unique need. They taught and preached with enthusiasm, dedication, and unction as if they were speaking to a group of hundreds. They gave themselves to prayer and fasting, and the Spirit of God was manifested day after day. There was one class in the morning, one in the afternoon, and then an open service for anyone in the evening. At the end of each class, the instructor gave time for questions and answers. I marveled at the depth of the Haitians' questions, considering the limited materials with which they studied and taught in their own churches and schools.

How we yearned to see these national teachers and overseers go back to their people on the remote mountainsides to preach the life-changing Gospel and be true spiritual leaders of indigenous churches. What potential there was!

Madame Moyiz's husband attended one service. After the service, Brother Mose challenged him about a report of an assembly at his place to call up demons against the Christians. He was very evasive, and when we asked to pray for him, he squirmed with fear and resolutely declined. I told him we would pray for him in our own houses. He said that was okay.

■ ■ ■ ■ ■ ■ ■

Spiritual Warfare

How my heart wells up with gratitude and praise, and throbs with excitement. I have just returned from a Friday morning prayer service. What a thrill it was, and what emotions stirred in my heart to see and hear about seventy Haitians and *blans* lift up their voices and hands to an almighty God. With fervor and intensity, we all prayed that the power and influence of voodooism and the works of Satan would be brought to naught in these mountains of Alègue. We were in close proximity to Madame Moyiz's house and the demonic cockfight shack. Alfred also lived nearby. During our meeting, Alfred stood off a ways and listened. What emotions must have stirred in his heart!

Using a bull horn, Levi shouted to all the heathen neighbors within hearing distance and to those passing by on the road to stop serving the evil spirits that destroy their lives. As I stood on a raised bank overlooking these dear people, the verse came to me, "I beheld Satan as lightning fall from heaven." Satan's kingdom was severely under attack. Praise God!

· · · · · · ·

Death—the Call of God

Before 5:00 this morning the wail of death came floating up to my ears. An eighteen-year-old Down's syndrome boy had died. Anna Joy had been at his home several times to nurse this sick youth. As a result, Pastor Rick was asked to preach at the funeral service.

I had often wondered what it was like high in the mountains behind the mission houses. We took one saddle horse and started hiking. First we went up one mountain and then back down. Then it was up, up, up. Finally it was so steep that we tied the horse to a tree and pushed ourselves on up the mountain on foot. At times we desperately clung to tall grasses and pulled ourselves up.

Finally we reached our destination. We sang for a while, and then Pastor Rick preached, calling men to repentance and very beautifully sharing comfort and hope with the grieving parents. Nearly all the neighbors and friends were heathen voodoo worshipers. To get them to think, Pastor Rick used the illustration of water, iodine, and bleach to show them their need of cleansing.

As we headed to the burial spot after the service, I saw an altar used for devil worship. Afterward we were asked to visit a neighbor, and again we approached the house where we had seen the demon altar. When some of the Haitian believers accosted the family about the altar, they said they did not use it, but an older son from Port sometimes did. "Go ahead and tear it down if you want to," they told us. "It brings us nothing but a curse anyway."

With sweeping gusto, the Christians flew into action. They whacked the cross off the altar, and in minutes the whole altar was in ruins. Machetes flew rapidly, cutting up the plants and shrubs used in demon worship. One man plunged a pick so deeply into the roots of a small tree that he cracked the pick handle. The job was not complete till they had removed the roots, leaving a deep hole. They then gathered straw and dried grass, placed it in the foot-deep cavity, sprinkled it with salt, doused the whole pile with kerosene, and lit it with a match. During the unique experience we sang "He is Lord." We then entered the house and searched the whole place to destroy anything related to demon worship.

On our homeward trek we passed the house of a Catholic priest Rick and Anna Joy had ministered to in the recent past. We stopped and visited with him. Pastor Rick beautifully pointed him to Jesus as the only way of salvation and gently but firmly showed him the error of infant baptism. I was amazed at his warm reception. I believe God is working in his heart.

. . . .

Anis and Madame Anis

Oh, the beauty of transformed lives! On Thursday afternoon I had the privilege of accompanying Rick and Cherry to a private wedding. It took place inside a small thatched-roof hut with two mini rooms for a family with four children. They had a private marriage because they were too poor to feed and entertain guests. How it thrilled my heart to sit on the little bed beside Pastor Rick as he performed the ceremony. The couple sat on chairs draped with sheer white fabric. The dilapidated mud hut was neatly white-washed inside and out for the occasion.

I well remember my first visit to this small shack. The husband, Anis, had fallen backward off a trailer and sustained a long, deep gash in his skull. What a bloody mess it was! Rick and Cherry had stitched and nursed him. Later I stopped by a few times to visit and pray with him and became quite attached to this warm, gracious couple. I was overjoyed to be with Rick when they were converted. They had become like family to me, so now I felt highly honored to be a guest and to sign as a witness to their marriage.

. . . .

Baptismal Service

I am certainly not vacationing in the Haitian hills of Alègue. Life has taken its toll and I have aged in body during the last several years. Nonetheless, I have had some unique privileges that defy description. I can walk up the mountain in such bright moonlight that it creates shadows almost like in the daytime, and I can lie on my back on a moonless night and see stars so brilliant that they fairly shout at you with their intense glistening and twinkling. They shine with an assortment of colors—green, blue, white, and red—never seen in Pennsylvania. I thrill as I sometimes see one dazzling meteor after another plummeting earthward. What a mighty God we serve!

But sweeter still is the Lord's Day service, especially when there is a baptism to conclude the service. Today when the service at the church concluded, close to two hundred people headed down the rugged trails to the riverbed. After about a forty-minute hike, we approached a unique spot. Here was a huge rock, perhaps seventy feet long and fifteen feet high, with layers of rock jutting out and forming natural bleachers. Between this rock and a similar rock was a stream flowing through a narrow ravine. Here Pastor Rick preached a simple baptismal message. Levi and Pastor Rick, aided by several Haitian brothers, performed the baptisms. Today there were nine more trophies for the kingdom of God. Other Haitian brothers and I prayed for them individually after their baptisms.

I stood in the shade of the huge boulder and scanned the audience. Welling up in my heart were sentiments of wonder, thankfulness, and humility as I saw one after another being baptized. Less than a year ago they were in fear, ignorance, and darkness. Now they were children of light.

Chapter 37

A New Man

• January 1999, written by Anna Joy Kauffman

Wilfrid has been here for about a month helping at the clinic. He comes from Port-au-Prince and is a former owner of a number of rank little gambling joints where they sell lottery tickets. Wilfrid was a very rich man, prospering greatly, but that was before God got a hold of him. One day, as riches always do, either by death or by misfortune, they came to an end. He was robbed and lost all his gambling joints.

Not having money to pay the lottery winners, he took to the mountains. It was not by chance that his wife's family lives near Alègue and he came to see them. I know it was all the hand of the Lord. While back here, he decided to visit our church one Sunday morning. He was deeply touched by God. During testimony time he stood up and started sharing his life story and all that had just happened. He broke down and wept as he told us of his need of Jesus and a new lease on life.

The owners of gambling joints have a reputation for carrying a lot of cash and defending it with guns, knives, and brass knuckles. They are known to be rough characters—they have to be, to protect themselves and their business. But now Wilfrid had lost pretty well everything, and his children weren't even able to attend school anymore.

Everyone listened in rapt silence as Wilfrid's story unfolded. When they saw his tears, a murmur went through the crowd; Haitian men seldom cry in public. But Wilfrid had found his Saviour that day, and what a difference it made!

When he became a Christian, he couldn't conscientiously live with his lady anymore, because they were not married. And with no money to pay for a wedding and a house, things looked pretty bleak. It was at about this time that we really needed help at the clinic, so Bruce asked Wilfrid to fill in for a time.

I know God allowed all these details to happen, and I know Wilfrid was "God sent" because he is proving to be such a blessing at the clinic. He is good with the people and he's good at keeping order. He works as our secretary, making the cards and bringing in the people one at a time. This makes it so much easier for me and helps everything run a lot smoother. He is living in the clinic for now till he has enough money saved up to buy a house for his family. He has two beautiful children in Port and is often sad that he cannot be with them.

God has done a marvelous work in Wilfrid's heart the last month. He doesn't even look like the same man anymore. When I see the hand of God performing such wonderful miracles, it just overwhelms me that I am called to be a daughter of such an awesome King!

Chapter 38

Controlled by Evil

• February 1999

E arly one Saturday morning as I sat at my favorite place for Bible study, I heard voodoo drums in the distance and a voice not far below me. At times it was a chant, and then a coarse, eerie laugh. Then it seemed to be a prayer, and finally it was just a babble of unintelligible words. Directly below me, in full view but at a distance too far away to see clearly, was a woman. Curious now what was going on, I got my binoculars.

The woman sat at the door of her hut and raised her hands above her head. Then, with decided rhythm, she pounded the ground with her hands, one at a time, screaming all the while. Without warning, she abruptly jumped to her feet and started gyrating so that her skirt flung outward, all the while moving rapidly in a large circle, sometimes bumping into her hut. In a flash she dashed down the trail, out of my sight. Minutes later she reappeared. This time she grabbed one of several brilliant red cloths nearby and draped it around her waist. Then she dashed around and around her house before plunging toward a nearby cliff. She stopped at the edge, but continued the gyrating movements. Finally, seemingly exhausted, she dropped down at the doorway of her house. As the scene kept repeating itself, a small child sat watching.

How sad! Obviously the woman had given herself over, body and spirit, to be controlled by a *lwa*. It was a vivid reminder of the need these people have for a Deliverer, and of our purpose for being here.

Another recent episode stands out in my mind. We were at Pastor

Rick's house enjoying an evening of singing and fellowship when we heard a *rara* group coming our way. Soon they passed Rick's house and went on back to Madame Moyiz's house. We decided to have special prayer against the forces of Satan and his demons and for the Moyiz family and other neighbors—Christian and non-Christian. We began singing "In the Name of Jesus" with fervor, including the part about conquering demons and witchcraft. We then decided to go out and invite the *rara* group into the courtyard and sing for them. I scurried out through the mud, opened the gate entrance, and invited them to come in. The main group started coming, but then their leaders sternly and emphatically forbade them to enter, and they continued on their way, chanting their ribald voodoo songs as they disappeared down the trail.

We learned later in the evening that they were angry because Madame Moyiz had closed and bolted her door and did not respond to them. Likewise, the recently converted neighbor, Mano, who formerly was their drummer, had closed his door and refused to go with them. Meanwhile, our whole group stood out at the road close to the cockfight shack and worshiped and praised God by singing in Creole.

Often those involved in voodoo have an extra, unused room in their house which they open only at midnight to invite the *lwa,* or evil spirits, into their house. After an event such as a voodoo ball, when they walk on the trails, they may see a demon manifest itself as a pig, goat, cow, or chicken on the path ahead of them. If that happens, they believe someone in their family will get sick or die. In this way the devil keeps the people in fear.

During a voodoo ball the parents will pour a bath water made from special leaves over their children to protect them from evil. At midnight the head witch doctor in the area calls all the evil spirits of his area to come to the ball. When the spirits do not come, they take a whip and crack it in the air over and over in an effort to entreat the spirits to come. Over the course of the next few days we heard the whip cracking again and again.

We rejoice that now it is finally quiet here in Alègue. It is so nice to just listen to the crickets again!

Chapter 39

A Bloody Baby and a Thief

It was Sunday morning. We were about halfway through our church service when John, a recent convert, came rushing into the service carrying his twenty-month-old baby boy covered with blood. Outside the church was a woman, Madame Onès, standing calmly nearby. She wore the typical garb of a voodoo practitioner— red, white, and blue sewn together in stripes. *What's going on?* we wondered. John explained that while walking on the trail, Madame Onès had begun cursing and throwing stones at him and his boy. So here he was with a blood-covered baby.

Bruce took both parties with two witnesses down to Judge Alsiyis's house. Bruce talked individually with each of the parties and convinced them to forgive and forget. So thoroughly did he convince them that Madame Onès helped carry one of John's children home.

Bruce was suspicious about what had actually happened and shared his doubts with us. We were horrified at what he suspected, but decided it was better to wait till God brought the whole truth to light.

The next Sunday after the message we gave an invitation for anyone whose conscience was not clear to come forward. Seven adults responded, including John. During counseling, he confessed that in a fit of anger he had killed two of Madame Onès's goats when he found them in his garden.

At this point we asked him about the incident with the bloody baby, and he revealed to us the whole truth. His wife and daughter had been at odds with Madame Onès, their next-door neighbor, for some time. They would yell at each other, provoking one another. On Sunday morning she lay in ambush. When John came by carrying the baby, she threw a stone which hit John in the ribs. Immediately she threw herself onto the ground and began injuring herself. She had done this once before and then taken him to court, with "proof" that he had hurt her. He had been forced to pay her a hundred dollars, a huge sum for a poor Haitian farmer.

So when John saw her flopping on the ground, he knew what she was planning to do. If she took him to law and was all covered with dirt and blood, the judge would believe her and not him. This motivated him to do the unthinkable. He took a sharp object and put a small cut on the child's head, causing blood to flow over him. When Madame Onès saw this, she began to scream in terror because she knew she would be blamed for hurting the child.

When we counseled John, we sensed a note of self-justification and shared with him how much God hated what he had done. To harm a defenseless child and to lie about it was an abomination to God. We asked him to think about what he had done and become broken before God. In his mind John didn't really understand, but in his spirit he was willing to learn. We challenged him to make a public confession of his sin, and he expressed his willingness to do that.

Again and again we need to gently but firmly counter cultural practices that are not based on the teachings of the Lord Jesus. The Holy Spirit, however, is working faithfully in the hearts of those who respond.

· · · · · · ·

Joslen

Joslen is a twelve-year-old neighbor boy, small for his age and an orphan. He has been in and out of our mission compound quite a bit and is a good worker. However, we were suspicious that he was stealing eggs and selling them back to us for a number of days before he was caught.

Since he was attending school here for some time already, he was taken to Bruce, the overseer of the school. Bruce dealt with him gently but firmly, talking to him as a father would to his own child. He admonished him to confess his wrongdoing, which he stubbornly refused to do. Bruce reminded him that all the children had been warned against the evil of stealing and had been told that if they were caught stealing, they would be punished.

In accordance with that warning, Bruce gave him twenty-five lashes with a belt, which is the normal punishment here for such misbehavior, and warned him that if he was caught again, he would be punished harder. Bruce then prayed with him, asking God to bless his life and help him. Our hearts went out to Joslen since he doesn't have any parents and doesn't seem to have much of a chance with the corruption around him. At the same time, we were amazed at the hardness of heart that we saw in him.

Joslen and his brother come regularly to Pastor Rick's house for evening meals. They come to his porch after dark so as not to cause jealousy in others. Being orphans, they have been given many privileges that simply can't be given to every needy child.

Since Joslen attends the Bible studies on Saturday afternoons, Rick also took the opportunity to talk with him. When he told Joslen that he knew about the egg-stealing business, Joslen finally acknowledged his guilt.

"Joslen, I am not angry with you," Rick told him. "But I am deeply hurt. I trusted you. You have privileges most boys don't have." Joslen looked down with moistened eyes as Rick further counseled and fathered him.

Chapter 40

Needy People

▪ April 1999

Demon Alcohol

We started up the mountain past my *kay*. Pastor Rick, Brother Norès, and I hiked together. Soon Nick and Anna Joy followed. It had rained a bit and the trails were slippery and treacherous, to say the least. I was "mudding" with Pastor Rick again, but this time on foot. Rick was ahead of me, slithering and sliding. I had a hiking stick and Tingley boots—a major advantage. We were on the way deep into the mountains for a funeral. Jira, Mama Matthew's younger 43-year-old brother, had died. Jira had sometimes come to the clinic in the past. He came as an emaciated man, just skin and bones. A victim of AIDS, he was paying a high price for his chosen lifestyle. The day before he died, Brother Norès shared the Gospel with him and he wanted to be converted. The outcome of this, we leave in the hands of God.

As we neared the courtyard of Jira's brother, we were greeted by the chanting of the mourners. We soon saw six men prancing, dancing, and chanting. One of them was beating a bucket lid on both sides with a stout branch. *Are they self-appointed pallbearers?* we wondered. In reality, unknown to them, they were "pall" bearers, bearers of death.

The stench of alcohol socked my nostrils time after time as I mingled with these poor, deluded souls. It seemed the demons of hell chose to obscure the reality and seriousness of death by strong drink.

As Pastor Rick opened the service, he appropriately asked the few men with hats to remove them, in respect to God's Word. Most of the men were respectful, but a minor ruckus arose as a few protested and others grabbed the hats from their heads and tossed them away.

Later one drunk said to another, "You are drunk and shouldn't be here," and started shoving and whacking him. Others soon jumped in and helped in the fray. Silence was called for, but soon they were at it again. Even Mama Matthew went to some guests to plead for quietness.

As Pastor Rick preached the Gospel in this disruptive setting, disturbers were crudely, physically hoisted from the gathering more than once. Satan's turf was invaded and he was not so soon to be ousted.

As we stood listening to the Good News and singing together about Jesus, it was so heartening to see those who had come from the Alègue church. Their beaming, open-faced, joyous countenances were a stark contrast to the hardened, fearful faces of the unconverted heathen who thronged about us.

When the service ended, the men hoisted the coffin to take it a short distance to the burial tomb. Ear-piercing wails and shrieks rent the air. These were wails of hopelessness and death, wails of futility and darkness, yes, demonic wails from the pit of hell.

We were graciously invited into the cook shack and served Haitian colas, coffee, and bread baked on the hearth of the House of Matthew. Meanwhile the unconverted men passed the bottle from lip to lip as they sipped and shared their "firewater." As we later wended our way home, a drunk man accompanied us. Once, he lost his bit of bread and it tumbled down a cliff so steep a sober man could barely climb down. But just like a monkey, he scrambled down after it and retrieved the morsel. After awkwardly stuffing it inside his shirt, he painstakingly worked himself to the trail again. He needs the true Bread of Life, Jesus.

"O Lord God of our fathers, art not thou God in heaven? and rulest not thou over all the kingdoms of the heathen? and in thine hand is there not power and might, so that none is able to withstand thee?" (2 Chronicles 20:6).

■ ■ ■ ■ ■ ■ ■

Eristan

Eristan was the deacon at Belamy, the most remote of the satellite churches we helped back in the mountains. He had been sick for some time and had previously been at Ti Goâve for medical help. When word reached us that he was very sick, Bruce, with a small caravan of interested nationals, went to visit him and returned with the news that he was close to death. The family was actually preparing a coffin for him. In the hope that better medical care would help him, they decided to transport him to Alègue. Bruce scheduled some Belamy locals to carry him on a litter about half of the way, and sent eight men from Alègue to meet them and carry him the rest of the way—a total of six difficult hours. The nurses would then oversee him. They thought he had amoebic liver disease. He was emaciated, ridden with horrible bed sores, and suffering unbearably.

. . . .

Madame Moyiz

Recently Kathy visited Madame Moyiz again. She told Kathy she knows God is going to show her that her heart is black. "I can't wait for that day!" Madame Moyiz exclaimed.

When asked if she liked when the *rara* groups come, she emphatically said, "No! But they are my gardeners, and if I resist, they will not take care of my fields."

Kathy also learned that many months ago when Madame Moyiz had been robbed in Port, her relatives had threatened to put a curse on her if she turned to the missionaries' God. Before leaving, Kathy asked if she may pray for her.

Madame Moyiz assented and fell to her knees as Kathy prayed for her deliverance from her sin. We must keep praying for Madame Moyiz. God is calling her, but Satan is resisting.

. . . .

More Stealing

After being reprimanded for stealing eggs, Joslen seemed to be doing

Remòn prepares my first meal at Alègue.

Alègue church gets a new roof.

Curious onlookers.

Grandpa Harold's rented *kay*.

My first burn patient on the left.

Remòn teaching music.

Market day.

Pastor Rick and Cherry arrive.

Harold Weaver making blocks.

The Les Reinford family—1997.

Pastor Matthew.

Yvette

Klomàn

Itanya

Madame Moyiz.

Madame Moyiz's family.

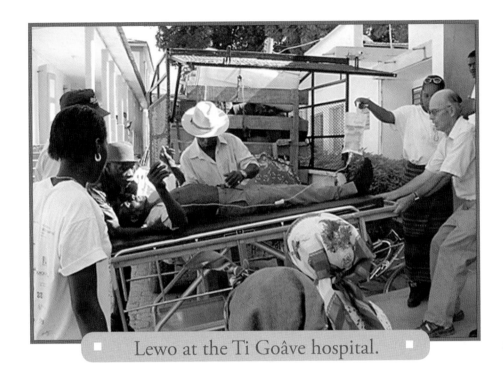

Lewo at the Ti Goâve hospital.

A clinic patient brought on a "Haitian ambulance."

Gospel Team.

Edgar's church house, an hour away from Alègue.

The nurses: Ada Fisher, Melissa Ewald, and Anna Joy Kauffman.

Communion at Alègue.

First feet-washing service at Alègue.

A mountain school.

Harold's meeting place with God.

Grandpa Harold and Raymond Burkholder
ready to visit the sick.

Trouble ahead!

2010 earthquake damage at Ti Goâve.

Mini motor home.

Bruce's lovely family—2011.

Yvette's lovely family—2011.

Mountains of Alègue.

well and we could see his heart softening. All was well until his brother sneaked into the mission house and stole some money. The local nationals were so incensed that both boys disappeared for fear of their lives.

Their fear is not an imaginary one, as apprehended thieves are often stoned to death or "necklaced"—a heinous practice. To do this, an old tire is placed about the guilty person's neck; then he is doused with gasoline and ignited. Graphically etched in my memory is the day I witnessed such a "necklacing" as I was driving through Port.

. . . .

Excited Pupils!

As I was walking the trail to Les's house, I rounded a curve and heard excited, happy conversation that sounded almost like the squeals of delighted children. There I found Mama Matthew, Bruce's mother, and several other ladies. They were returning from an adult class where they were learning to read. Bruce told me his seventy-one-year-old mother was overjoyed that she would finally be able to read the Bible herself.

I visited the classes yesterday. It was exciting to see Judge Alsiyis instructing the women, and his deputy teaching the men. Both are certified instructors. They are helping about forty eager students with the simple letter sounds. Their faces beamed as they repeated sound after sound in unison. Indeed, God is again doing way beyond what I could have dreamed.

. . . .

Madame Ogitè Attacked Again

As I arrived at the mission, it was easy to see that something was wrong. There were angry voices, shouting, pointing, and jostling. Levi and Les were going through the adjacent three-foot-high cornfield as though searching for something. Les came and told me that Dejoni, Madame Ogitè's previous assaulter, was at it again. I later saw Madame Ogitè's arm ripped open in several places, with blood oozing out. The mob continued to grow as Levi calmly tried to pacify them. Earlier, some had knives and wanted to kill the assaulter, but when Levi came, the knives had been thrown into the cornfield.

The story, though sketchy to me, slowly emerged. Madame Ogitè, it seemed, had a pig which she had given to Henry, a neighbor boy, to care for. Dejoni, however, thought he should be in charge of it. In a fit of jealousy, he had assaulted Henry with his fists and bitten him. A short time later, when Madame Ogitè and Henry were on their way to talk with Pastor Rick, Dejoni came upon them again and assaulted Madame Ogitè by biting her and ripping open the flesh on her arm.

By now the relatives and neighbors were inciting each other to take revenge and kill him. Dejoni hid in Mano's courtyard while Levi sought to calm the angry mob. After a bit the air cleared, and the extreme ire diminished.

Judge Alsiyis came later in the day. Again the group became riled, but the judge's authority commanded silence and submission. After Dejoni was charged by the judge, his hands were tied behind him and he was placed in charge of the local constable to walk him to Ti Goâve to be jailed. The next day we learned that they stayed overnight nearby, intending to continue the next day. But Dejoni, who was tied to the bed, chewed the ropes loose and escaped.

There are few dull days in Alègue.

Chapter 41

Why, God?

• April 1999, written by Anna Joy Kauffman

On Sunday night our dear brother Eristan passed on to meet his Maker. On Friday afternoon I had started noticing that he sounded a bit congested. I listened to his lungs but didn't hear anything unusual. I kept watching for anything unusual, but then he seemed to be taking a turn for the better, so we decided it was nothing to worry about. By Saturday afternoon, however, he was getting worse again.

On Sunday morning he was very alert. I was sitting by his bedside giving him some soup when Les called on the radio. He told me to ask Eristan if he'd like to go to church and share a testimony. He got a big smile on his face when I told him, knowing that Les was joking. Later I went to church for about an hour and a half, and when I returned, I thought his breathing sounded worse. That afternoon Les and Kathy came and we talked about putting him on an antibiotic, but it just didn't seem as if he had pneumonia. We decided to wait another day and observe him a little longer.

By late Sunday afternoon I was getting a bit worried. Once in a while his breathing would get very rough, but there was not much to do, so I just committed him to the Lord. That evening I went home for a bite of supper and to put on some clean clothes. I returned to find Eristan a lot worse. When I knelt beside his bed, he saw me and gave me a beautiful smile.

I spent some time in prayer beside his bed before I went to lie down. I had a sinking feeling in my heart. I knew he could not last much longer if his breathing did not clear up soon. A tremendous warfare took place in my heart; I so desperately wanted this man to live. He had a sweet wife and three lovely children. Then there was his church group at home and the school he was directing. "Lord, surely you know how much this man is needed here," I prayed.

I finally was able to commit him totally to the Lord. I wanted to stay by Eristan's side longer, but I was getting very weary and decided it would be better for me to try to get some sleep.

I lay down and was just beginning to doze off when I woke to see his wife giving him a few sips of water. Suddenly she gave a loud exclamation and rushed across the room calling, "Miss Anna, Eristan is dying! He's dying! He's dying!"

I jumped up and ran to his side. His breathing was tight, as if he were strangling. He did not gasp at all; his breaths just got farther and farther apart. This was my first experience with death, and I felt panic rising within me. I tried to sit him up, but he was so limp I couldn't support him. I laid him down again and tried to open his airways so that he could get another breath, but it never came. I did CPR, but dead silence was my only answer.

"Oh, God, is this the end?" I moaned. I quickly called Les on the radio, and he said he'd come immediately. I checked Eristan again and found his heartbeat had stopped. His spirit had taken its flight.

Madame Eristan was going into hysterics in the other room. She was wailing and yelling, "Eristan is dying! He's dying! Oh, what shall I do? Oh, Eristan, what are you doing to me?" My heart broke as I tried to comfort her, but my tears were falling so fast I was not much comfort. I kept going back and checking him, finding it hard to believe that this man had actually died.

The rest of the night was a blur of people coming and going, of weeping and wailing and crying. A few times Madame Eristan got so hysterical that we had to hold her down. As time went on, she started calming down and thinking a bit more rationally.

After discussing our options, we decided it would be best to send Eristan's body back home as soon as possible, so we rounded up a group of strong men to carry it. Two of the church sisters also agreed to walk with Madame Eristan. The group started out around 1:30 that night.

The next morning a group of us set out for Eristan's house for the funeral. We had a caravan of about fifteen people with three mules and one horse to ride. God blessed us with beautiful walking weather. The sun was out, and we had a nice breeze most of the way.

We arrived at Belamy around 12:30. It tore at my heart to hear the wailing and crying, which we could hear a good ways off. I went into the cook shack where Madame Eristan and the children were. When I entered, Madame Eristan started wailing and calling my name. Seeing me was a fresh reminder of the reality of Eristan's death.

There were many people at the funeral. Eristan had been loved and respected by many. The church house was full, and people were standing in the doorways and at the windows. Rick shared a beautiful message and also challenged them to continue with the work of the church and school that Eristan had been doing, and to share the load Madame Eristan now had to carry.

After some tea and bread, we headed out again at about 3:30. The way home was a bit more difficult. The walking was actually easier, but everyone was so tired. About three-quarters of the way home, darkness overtook us, making it a challenge to pick our way home. Most of the time I was walking by faith; I could barely see the path at all. We had only two flashlights, so it was a welcome sight to see the lights of home. We were inexpressibly weary and our bones ached, but God had been with us each step of the way and granted us safety and strength.

We think Eristan's death was caused by heart failure. He had severe anemia, which made his heart work extremely hard, and then his lungs filled with fluid. It was a gradual process, but finally he could not take another breath.

It's hard to understand an experience like this, but I don't need to. My flesh wants to argue and asks so many questions, but I am confident that God is in control, and I am willing to learn whatever He wants to teach me through this. May He continue to have His way, however and in whatever way He chooses.

Chapter 42

Trust in a Sovereign God

• April 1999

Pastor Rick recently led a hike to Ogitè's old homestead to get rid of the demon altar in it. All about the property were many items dedicated to Satan. Close to the old house lived some ungodly voodoo worshipers. Pastor Rick stopped to witness to them. The lady hid her face in her hands as they invited her to the nearby service to demolish the devil's altar. Surprisingly, she decided to go with them.

As they approached the altar, the group paused and fervently sang several Creole hymns, including "There Is Power in the Blood." A lovely testimony was shared by both Ogitè and Madame Ogitè. After a prayer, the group proceeded to destroy the altar. The words of Jesus, "The zeal of thine house hath eaten me up," were very fitting as with zeal and determination they completely destroyed the altar. They discovered a red turban used in voodoo worship, and with carefulness, lest the wind blow it away, they stomped on it and kept it on the trail till it was covered with dry grass. Then they doused it with kerosene and burned it.

On the way home they again stopped to share the Gospel with the voodoo neighbors. Pastor Rick read the Word to the husband, while his immoral daughters gathered and listened with rapt attention. In parting, the man said, "Maybe your God will come to me and show me this way."

· · · · · · ·

Humbling, but Special

Lord willing, I plan to travel to Pennsylvania to take in the missions conference and some other meetings. On Sunday Pastor Rick asked me to share some thoughts, since this would be my last Sunday in Haiti for a while.

The hearts of the nationals knit with mine as I shared the moving story of Abraham's call to offer his beloved son Isaac. With their simple, uncluttered hearts, the Haitians drank in every word I said. Again and again they have challenged me to a simple faith in God.

At the close of the service, they individually came to bless me and tell me they would continue to pray for me while I was gone. How I will miss them!

Chapter 43

Heart Tugs

· June 1999

The tug for Haiti stayed strong all during my absence, and it was with great excitement that I prepared to return. Along with the excitement, however, was a bit of foreboding.

For the last while there had been some struggles among the missionary workers and among the national workers. The fiery darts seemed to be flying with intensity. As I returned, it was with a sense of unworthiness, but I trusted my heavenly Father to work in all our hearts. Oh, for wisdom, for grace, for brokenness!

· · · · · · ·

First Night Home

Most of my Haitian friends did not know I was returning, so their surprise and gracious reception was indeed overwhelming. I don't think I received any bruises from their embraces, but their blessing was so warming.

Brother Galen Yoder and his family also arrived in Haiti to spend the week at Alègue with us. Bruce was especially delighted to have his two white "papas" here—Galen and myself.

Haiti has not changed. Our truck has an engine problem and is in Port at a garage, my e-mail refuses to function, my printer is rebellious and will not print, and both ATVs are out of order.

Below me in the valley, the voodoo drums were again echoing out the call of the enemy, and my thoughts about problems were cut short as the reality of why we were here suddenly hit me. Yes, I had been meeting my Haitian friends and entering their lives. Yes, I knew many of them were in bondage, fear, and superstition. But all our needs as missionaries, the work responsibilities, and the busyness of our work here had overclouded the need of bringing Jesus to these dear souls.

. . . .

Sit Where They Sit

They came one after the other, both the converted and unconverted—my black friends. The crude benches were soon packed full. It was the Lord's Day. The heat was stifling, and the perspiration poured. I saw Selès, his face aglow after being delivered from intense evil powers. He shared with joy that he will be married before long. Then there was Brother Jil, the Banav family, Mano, and many more.

Converted just two days ago, Mèjil stood to share the memory verse. He is Bruce's half-brother and a special friend of mine. He gardens the little plot of ground surrounding my hut here on the mountainside. While I was in Pennsylvania, he lost his temper and killed a goat that had been tethered in my garden by a neighbor. Yesterday he came to the end of his resources and bared his heart to Pastor Rick and Bruce. He confessed his sins and cried out to God for forgiveness. How beautiful it was for Bruce to help lead his brother to Jesus!

Later he publicly shared his testimony. His father was an important *bòkò*, a wealthy man feared by many, and Mèjil was being groomed to follow his path. Now he has chosen to follow Jesus.

The service was long; it lasted till after 2:30. Pierre, a young man who had gotten into trouble and was publicly disrespectful to Bruce, came to the front, shared a confession, and stated his desire to walk the straight and narrow way.

After the service, Mano shared a new concern with us—a painful, swollen knee which so far has not responded to treatment. We prayed with him and encouraged him to see the nurses at the clinic again.

Building Projects

With our clinic work growing by leaps and bounds, we had reached a decision to build a separate clinic facility. We had hired a local builder to build a stone clinic which would include a waiting room, two exam rooms, a pharmacy, a storage room for medical supplies, and a restroom.

Although the project has been underway for a while, it seems things are progressing at a snail's pace. Right now local ceramic tile is being laid on the floor. Another thing that takes a lot of time is making all the jambs, doors, shelves, and examination tables from local wood. That means ripping, sizing, planing, cutting, assembling, staining, and varnishing in our crude woodshop. When we finally get everything completed, we'll need examination and approval from the head doctor at Ti Goâve.

We're also building a clinic custodian's house. Although this house is coming along well, there are still many things to do. Besides that, we also have fences and gates to build. There are so many things to do that I sometimes wish I could be at two places at once! But God is in charge and I have chosen to live one day at a time, let come what may.

Yes, I returned to Alègue in the midst of deep needs and an overwhelming work load, but God is working in our midst. Healing, restoration, and openness are prevailing. Indeed, when we bow our hearts to God and to one another, God is able to draw us more closely to Him and to each other.

Chapter 44

God Says, "Stop!"

· July 1999

It was one of those really hot, humid days we often have here in Haiti. Rick's family had gone to Port to bring home our repaired truck and pick up Nurse Melissa Ewald, who was coming to help Anna Joy at the clinic. I was pouring concrete in the rear room of the new house we were building for the custodian of the clinic. As the afternoon progressed, the heat really started to get to me. When six o'clock came, I felt I could hardly walk up the steep mountain trail to my *kay*.

The next day was again hot and humid. Six Haitians carried materials and hand-mixed the concrete for me. The concrete was a bit stiff, so I had to work extra hard. I finally finished pouring the concrete by noon and started troweling. I was sweating profusely since I was inside the hut with little ventilation.

Suddenly my face started burning and my heart started getting all fluttery. I also developed a severe headache. I lay on the floor for a bit, but soon got someone to help me limp to the mission house. I felt so terrible that I wondered if maybe my time was here to meet my dear Jesus. "Hurry!" I told Nèli. "Go get Anna Joy at the clinic!"

He rushed up the hill at full speed. "Anna, Anna!" he said excitedly. "You must come quickly. I think Grandpa Harold is dying!"

After checking me out, Anna Joy decided I probably had a mild heat stroke.

Later that evening many of my friends came to visit me and pray for me. They sang and prayed so lovingly. I greatly appreciated Anna Joy's diligence and helpfulness. She walked to my hut and brought down my clothes, Bible, and other things.

It seems God has told me to slow down for a while, and I intend to listen to His sweet direction. May He get much glory from this.

Refreshment

Dear Edgar, his wife Anna, and their five children live an hour away, high on a mountain. Their dingy little hut has only two tiny rooms. There is one table, one bed, some mats, and bags stuffed with rags to sit and sleep on. He is a poor, humble, gray-haired man of God. His vision has always been to have a church and a school for the people. Although he lives in squalor, Edgar is a generous man and recently donated some land on which he built a church/school house.

Today Levi and I decided to go with some others to visit him and hold a worship service. Since I was still a bit weak from my mini heat stroke, I was so thankful it was a cloudy day and not so hot. I drove an ATV part of the way, and then I mounted a mule till it was so rugged I had to dismount and walk. But what a treat it was—like a beautiful vacation. I surveyed God's lovely mountains, viewed the plants and flowers, and talked briefly with the people enroute.

When we arrived at the church house—the beautiful "temple" Edgar had constructed—I was overjoyed. The building was about 16 x 22 feet in size, and the crude posts were strapped together with date branches. The roof was covered sparsely with banana leaves, making a slight shade.

To prepare for the service, boards were placed on stones to serve as benches. As I sat about seven inches off the ground, my legs hurt because of the continued squat position. But how my heart resounded with joy as Brother Levi vigorously declared the Gospel of Jesus.

Here, amidst the banana plants on the mountaintop under heaven's canopy, we sought to worship God in Spirit and in truth. No Sunday clothes, no padded benches, bare-footed, with God's air-conditioning—how the simplicity drew my heart heavenward.

After the lovely worship service, we started to walk toward home but were intercepted by Brother Edgar. "Please come to my house for supper," he invited. His wife and others had prepared a meal of plantain and bean sauce. Deeply humbled, I partook of the most generous meal possible. Before I left, I embraced Brother Edgar and blessed him for his unstinting hospitality.

Chapter 45

A Day With the Nurses

· September 1999, written by Anna Joy Kauffman

On Wednesday we were asked to go see a lady named Ti Klis in a little town called Larifi up in the mountains. It was one of those vague cases where we weren't exactly sure what we were going to encounter. When Madame Moyiz found out that we were going, she said she'd go with us. She knew Ti Klis well. Before we left, we found out that Ti Klis had gone "crazy" that morning.

It was a good climb to Ti Klis's house, and we were all dripping wet till we got there. When we entered the courtyard, I noticed that a lot of people were there.

Great, I love being observed when I diagnose a case! I thought. Madame Moyiz had to ask some people to leave the house so that we could fit in. About two dozen people were squeezed in that one room and plenty others were standing outside. They did not want to miss anything.

We found that Ti Klis indeed was "crazy." They had to hold her down constantly so that she wouldn't take off or hurt herself. I just sat and observed for a while. She talked and talked and talked. She talked so fast I couldn't understand everything she was saying, but what I did pick up was pretty weird. One thing I noticed right away was that she was always talking about demons and death.

Suddenly she looked at me and muttered, "My throat. Oh, my throat!"

"What is wrong with your throat?" I asked.

She clutched it and with a wild look in her eyes said, "Demons. There are demons crawling up my throat." And quite a few times she'd fasten her eyes on someone and say, "Demons are going to come eat you tonight!"

Sometimes she would come back to sanity for a few brief seconds, but then she'd start talking crazily again. Every few minutes her eyes would get huge, and with a wild look she would say something about demons or Satan. She was shriveling in fear and agony.

A few times she just stared into my eyes, and I felt a strong sense of an evil presence. One time she suddenly said, "Look at the nurse's eyes. See what's in them!" It almost gave me the chills, but I had a strong calmness in me that I knew was straight from God, and I stared right back at her.

I felt so tied. How I wished I could talk Creole more fluently. I was praying earnestly all the time, pleading for wisdom and discernment. Ti Klis was only twenty-eight years old and had been sick for some time. She was known to be a quiet, sweet, loving person, so it was unlike her to act this way. Soon after we arrived, Madame Moyiz stationed herself behind Ti Klis to hold her and help calm her down. Quite a few times I saw Madame Moyiz wiping tears; she seemed deeply touched with the whole scene. A few times while I was telling Ti Klis that she doesn't have to fear Satan if she has Jesus in her heart, Madame Moyiz chimed in, emphasizing everything I said.

Melissa and I talked it over and finally decided to go home to get an injectable sedative and also to ask counsel from Rick. It was about 5:30 by this time and the sun was beginning to set. We quickly got what we needed and hurried back. After we gave the medicine, Melissa and I prayed for her. Most of the others in the room were staunch Catholics and looked on in silent observation.

We left with mixed feelings. I wasn't sure we had handled it the best way possible, but I wasn't sure what else to do but continue praying. She was so crazy, it was impossible to even communicate with her. I went up to see her on Thursday again, and she was quite a bit calmer. But I am convinced that we are not at the bottom of this one yet.

This experience opened the door with Madame Moyiz. We talked almost the whole way home. She told me more about Ti Klis and her family. Ti Klis had gotten into a fight with another woman, and Ti Klis's family ended up putting this other woman in prison. While in prison, the woman supposedly sent evil spirits on Ti Klis.

From that subject we got onto other subjects. Quite a few times we stopped right in the middle of the trail and just stood there and talked. Under Madame Moyiz's hard, almost cruel looks and the rigid, calloused face is a soft, tender heart. And she seems to be opening and exposing that soft heart more and more.

Chapter 46

Spiritual Warfare

• December 1999

This morning I felt like the Apostle Paul in Acts 17, where it says ". . . his spirit was stirred in him when he saw the city wholly given to idolatry."

Yes, there was "fight" in my heart this morning—that deep struggle against the forces of the devil. We have prayed earnestly against the inroads of Satan through Alfred, who seems to be a most cunning *bòkò*. It seems he is doing everything possible to weaken the followers of Jesus. He tries to stir up fear and lure them back to Satan's control. We pray for his conversion and that the principalities and powers over him would be overthrown.

This morning my heart was burning for our dear people. I had just talked with a young girl named Michline and encouraged her in the Lord. Before I left, I invited her to come to our church services. As I walked, I wished for an opportunity to counter Alfred with the truth and power of God. Approaching his house near the trail, I saw him sidle behind a tree to hide. He held a rooster that he was washing and grooming. I called to him and he came out to the trail. Looking him squarely in his flashing eyes, I kindly but emphatically told him that he needs the Lord in his life. I told him I was praying for his conversion, that God knows his heart, and that if he died he would be lost. "Do you understand?" I asked.

"Yes," he replied. "I will come to Jesus later sometime."

Alfred is a sly, powerful man with much influence, although more out of fear than respect. He has several wives and is in demonic control.

Later this morning as I walked and prayed, God again sent Alfred on the same trail I walked. I had a sharpened sword from corporate and personal prayer for him. Again I pointed him to his need of changing his life from serving Satan to serving the true God before he dies.

I then walked on to visit Sove, Klomàn's uncle. I talked with Sove and encouraged him in the Lord. His mother, who is ill, lay on the damp, musty floor. She was bedecked with the traditional red voodoo clothing. Outside, a mere fifteen feet away, was an altar with a bottle of some concoction offered to appease the devil. After meeting the family, I knelt on the floor and first prayed a simple prayer in Creole. Then, with an intense burden for her and her family, my heart ruptured and I earnestly prayed in English that God would speak to their hearts and deliver them from the clutches of Satan. Also present at the house was Sove's brother Towo, who is deeply bound and needs Jesus. Indeed the warfare wages.

■ ■ ■ ■ ■ ■ ■

Jiryòn

On my way home I met Jiryòn, a very sick man. His small, rounded face and cheeks were so puffed up that he resembled a chipmunk bulging with nuts. Nurse Melissa diagnosed his disease as anthrax, which is often contracted by eating contaminated meat. In their poverty they eat almost anything; precious meat cannot be wasted.

On Monday the nurses and I went to see him again. He lay on the floor on some rags, and his eyes had the pitiful look of despair and death. I knelt on the floor of the hut and placed my hand on his frail shoulder. After telling him about Jesus, I offered a prayer to God on his behalf.

At 3:30 Tuesday morning as I was preparing for a trip to Port, the sound of wailing from the valley below struck chills to my heart. It was eerie, hopeless, despairing—a reminder of eternity. Jiryòn was gone. Gone into the life beyond—probably without Christ.

Jiryòn had no family of his own, so he had lived in the same home as Michline, who now comes to our church and has given her heart to the Lord. This openhearted teenager faces heavy demonic influence since her blind mother has turned back to Satan. There is an ongoing, intense spiritual warfare on behalf of her and the rest of her family. I am sure Satan is drooling and licking his greedy chops in his desire to see her stolen from the kingdom of Jesus.

. . . .

Weep With Me

I first saw her at the House of Matthew—a gracious, gentle fifteen-year-old mountain girl named Gèline. She greeted me with a smile and a customary peck on my cheek. I wondered who she was.

Anna Joy soon answered my questions. On one of her adventurous house calls up the rugged, grueling mountains, she had gone to see Gèline's mother, who was very sick. This lady's extreme poverty often caused her to go foodless so that her children could eat. Her health was so critical that she had to be rushed to the hospital in Ti Goâve. Unfortunately, her malnourished body was dissipating and she died not long afterward.

Anna Joy learned that the mother, in her desperation, had given Gèline to certain men to "earn" a little food to prevent starvation. Now, sadly, Gèline was expecting a child. At first she did not tell anyone who the father was. Later we learned why. The father is her wicked uncle, a *bòkò* who threatened to kill her if she divulged that he was the father.

Homeless after her mother's death, Gèline was taken by the hospital staff to the home of Levi's brother-in-law. Levi, in the kindness of his heart, then brought her to the House of Matthew.

. . . .

Nereyis's Bible

I watched with joy and amusement as fifty-four-year-old Nereyis and many others went forward when their names were called. Nereyis smiled from head to toe, and his face beamed like a triumphant child as he grasped the new Bible in his hand. No, he could not read, but it was a treasure to him. His children were learning to read and would read the Bible to him. He, like the others, earned the Bible by attending an eight-week Bible course and passing a verbal test at its completion. Those who already had a Bible received a songbook or a zippered cover.

■ ■ ■ ■ ■ ■ ■ ■

Surprise

One day not long after I visited him, Sove was seriously injured by a falling tree. A quick diagnosis in Ti Goâve indicated several fractured ribs and internal injuries. Many of his friends and relatives expected him to die. In fact, his brother Towo told Sove that if God heals him, he will get converted.

Yesterday afternoon some Haitian children came walking up the path past Rick's house. "Sove is coming home from the hospital," one of them said, pointing up the steep mountain trail.

"No way," I said. "He couldn't have walked from Ti Goâve. That's fourteen miles away!" Imagine our surprise some time later when we went to see who was coming. There was no doubt about it—it was indeed Sove.

Rick met him at the base of the mountain. Sove spoke excitedly, "The doctors didn't heal me. God did. I am so much better!"

God, in His mercy, was showing His power and was giving Sove's family another opportunity to repent. Except for Klomàn and her parents, all of Sove's family and close relatives remain staunch voodoo practitioners. Now they can truly see that God is calling them.

"Towo, where are you?"

Chapter 47

The Power of Evil

· December 1999

Sunday is a good time to visit the locals. On an early Sunday morning stroll, I visited with Sove's mother. "Please pray for my son Towo," she said. "He is very sick." Surprised at the news, I promised to visit him as soon as possible.

That afternoon after church I hurried to Towo's house to see how he was. He did not appear to be very sick. When I told him his mother had sent me to pray for him, he gave a hearty assent. With a burdened heart for his soul, I cried out to God that he could be saved from his devil worship. I told him I would come to see him later, and he thanked me for coming. Little did I realize when I left that within hours Towo would stand before the great Judge of the universe. His time for repentance was drawing to a close.

We'll never know exactly what happened, but later that evening his life had fled. And once again the blood-curdling wails pierced the blackness of the night. Another Haitian had met his Maker.

· · · · · · ·

Voodoo Service

The next afternoon I trudged up to Towo's mother's *kay*, where men had dug a grave down to solid rock. They were laying a perimeter of stone with mortar. Earlier in the day I had stopped by amidst wailing, drunken men who were using dried banana tree sheathing to simulate drums, beating their native rock music with crude sticks to draw in the demons. Drunken, raucous laughter split the air again and again. But now not many people were there. Where were they? I soon found out.

A friend stopped by and told me to follow him to the house where I had prayed with Towo the day before. There they were, hundreds of voodoo worshipers, many unknown to me. Blast after blast of pungent, sickening booze attacked my nostrils as I passed through the noisy, milling throng.

Moyiz was "Master of Ceremonies." He personally led me into the house where they were preparing to place the body into the coffin— an expensive, fancy, spatter-painted one. It seemed I wasn't very welcome there, so I quickly retreated. In minutes they carried the coffin outside and placed it on two chairs. At Moyiz's request they opened the lid for me to view the corpse; then the voodoo service began. Yams, plantains, coconuts, and much more were placed under the coffin to feed and appease a demanding, greedy devil. They lit small candles and placed them on the ground at either end of the coffin. Their incense rose to call the demons.

All who handled the corpse washed their hands, arms, and face with a strong-smelling, pungent solution. Moyiz then took a small bunch of leaves, dipped them in a "sacred" solution, and sprinkled the coffin. Ritual after ritual took place. Then Moyiz, waving his arm like an experienced song leader, led the worshipers in singing, chanting, and praying for quite some time. He and his fellow cohort read from an aged book with tattered brown edges resembling something you might see under glass in a museum. I was in the midst of deep spiritual darkness, demonism, and despair.

Then came a surprise. Moyiz asked me to pray! I floundered through a simple Creole prayer. Then in English, no longer able to restrain the deep burden and hurt of my heart, like an erupting volcano my heart let loose as I pleaded to God for these dear deceived heathen. Though my words were Greek to them, I trust God took the burden to their hearts.

Small children, relatives of Towo, were handed back and forth over the casket, a ritual supposed to prevent nightmares and fears in the hearts of the children.

Suddenly pandemonium erupted. There was a disagreement as to how they would carry the coffin to the burial site several thousand feet down the road. Finally several men hoisted the coffin on their heads and pranced off, a parade of hundreds of screaming, wailing people following.

Upon arrival they attempted to place the coffin in the prepared site, but the place prepared for it was too short. Amidst much shouting and confusion they demolished the end wall, placed the box, and then rebuilt the wall.

It was a day to remember, a day to burn in my heart, a day to remind me to fall on my knees in prayer. There are times in life when one is completely overwhelmed with inadequacy and failure, but at the same time filled with love, concern, and soul travail. One thought keeps going through my mind. *I was in a position to lead Towo to Jesus when I visited him a few hours before his death. Now he's gone—eternally gone!*

. . . .

Behind the Scenes

The consensus seems to be that Towo was truly seeking the Lord and was a victim of Satan. In an area where Satan worship runs rampant, any follower of Satan who seeks the Lord becomes vulnerable to attacks from the enemy. He is not about to let his followers go scot-free.

"Does the devil have power to snuff out the lives of men?" you may ask. My own theology has altered as I live among devil worshipers, and many times my skepticism has turned to simple belief. Is it possible that we at times underestimate Satan's power? We don't know the answers to all these questions, but one thing we do know: it is a dangerous thing to give oneself over to the power of Satan. We must keep ourselves under the blood of Christ.

. . . .

Gèline

We all rejoiced that Gèline, the innocent victim of wickedness and poverty, was converted a few weeks ago. She is being nurtured in a godly Haitian home. On Wednesday she gave birth to a little boy. Gèline's new "mother," Madame Dodo, is nurturing and blessing her. We thank and praise God for meeting this urgent need.

Late on Sunday afternoon a few of us hiked up the steep mountain behind the mission to see Gèline and her new baby. The spirit I found was encouraging. Gèline loves her baby dearly and cares for him as a faithful mother should. Though a few weeks old, the child still had no name. They asked me to name him, so I suggested David.

On each hand David had a tiny extra finger. The protective new mother struggled with having anything done to hurt the child, but we persuaded her that now was the best time. So Madame Dodo found a string and performed the tiny "operation" by tying it tightly around the growth. The tender-hearted mother's eyes grew big with concern as little David whimpered plaintively in pain.

We blessed the home, prayed for them, and encouraged them in the Lord. It thrilled my heart to hear Madame Dodo say that whenever Gèline goes out, she will go with her and never let her out of sight. Madame Dodo is a godly mother over the two, looking out for their best in every way.

Chapter 48

Trying Times

• December 1999

We are in the midst of some grueling times. Really, it is little wonder in a land dedicated to Satan, the father of lies. He is constantly trying to deceive and destroy anyone he can. "He knoweth that he hath but a short time" (Rev. 12:12b).

Covetousness, direct lies, slander, suspicion, cultural misunderstanding, and you name it have really rocked the boat recently. For a while the basic attacks seemed to be against the missionaries, but now there are also accusations against the national workers, especially Bruce. All this has drawn us to our knees again and again in earnestness and brokenness.

The most delicate situation involved a head teacher from an outlying school who wanted more teachers and more wages. He resorted to some outright lying against Bruce about the use of funds and Bruce's integrity. He claimed not to have received all his wages. (The matter was recently cleared by the school supervisors and deacons who heard the allegations).

The water then got deeper as other rumors came out about Bruce. The local Catholic priest is working against us because so many of his sheep are now feeding in our pastures. He started the rumor that he gave $12,000 Haitian to Bruce for some other workers and Bruce pocketed it all. They are furious, and some have threatened his life. Such a threat here is no light thing. We hear more and more rumors and gossip.

▪ ▪ ▪ ▪ ▪ ▪ ▪

Communion

On Saturday afternoon we congregated for a time of preparation for communion. The group of believers sang for a while as the deacons and Pastor Rick did some last-minute counseling. Then the assembly was given the opportunity to share needs, confessions, and whatever it took to clear their hearts.

Several people shared and cleared bad attitudes. In the process, some very intense moments ensued. If I had not been accustomed to Haitian culture, some of it might have blown me away. But the air soon cleared and we had a beautiful time of exhortation. How my heart rejoiced as we worshiped together. Over fifty-five of this group of seventy-some believers have come to the Lord in the last year and a half.

On Sunday morning the service began at ten o'clock and lasted pretty well all day. We Americans are like wiggly children compared to the Haitians. The long hours mean little to them. We had a sweet time of fellowship as the nationals and the *blans* shared together in the death and suffering of our dear Jesus. It was a sacred and serious commemoration for them. Whether it is praying publicly as a group, confessing and clearing sin before the congregation, joyously adoring, or singing and clapping before the Lord, they do it with all their might.

It was a beautiful experience to wash the feet of my beloved black brothers. I was at the end of a row of about twenty-five brothers. The floors were dusty and grimy, and by the time the basin came to me, the water was the same color as the black feet. I confess I had to deal with my heart and my thoughts, but then I thought about the intense suffering of Jesus and my heart smote me. This was nothing, absolutely nothing! With shame I repented and saw myself as God sees me—a dirty, filthy, sinner who daily needs the cleansing blood of Jesus. Yes, the water was dirty, but it didn't matter.

On my left side on the backless bench sat dear old gray-haired Deacon Edgar. I had the blessed privilege of having him wash my feet. On my right sat little Brother Selès. A year ago he was pitifully demonic. Now I could bless him as my dear brother and wash his calloused feet as our Saviour taught us.

Chapter 49

Murder!

• February 2000

One day Anna Joy and Melissa were asked to check on a gravely sick man. Pastor Rick was also called since the man wanted to become converted. The home had been steeped in voodoo and Catholicism. Several deacons and others went along.

After some counseling, the voodoo paraphernalia was gathered on a heap and burned amidst much rejoicing.

Among the crowd present that day was a man whose last name was Lejitim. Years ago, before his conversion, he had been a part of a coup which overthrew the government. Because of this, he was still a mistrusted, despised, and hated man, and some people would not even buy his corn. Being a talkative man, he soon got into a heated discussion with others who were there. They got so angry at him that they started to pelt him with rocks, with intentions to kill him. Even the presence of Pastor Rick did not hinder them. Finally Pastor Rick stood before them, shared the message of peace, and told them if they must stone someone, they were to stone him. One by one they let their rocks fall to the ground.

■ ■ ■ ■ ■ ■ ■

Death Valley Again!

The news came as a blow. Lejitim and his wife had been brutally murdered. Members of our church, they had seemed so sincere. Now this. Seemingly, some people just could not forgive him for their past disagreements.

As soon as possible, a group of us headed up the trail toward the Lejitim house. When we got there, scores of people were milling around the house. I will never forget the scene that met our eyes.

On the floor, untouched since the murder earlier that morning, lay Brother Lejitim with a bloody bullet hole close to his heart. Beside him lay his wife, her head a bloody, gory sight. She had been killed first as she tried to defend her husband. After killing her, they had asked him to pray, and then shot him on the spot.

In the next room were two of his sons. The one, an eighteen-year-old, suffers from autism and cannot speak, while the other is about fifteen years old. They had kept quiet during the horrible episode to protect themselves. An older sister, Madaline, was at school in Ti Goâve. When she learned about the killings and arrived home, she went berserk, shrieking, flopping about, and yelling, "I've got no father or mother! I've got no father or mother!"

We needed Levi to make funeral arrangements, so we headed to Ti Goâve and took Madaline along. She immediately bonded to Anna Joy and quieted down somewhat. At Ti Goâve Anna Joy gave her a sedative to calm her down some more.

On the way to town, we met a truck packed with about six uniformed policemen and some other officials. They were headed to the murder site. We learned that this was indeed the talk of town. Nothing like this had ever happened before in this area.

When we returned from Ti Goâve, we met streams of people coming down the mountain. We learned that five suspects had been rounded up, supposedly family relatives. Thankfully, the bodies of Lejitim and his wife had been taken to the morgue in Ti Goâve.

We were asked to take Madaline to a nearby Catholic church, and on the way we picked up the other children also. At the church, hundreds of spectators were noisily milling around. Madaline was shrieking again, and the people pushed and flocked about our truck cage where Anna Joy was caring for her. The whole scene was like a zoo. The people just gawked and gawked.

Lejitim Orphans

Crissy Ann, the oldest of the Lejitim children, has had emotional struggles stemming from a politically motivated attack on their home two years ago. Nurse Anna Joy has worked with her in the past, so she is now caring for her. Although devastated and depressed by the death of her parents, Crissy Ann has responded quickly and beautifully to Anna Joy's care.

Four of the Lejitim children are going to school, and these have been temporarily placed in a Seventh Day Adventist pastor's home in Ti Goâve. The situation is so loaded and volatile that the relatives are scared to take the children into their homes.

We have learned that several of Lejitim's brothers are paying the bill at the morgue to release the bodies. The sad part is that legally the one who pays and cares for the funeral and burial can oversee the disposal of the deceased's property. Brother Lejitim had much land. These wicked and unscrupulous men seem to be plotting to take possession of everything belonging to the wounded, heart-bleeding orphans.

. . . .

The Drama Continues

How blessed to be free in Jesus! How privileged I am! My heart continues in deep pain and turmoil as I contemplate the happenings of the last two hours. As always, the picture I paint is so blurred, crude, and incomplete. Why are we involved? What are the purposes of God in these mysterious happenings?

On the morning of the funeral, we picked up the four children who were staying at the pastor's house and took them to the church in Ti Goâve where the funeral was to be held. Anna Joy sat on the front bench with Crissy Ann on one side of her and Madaline on the other, both claiming her as their adopted mother. I initially sat on the next bench, but Madaline requested I sit next to her as substitute Papa.

As we waited for about forty minutes, Madaline became restless and sometimes grabbed either my arm or Anna Joy's arm. My heart went out to all the children. As I sat there, I relived the experience at their home when I first saw the murdered bodies and heard Madaline's uncontrolled screaming. Tears began to trickle down my cheeks. What painful memories, what agony these dear young people must be experiencing at this moment.

Suddenly, like a gunshot, Madaline jumped to her feet, writhing and shrieking, "Papa! Papa!" The first casket was being carried down the center aisle. For most of the time after that, three or more men were needed to restrain her writhing, jumping, twisting body. All the while sweat poured profusely from her and from the men attempting to restrain her. At the same time, a huge group of protesters marched past, chanting as they went. Each carried a poster picturing the head of Lejitim, the date of the assassination, and a statement saying that he died a political martyr. Somehow Lejitim had been the target of political turmoil. Thankfully, Madaline finally calmed down somewhat.

Only the children and a few of us were permitted to view the dead parents. Pictures were taken, however, and even videos. All the while Madaline was in deepest agony and erupted with regularity. Nevertheless, the singing and preaching continued amidst the bizarre confusion and disruptions.

Before the service finally concluded, the pastor's wife came to me and asked me to start the truck and quickly escort the children from the scene. With the protesters still marching, we were aware that the children's lives were at risk. Ours were too, but we had a responsibility to fulfill. By this time several of the children were writhing in distress. With difficulty they were placed in the caged bed of our truck, and we took them to the pastor's home. I was then also asked to transport the boys and several men to the burial site in the town cemetery while Anna Joy stayed with the girls.

As I drove, I got ensnared in a huge parade of hundreds of slowly marching people. I finally found a back route to the cemetery, entered the narrow drive, and continued. Suddenly I was halted by a parked car. Farther ahead I could see a police pickup and many policemen milling about. Five of them held huge rifles while others brandished handguns. I had been asked to take the boys to their parents' burial, so I approached the police to let me through. They ignored me, deeply occupied with several shouting men. Soon tussling began, and angry shouting came from the dissidents. Uncertain what to do, I started to walk toward our truck.

Bang! Bang! Bang! Loud shots pierced the air. Everybody ducked and ran. I, too, ran and ducked behind a nearby car. Several men were seized by the police and forcibly thrown on a pickup, all the while struggling like wildcats. Then there were more shots, and I was told to get out of there. I gladly left!

I was about to back up my truck when the stranded vehicle in front of me drove off. Away I sped, but I wasn't sure how to get out of the large cemetery. When I slowed down because of uncertainty, Judge Alsiyis's son ran up to me, yelling, "Why aren't you driving faster? Don't you know this is a dangerous place?"

"Jump in and direct me out of here!" I begged. Off we roared. Once out of the cemetery, I took the boys back to the pastor's house, secluded in a back street.

Later on I learned that thieves had broken into the Lejitim house and stolen everything, even the legal papers for the land that should be going to the children later. Oh, the wickedness of the covetous scoundrels who oppress the poor and fatherless! God will judge them!

∎ ∎ ∎ ∎ ∎ ∎ ∎

There is much turmoil in Ti Goâve at present, as next week is election time. There were deep political overtones in the Lejitim murder, and now the children's lives continue to be at risk. Things became so volatile at the place where they were staying, with even the pastor being attacked, that they are now with another family. We have been told not to visit them, lest we draw attention and further endanger them. They do not go out during daylight hours. They have even been threatened by the same man who killed their parents. This wicked man apparently has political clout and has been left untouched by the local authorities.

Chapter 50

Reflections

• March 2000

Off to the Mountains

It finally happened. Levi and I mounted our steeds and went off to visit some church schools. As we traversed the rugged mountains, I was overwhelmed with the poverty along the way. The raggedly clothed children were potbellied and so malnourished that they often had orange-tinted hair. I was struck by the purposeless expressions on many adults, as well as the bony, ragged cattle. The people lived in ramshackle huts with only the most meager of possessions, and the barren, lifeless fields were awaiting water from above.

In one school, we found nearly seventy children and four teachers packed in a little make-shift building with tattered canvas for walls. There were usually about ninety pupils, but because of sickness and deaths in some of the families, many were absent. To test their skills, I asked some pupils to read. For their age they did only average, but at least they were learning to read. My teacher heart resurrected again.

We had a hurried meal and rushed off on our horses to the next school. Here I was amazed at the ability of the head teacher as he taught with skill and authority. Needless to say, when these pupils read for me, they came through with the highest honors.

Yes, progress is being made, and I am so grateful. Of all the blessings these schools bring to the children, one stands out above all the rest—these children will be able to read the Bible.

Clinic

Bruce literally spent days and days going from government official to government official and from office to office to get our clinic approved. The officials finally arrived at Alègue with Bruce on Tuesday.

Later that day, an exuberant Bruce told me we could finally open the clinic—after some more paperwork, of course! It seems unreal after months of difficult work, delays, and disappointments.

Lord's Day at Alègue

Brother David, visiting from the States, shared an inspiring message about the return of Jesus and the need to be prepared. I had slipped up to my *kay* for a while during Sunday school and exhortation time because of stomach cramps and nausea.

When I returned, I learned of a major eruption in the service while I was gone. Amidst much confusion, thrashing about, and commotion, Gèline had passed out and was carried down to the House of Matthew immediately below the church. Droves of people flocked down after them to see what was going on but were sent back to church, where the whole congregation then knelt in prayer.

They laid Gèline on a blanket in Mama Matthew's courtyard while Nurse Melissa and others checked her out. When they couldn't get Gèline quieted down, they sent word to Pastor Rick that it looked like a satanic attack. When Rick arrived, he found Gèline being held down by four or five people, but still in a seeming state of unconsciousness.

Gèline's teeth were clenched, which is sometimes the case in demonic possession. Rick knelt down beside her and called her name, but got no response. Then he began to ask her, "What is your name?" There was still no response, but it was evident she heard him and was trying to respond. He then commanded that in the name of

Jesus the spirit must speak. Finally her mouth was opened and the spirit began to speak.

They soon learned the spirit's name and also found out that it was the girl's uncle (the alleged father of her little child) who had sent the spirit to take Gèline back. The evil spirit said the uncle wants to "eat" the girl for meat (meaning he wants complete control, even to bring death). Rick told the demon that he has no authority over the girl and must leave and go back where he came from.

Suddenly Gèline's eyes opened and she sat up. It appeared as though the demon had left and she was in her right mind, but Rick had some doubts. Often the demon pretends to leave someone, but is only hiding in the deep recesses of the person's being for a time until the person acts sane and the people stop praying.

When Rick asked Gèline, "Who is speaking to you?" she was confused and could not respond. Then her eyes got glassy again, and they knew the demon had not left. They went back to praying and commanding the demon to leave in the name of Christ. Praise God, the demon then left her, and Gèline sat up and confessed some satanic adoration she had been involved in throughout her life, as well as a real weakness in telling lies.

Rick then probed into what exact involvement Gèline had in the demonic world. As it turned out, this meek young girl had an experience much like the maiden that is spoken of in the book of Acts. Like the girl whose master made money off her soothsaying, Gèline's uncle made money from Gèline's demonic possession. She said they lived in the section of Port-au-Prince called Bon Repos. There, many people had come to find healing at the hand of the demon that dwelt in Gèline, and the uncle got the profit. In reality, Gèline was a *manbo,* a lady witch doctor. It was now clear why the devil seemed to have such a stronghold in her life and why the uncle was so upset.

Gèline was an exhausted girl when the demon finally left her. Melissa and I later went down to pray for her and encourage her. The girl will need lots of support to remain free.

. . . .

Levi and Rose's Wedding

We are so excited—Levi has finally gotten married. His wife is Rose, the only daughter of Judge and Madame Alsiyis. She is a dedicated Christian woman who has spent a number of years in Ti Goâve as a teacher. We have learned, through Anna Joy's close contact with her, to respect her Christian ideals. Her father is a very able and much respected judge here in Alègue. For a while her mother attended our services, but she has a staunch Catholic background and is a very strong-willed, determined person.

I knew that Anna Joy had been asked to be the maid of honor for Rose. I could understand this, as she was a close friend. I was surprised, however, when I learned a few days before the wedding that I was to be best man. Wow! This bald, gray-haired, sixty-five-year-old was to be an attendant!

Strong cultural patterns demanded a wedding which indicated their social and economic level, and both families are close to the highest rank here. The wedding was an experience I'll never forget.

. . . .

Heart Musings

As I trudged up the road from the mission toward the church, my heart burned within me. I had just heard the news that the Banav family was struggling and had been involved again in some voodoo. Also, Sove had been drunk recently.

I first met the tall, angular, six-foot-six Sove. As he grasped my hand, I held to his and gently looked up into his eyes. My heart was deeply burdened for him and his family, and I let my concern spill onto him.

I then walked on to the Banav residence. Only the younger children were there. The parents had gone to visit their son. Disappointed, I trudged off to the morning service.

As I walked and visited with other churchgoers, I became overwhelmed with my inability to converse well in the native tongue. I failed to hear their hearts keenly and truly "sit where they sit." During the service, my lack of language mastery loomed big over my head and even bigger in my heart as I failed to grasp the full impact of Brother Levi's teaching. A deep sense of inadequacy and failure overwhelmed my being. Later, we knelt for prayer, and amidst the loud outpouring of my beloved Haitians, I was able to unburden my needy, hurting heart.

Adding to my sense of inadequacy was the looming departure of Pastor Rick, who will be returning to Pennsylvania in the near future. This was decided after much counseling and prayer. He desires to be able to spend more time with his family. Levi, former Pastor Matthew's son, has been ordained to lead the church. He has been discipled by Pastor Rick's teaching and has tramped the trails with him as he counseled many people.

How grateful I am for the work of God's powerful, yet gentle Spirit as He delves deeply into my needy heart. I have been longing and praying for revival. Revival comes when we see ourselves as we really are, when we break our hearts before God and one another, and when we repent and truly submit to Jesus and each other. When I see myself in reality, the illusions broken, it is devastating. But oh the joy, the strength, the freedom, the healing, and the peace of mind that comes with true surrender! Missionaries truly are needy, vulnerable human beings.

Chapter 51

Assaults of the Enemy

• April 2000

Deceiver at Work

God is doing a work here against the works of darkness, but the devil is working overtime to try to harass, hinder, and halt everything that is good.

On Saturday night I awoke to the *tom-tom* of the drums, the escalating noise of mournful voices, and raucous singing and shouting. As the noises continued, I put in my earplugs and went back to sleep. I learned later from Levi that it was a mini voodoo ball, a devil service. Moyiz, Madame Moyiz, Alfred, and their motley band were calling down the evil spirits.

On Sunday while Pastor Levi was preaching, Sove came shuffling past me as he entered the back door of the church, nearly falling as he stumbled his way down the aisle toward Levi. He handed him a paper before he was told to sit down. He plopped his tall body on a bench and blurted out some words.

Poor Sove had been at the Saturday night ball and was drunk. Someone led him to the rear, where he kept shuffling around and saying, "Amen," or, "That's right, Pastor Levi."

I have worked with Sove different times in the past, so as others tried in vain to quiet him, I went to him, took him by the hand, and offered to take him to his hut. With my small hand I grabbed his huge one, and we plodded off toward his house.

At his house I found Moyiz and others. Sove's son came on the scene and seemed embarrassed with his father's drunken muttering.

The next day I met the same son on the trail. He called me aside and in shame he said, "My father is bad."

"I understand your feelings," I told him, "but I still love your father and am praying for him."

. . . .

Mano Is Healed

It was dusk. I had just left the mission house and was walking up toward my house when I met Mano coming down the trail. Eagerly he started talking to me, his voice emanating joy and excitement. Little wonder! He no longer used his crutch! He pulled up his trouser leg. The huge painful growth on his knee was indeed subsiding. He could again work in his gardens and walk around without excruciating pain. We rejoiced and thanked God together.

For many months Mano had suffered from this grapefruit-sized, hard growth on his knee. He could hardly get around, and therefore could not support his family. We had helped him get some X-rays and medication to treat the painful growth on his knee, and now it was a blessing to see him again fill his God-given place as supporter for his family.

Mano lived across the trail from the cockfight shack. He had been a major music player in the *rara* groups in past years before his conversion, but now he and his family served the Lord.

. . . .

The Battle Rages

My heart is full. It's bursting. The burden is great.

It's Sunday morning at about 10:30, and I should be at the service. I was earlier, but after the meeting with Pastor Levi and the deacons, my tears flowed so deeply that I needed time and solitude to cry out to God and unburden my heart. I decided to return to the mission house for some solitude.

It's about the girls, Yvette and Itanya. After they successfully completed the highest grade in our school, Levi and Remòn asked the mission board to start a small-scale high school to train some of the young people in skills to be able to help as teachers in our school.

Levi and Remòn did not want to risk the influence of having the girls in Ti Goâve or at the Catholic school, as youth are so often trapped by the tactics of Satan and lose out in such situations. Many girls become pregnant, and the boys become worldly.

The board felt our primary mission was church planting; therefore they could not lend support in that direction. This hurt Brother Levi deeply, but with the help of Bruce, he was able to sort through and accept this decision. In fact, just last evening he explained to me that he wants to be under the authority of God, the board, and myself. He had such a humble, sweet spirit. He also said that the girls' parents are on their case about placing them in high school.

This morning before the service it happened. Yvette's mother and her older sister Edline, who is the third "wife" of Valsiyis, came and spoke with Remòn and Bruce, telling them that Yvette and Itanya must go to Port, live with their father, and go to high school. Yvette, in tears, said she does not want to. She said her father worships the devil.

The enemy of our souls is out to destroy these dear handmaidens of God. Strong in my memory are the first times I learned to know Yvette and Itanya. They were bound deeply with demons and were struggling with fear, wanting freedom. At first I thought the attacks which overwhelmed them were artificial, but God so graciously freed them. Their deliverance became a strong testimony to the heathen voodoo worshipers of the truth and power of the true God.

Now the enemy is assaulting these girls again. When I heard that their mother wanted them to go to school, I thought it could never happen—she was too poor. But Satan is using wealthy Valsiyis to work against the Gospel here at Alègue.

After committing everything to my kind heavenly Father, I trudged up the hill to the church service again. Sweet, beautiful singing wafted into my hungry ears as I got close. "Jesus is King, Jesus is King; Jesus is King of Kings." How encouraging and uplifting! God will make a way. He is in charge.

I choose to believe that God will make a way for Yvette and Itanya. He has worked in mighty ways in the past, and He will do it again.

Chapter 52

Robes of White

• June 2000

On Sunday morning, visiting Pastor Filibè from Ti Goâve preached a powerful message. Emmanuel, an unconverted seeker present for the first time, stood and asked counsel for salvation. "My wife and mother are not here, but they want to come to the Lord too," he declared. For years they had been deeply entrenched in voodoo. After hearing his heart after the service, Pastor Levi decided we'd better go to his house immediately, since his wife was ill and the household seemed to have voodoo entanglements.

That afternoon a truckload of us wended our way to the little ramshackle hut of these poverty-stricken people. As always, others amassed to observe.

The pastors dealt first with Emmanuel's wife Annette, who was illiterate and so ignorant of the Word and the Lord that she didn't even know the name Jesus. The only spiritual name she knew was the name of her personal demon who gave her advice. There on her bed of affliction, in a cramped, filthy hut, sweat poured from her, and her countenance emanated deep uncertainty. But there was a deep desire and hunger written all over her face too.

Gently, yet powerfully, the Haitian pastors shared the liberating truth of Jesus. They helped her see her personal sin, and she expressed her desire to have her heart and hut cleansed from all her fetishes and other items used in devil worship. In accordance with her wish, several church brothers diligently probed the far corners of the hut for all possible items and stacked them outside for burning.

They then dealt with Emmanuel, who seemed to have more understanding. He was able to understand the simple saving Gospel better than his wife and soon found forgiveness and peace.

Next came unkempt Grandma Susan, who seemed hopeless and in the deepest of ignorance. Could she even faintly understand the Gospel? Not clear with her responses, the pastors went back to Annette again. She had changed her filthy dress and was wearing a crisp, clean, yellow one. But the greatest change came as she publicly renounced her controlling demon and finally understood the reality of Jesus. Her eyes seemed to warm and her countenance spoke of peace—the peace of Jesus. Songs and expressions of joy rose to heaven from all of us. What rejoicing we shared! What joy the angels must have felt in heaven.

Then we went back to Grandma. She, too, had a change of dress—now she wore a clean, white one. She now seemed open to the Spirit of God as the pastors counseled and prayed with her, and after a time she knelt down and committed her life to God.

The drama continued to unfold as Emmanuel appeared with a pick. With a sense of urgency, the pick plunged down with vehemence, blow after blow, crumbling the devil's altar to pieces. No more offerings to demons!

After a few dabs of kerosene were put on the pile of voodoo items outside, a match was held to it and the smoke started to ascend. The flames burst out, slowly at first, then with vigor. That which was formerly incense to worship the demons of hell now wafted heavenward as sweet incense to the eternal God. Times like these draw the hearts of the local church together. They help us in the many struggles and weariness of mission life.

This deliverance was a powerful testimony to the many curious onlookers, among whom the power of evil was evident. The brothers and sisters witnessed to the young people milling around the house, but unfortunately, they refused the invitation to come to Christ. One person said of two of the young women who milled around, "They were born in red kerchiefs," meaning they were born into voodoo-practicing families. In a sense, all of Haiti was born in a red kerchief. Oh, for a continued breaking of the power of evil.

Chapter 53

Medical Excursion

· July 2000

La Gonâve is a large island a few hours by boat from the Haiti mainland. Thousands of people live on the island, most of them very poor. They are also quite isolated from the mainland. For weeks, Lamar had planned a trip to the island with some doctors and nurses for a week of clinic work.

When I awoke on Monday morning, eager to go, Lamar told me that if I wanted to, I could go with a much smaller boat that would also be going. We would be traveling twice as fast as the ship and would stop at some smaller islands enroute and do some snorkeling, etc. This sounded exciting to my adventurous mind, but should I go? What about that pain and ache in my legs and lower back this morning? Despite some misgivings, the lure was too great to resist. I would go with the small boat! I couldn't miss this once-in-a-lifetime experience.

The speedy little craft parted the water as we took off, but the waves started becoming angrier as we got farther from shore. The boat rose and fell with a slap and a sharp crack that shook my already aching body. The four-foot-plus waves kept tossing us freely, and my glasses became coated with saline crystals as I held tenaciously to the grip bar and boat rail. I pondered the fate of Haitians fleeing the country in frail, vulnerable, delicate skiffs. I thought of the story of Jonah and remembered that I couldn't swim. My headache, nausea, and aching limbs began to intensify. Yes, the adventure was a little more exciting than I had bargained for, but there was no turning back!

We finally beached on a little island midway. Lamar and the rest prepared to snorkel, but I had lost all desire. I rushed into the foliage—diarrhea! I gulped some Tylenol, took out two life preservers for pillows, and lay down in the shade. No question, I was sick! As I tossed and turned, I longed for the comfort of the bigger ship. But it was too late. I realized I had made a foolish decision.

An hour later the men returned, and we took off again into the deep, turbulent ocean. Suddenly we discovered we were in the midst of a school of porpoises. Enèl, a Haitian pastor who works for CAM, was with us. Like an excited, exuberant lad, he jumped up and down, clapped his hands, and shouted with ecstasy. The rest joined in the adventure like delighted children. In their excitement they stood up in the little skiff, and I was afraid one of them would tumble into the furious, swirling water. Lamar guided the skiff around and around in huge circles while we enjoyed what for me was probably another once-in-a-lifetime experience. One after the other, the porpoises gracefully jumped three or more feet into the air and then plunged once more into the billowing ocean. They seemed to know they were performing for an audience.

By noon we arrived at the large island. The bigger ship had just arrived. We clambered aboard and I managed to eat some lunch. Afterward, however, I lay down on a bunk on the lower berth and felt worse than ever. Sweat poured from my aching body, and the rolling of the ship added to my misery. I longed for my little *kay*.

Experiences like this help me to feel for my oft-sick fellow Haitians. Sometimes the rough sea made me totter and sway just as I have often seen drunken men do. It was not until Wednesday morning that I trusted going ashore and helping with the work in the clinic for a half day.

The clinic was set up in a small church in this remote shore village. The medical staff consisted of two doctors and several nurses. We served over 450 people those few days—and what days they were! At times the noise and confusion were so great that it was difficult for the nurses to obtain the vital signs with the stethoscope. As the time drew near for wrapping up the project, the pandemonium increased to the point of a slugging fight among the aggressive ones. Some feigned serious sickness to increase their chances of being consulted by a doctor.

We had a service on Wednesday evening in a crude school building, where Brother Enèl preached a message of salvation. He has a deep evangelistic interest and would like to see an evangelical church emerge in this very needy area. It was certainly a delight to be able to share medical and spiritual help on this remote island of Haiti.

Chapter 54

Mugged!

• October 2000

O n Sunday evening I returned from Port-au-Prince with a full load, including funds for the mission. We pulled the truck into the shop to await unloading the next day, and I put the funds away in the mission office. After the evening meal with the mission staff, Pastor Levi took me up to Mama Matthew's house on the ATV. It was already quite dark. As always, I toted my things in a pack strapped to my back. As I slowly tramped up the rest of the steep, muddy trail toward my house, I met a man coming down the trail. "Good evening," I said. He grunted only a feeble response before he was beside me.

At that moment he turned, lunged at me, and forcibly seized the pack strapped to my back. So intense was the lunge that it tore both straps. The impact instantly and violently threw me down the bank into the rocky cornfield. Before I came to a stop, I felt a sharp pain as my chin hit a rock and my arms and hands were lacerated on the sharp rocks. I was momentarily dazed. Finally I sat up and discovered to my chagrin that my glasses and flashlight were both gone. My backpack was also gone—as was the robber!

Hoping to get people's attention, I started yelling loudly, "Thief! Thief! Help! Help!" Madame Moyiz heard my desperate cry. Trembling with fear, she ran to the nearby mission house.

"Grandpa Harold is being killed!" she blurted to the missionaries.

Immediately they clambered up the trail toward my house. Ahead of them the Haitians were coming in droves. They found me banged up and bleeding a little here and there but not seriously hurt. My biggest concern at the moment was my expensive glasses. I couldn't read a stitch without them.

After someone finally found my glasses, twisted and dirty, they carefully helped me to my house. My face and arms were smeared with a mixture of mud and some blood. You would have thought I was half dead, like the man in the Good Samaritan story, the way they hovered over me.

As for the stolen backpack, most likely the robber was disappointed. Instead of the money he was hoping for, it was full of dirty laundry, a two-way radio battery, an electronic date and address book, my mail, and other personal belongings.

Later that evening, after everything had been thoroughly discussed, we had a lovely time of singing, and Bruce led in a prayer of thanksgiving that my life had been spared. The nationals were shook up, to say the least, and insisted it is not safe for me to live alone up on the mountain in my *kay*.

As we discussed the robbery, it became clear what had probably happened. The cockfight building at the entrance to our mission house had been packed with gamblers. Likely, several men who assumed I was loaded with funds and were hoping for big loot had trailed me. Fortunately, I had little money on me. In the future, if I return after dark, I will not head up to my house but sleep at the mission base. I do want to be careful, but I realize I must also trust my heavenly Father.

▪ ▪ ▪ ▪ ▪ ▪ ▪

Deep Sorting Out!

God gave me a peaceful sleep after my mugging Sunday evening. I really thought I was doing okay, but to my disappointment, I learned I had much more to work through. The next day we drove about three hours to an optometrist to get my badly twisted glasses in shape.

I returned late, and it was starting to get dark. I wondered whether I should stay at the mission or go on up the trail to my *kay*. *Surely, it's not that dark yet,* I thought to myself. *I think I'll go on up.* But then fear started to loom in my heart, and I longed to have someone go with me. While I was battling my fears, Bruce came to meet me and kindly placed his hand on my shoulder. "There's no way you're going to walk to your house alone. I'll go with you," he assured me.

"Thank you so much. It's so kind of you!" I exclaimed. Once again God had seen my need and had met it. He is so good.

As we slowly walked up that steep, rocky path to my *kay*, I felt so vulnerable. When we came to the spot where the stranger had lunged at me, I relived the attack by the mugger—his hardened face, the sensations of the violent plunge on the knife-like rocks, and the pain in my arm. How thankful and encouraged I was by the presence of my friend Bruce.

I had to ask my co-workers for special prayer on Tuesday. I also learned that many Haitians thought I would return to the States. I chose to put it all under the blood and protection of my dear Jesus. I know His grace is sufficient. God is with me!

■ ■ ■ ■ ■ ■ ■

Painful Void

Brother Rick has left. He is missed sorely, not only by the converts, but by many heathen neighbors far and wide. They loved, respected, and obeyed him; he was indeed their "papa." Not only do the Haitians miss him, but for me the void is intense. For months, I had sought to work through and accept his coming departure. We had worked together closely, and Rick became as a son to me. He understood and spoke the language well and also understood so many of the intricacies of the Haitian culture. He seemed to have a photographic memory. As for me, I can't even remember where I put my passport! Rick knew the foods, the plants, the numerous trees, the animals, the farming methods, and much more. Nationals would daily wait by the hour to have a chance to ask for counsel or help from him. He lived and identified with the people in so many respects.

I realize I am not called to be a Rick. But nonetheless, the void is huge! The questions about spiritual needs and problems now fall upon Pastor Levi. He feels it heavily but is rising to the challenge.

With Rick gone, we are especially thankful for Lowell and Rosanna Auker, who have arrived to help out at the mission. They couldn't have arrived at a better time.

190

Chapter 55

Nightmare!

• November 2000

"**B**rother Harold! Brother Harold!" I was in my first deep sleep. Groggily I tried to listen. "We need you. It's Levi, Bruce, and Remòn." Still somewhat dopey, I fumbled for my flashlight and shuffled out to the porch. Even though I was tired, my mind was spinning in overdrive. *What's up that I am awakened at 11:30 p.m.?*

Once they had me fully awake, they spilled out the story. In pitch darkness, a large truck had stalled on a hill. The engine would not restart and the truck had no backup lights, so the driver asked the people to get off. Many did, but others chose not to. A rider was asked to use a flashlight to direct the driver as he attempted to start the engine by rolling backward. Naively, the man misguided the driver and the truck shot out over the ledge. It tumbled, rolled over several times, then landed on its wheels and careened a short distance to the bottom, where it jammed into the nearby bank. The report said some were dead and many were seriously injured. They needed trucks to transport the wounded to a hospital.

Dazed and weary, I sat a moment and then said, "Okay, I'll get ready." I called down by radio and awoke Anna Joy so that she could go along. Hurriedly I gulped down a cup of coffee and, using my hiking stick, slithered down the muddy mountain trail, my mind racing way ahead of my body.

We decided Bruce would drive the Toyota and I the Mitsubishi. We took along stretchers, beanbags, lots of flashlights, and Anna

Joy's medical things, not knowing what to expect. The accident had occurred beyond Girard. The driver, though injured, had walked miles to our mission to beg for help. We picked him up and headed out into the black of night. We soon learned that he was fearful for his life, lest he be killed by angry riders or their friends in angry protest. Killing the driver after a serious accident is not uncommon in Haiti. Each time we met a group of people along the way, he fearfully slouched down in the back seat.

By the time we arrived, the injured had been carried or dragged to various huts on the mountainside. We found seven people seriously injured and needing a hospital. A mother of seven children had been killed in the accident. There were two broken legs, as well as multiple cuts and serious bruises. One shoulder bone was fractured, one arm broken, and a lady with a horribly lacerated face had a popped eyeball dangling on her cheek—a gruesome sight to behold. We found a little boy with internal injuries who was vomiting. Others with minor injuries were left on the mountain.

After sorting out who should accompany the injured, we finally started the slow, tedious drive to Ti Goâve hospital. There were no sirens, no advance radio or phone calls, and no waiting doctors or nurses. We arrived around 3 a.m. to find everything dark and, of course, the nurses sleeping. With the aid of flashlights, most of the injured had been unloaded and placed into the dark hall when a nurse finally showed up and gruffly stated, "We have no lights, no rooms, no facilities; you need to leave and go to some other hospital. Take them to Léogâne or Port."

What! Load them up again? It was a little after 4 a.m. I knew that my emotional and physical resources were nearly exhausted. When Anna Joy came and kindly suggested that I rest at the house of Levi's brother-in-law while Bruce and Levi transported the injured, I soon acquiesced.

We soon reached the brother-in-law's house and roused him for my sake. Even though it was still nighttime, swarms of onlookers swarmed about the truck, pushing tightly against the truck cages, gawking, squawking, and exclaiming. The news had spread far and wide already.

I finally lay down at 4:30, but even my faithful earplugs could not stop the multiple shrill, insistent *taptap* horns, the gear-shifting, and the people yelling. I dozed fitfully until 6:30, at which time I was able to contact CAM personnel with my handheld radio and asked them to report to Lowell Auker at the mission.

The injured were transported by ambulance to the Léogâne and Port hospitals. Family members had to be located, so it was a most grueling time for Anna Joy, Remòn, Bruce, and Levi. They didn't return to Alègue until six o'clock that evening. Truly it was a nightmare.

■ ■ ■ ■ ■ ■ ■

ATV Accident

It happened in moments. It seemed like a bad dream, but it was real. I was heading down toward the mission house for lunch. At a sharp curve and steep descent, as I tried to avoid some rocks, the front wheel of my four-wheeler dropped into a washout and the ATV started tipping. As I dropped my leg to stabilize the machine, I was thrown off. The ATV continued across the road and up the side bank. Getting to my feet, I quickly ran and grabbed the culprit. As I started to seize the bars, it capsized and rudely threw me down—this time with the machine on top of my body! The rear carrier knocked my head against the rocks. The beast then rolled over onto its wheels and kept going down the steep road, which had a sharp turn. Finally it plunged down a four-foot bank and ended upside down against a banana tree.

I was dazed and in shock, with my head, shoulder, and leg badly bruised. I radioed to the mission for help. In the meantime Haitian friends, hearing the excitement, came from far and near. After a while Lowell, Melissa, and Ada Fisher, a nurses' aid who had come to help at the clinic, came with a truck. Under Lowell's direction, the beast was soon righted and hauled through a wooded lot to a lower spot on the road. It easily started up, seemingly not much the worse for the

Nightmare!

193

scenario. It seems I got the worst of the bargain. I was so thankful I had no broken bones or other serious injuries.

■ ■ ■ ■ ■ ■ ■

Brotherly Aid

The Haitians were so concerned that sometime I might be killed at that sharp curve that they decided to correct the problem. Over a hundred men showed up to get the job done. All day long they labored industriously with picks, shovels, hands, and wheelbarrows. Judge Alsiyis supervised the diligent men. It was humbling. How grateful I am for their love and concern for me.

Chapter 56

A Broken Heart

· December 2000

A n ancient poet of the nineteenth century sat in his padded pew in an orthodox church. In front of him sat a sophisticated, proud matron, with not one wrinkle upon her dress. Her bonnet covered her stoic face and her bonnet ribbon was starched to perfection. But, marching up her starched bonnet ribbon, unbeknown to this prim lady, was a train of lice. In response, the poet penned these lines:

> *Would that God some gift would give us,*
> *To see ourselves as others see us.*

Yes, it might be revealing, embarrassing, and humbling to see ourselves as others see us. But let's go deeper. I'd like to change a few words to read: "To see ourselves as *God* sees us."

This is not only humbling, it is grievously crushing. As with Isaiah, I need to cry out, "Woe is me!"

■ ■ ■ ■ ■ ■ ■

Beyond the "Lice"

In my situation as a missionary on the field, God has helped me to see myself as others see me and as He sees me. Oh, the rottenness of my sinful, proud heart! The "lice" in my life which others see are very real and offensive. What then does God see?

God gives us many burdens in life that are necessary burdens—the care of families, of churches, and of missions. These should drive us to our knees in prayer and fasting. Many times we do not take this seriously enough. God wants us to bring these necessary burdens to Him. We need to release them and roll them on Him in trust. Then we can find the rest Jesus invites us to receive. If we do not, the very proper burdens and responsibilities given to us by God will finally crush, wound, and disable us. Then we start to fret—the very opposite of resting, committing, and trusting. "Cast thy burden upon the Lord, and he shall sustain thee" (Psalm 55:22).

Haiti is indeed the land of the unexpected. The demands of life, the requests, and the need to make decisions plunged in on me day after day. I knew, and most of us know the words of Scripture, "His grace is sufficient," and "I will give you rest." But I was not experiencing that rest. I worried about the finances, the daily demands of mission life, and the responsibilities, and I started to fret. Indeed, it started to eat as leprosy.

Someone always gets hurt in such situations. In my case it was my missionary helpers, the national laborers, and others in my path. I say this to my shame. I would see it sometimes and seek release, but would stumble again and again. I did not want to go on in this way. I struggled and prayed, but failed again and again.

I struggled with the frequent medical trips to Ti Goâve, with too much wear on the trucks, and with too many dollars spent. I overshadowed the missionary workers in their routine decisions and thought the Haitian laborers did not produce enough or well enough. As a result, I became curt with them in their many requests and expectations of me. I would become aware of it and ask forgiveness at times, but like a tire taking a deep, muddy rut, I was soon back, wallowing in mud again. How I wanted out of this trap—or did I?

In the midst of the flurry of many medical trips, I was returning one day from Port with supplies on the Toyota. On the rugged road from Ti Goâve to Alègue, I met the other mission truck coming my way, loaded with workers. Yes, as you might have guessed, it was another medical case. I sensed my spirit rising up. Not another case! I sought to conceal my feelings, but couldn't. What is in the heart comes to the surface sooner or later. I asked a few questions and made some remarks. I forget the exact words I said, but I'll not forget the wounded look on their faces. How this haunted me!

As I left, I cried out to God, "Give me another chance!"

I pondered deeply, *"This dare not continue. I will not keep hurting my friends. If I cannot find rest and freedom, I must go back to Pennsylvania."*

That night I climbed the steep hill to my little *kay* with resolution. I was determined to go the whole way, whatever the cost. The next morning I was up early, crying out to God for mercy and deliverance.

"God," I cried out bitterly, "I can't go on like this!"

I knew I needed to apologize, so I sent a letter down the mountain to the other workers via e-mail, asking for a meeting. Before the meeting, I went to the house nearby where Levi, Bruce, and Remòn were staying. I wanted everything clear. There I confessed my impatience, my curtness, and my lack of love. With tears we all shared together. I repented. I confessed. I was a broken, wounded man.

This was but the beginning. I then met with my loving fellow workers. I told them to be very frank and share their hearts where I had hurt them. It was difficult at first for these dear younger people to expose and rebuke me as an older grandpa. But I wanted God's knife to go deep. We had a painful but healing time of sharing, praying, and weeping. God was indeed cutting deeply.

The next morning I was still struggling. I went down to my little prayer place on the concrete slab over the cesspool and tried to find direction and comfort from Psalm 51, David's prayer of repentance. It was difficult to read it and receive it for myself, but God kept revealing my heart in its true state.

For two days I struggled to find total clearing. My heart was shattered. I went to each of the missionaries and told them I want everything to be clear.

God then went deeper. I felt a need to publicly share sins and failures with the nationals at the morning service. I wanted no stone unturned. That afternoon I met with the deacons and opened my heart to them likewise. I was finally casting my burden on the Lord.

There were some Haitians who I thought were a continual pest to me. Their requests drained me, and I had trouble accepting and loving them. I asked the Lord to give me a special love for them—and He did. I had offended a deacon's son at Ti Goâve one time. I had tried to clear it in the past, but in vain. But that very Sunday afternoon he walked into my courtyard. When I saw him coming, I thought, *God, whatever he says, whatever he asks, I want to take it. I will make no defense.*

There was nothing to take; God had already worked in his heart. We embraced and forgave each other. Oh, how lovely are the ways of God.

In the midst of all this I told God, "I want to surrender everything to you. The trucks are yours. The finances are yours. If you want me to go back to the States and give up the work, I am ready."

I was more concerned about peace, rest, and the grace of God in my life than anything else. Yes, my life was shattered, but I sensed God picking up the pieces. May He put it together as He chooses, for His glory.

Chapter 57

Ominous Clouds

• March 2001

Although Bruce has been a tremendous asset to our work here in Alègue, there have also been many struggles involving him lately. The involvements are too fragile to easily explain, but Bruce has gone out from us. Sadly, he seems to be working against Pastor Levi and the work here and has written some threats against the work.

Levi is deeply burdened and is struggling to cope with everything. Bruce had been in charge of the schools, and this weight now falls on Levi and Remòn. There are so many problems to try to solve. Other schools are trying to nab some of our teachers, and the school budget will not stretch far enough to cover inflation. To top it off, there are pressures from the government about our present school buildings. The load is very heavy for a young pastor. He is looking forward to the coming visit of his beloved Pastor Rick. We are at a new juncture of the road for the work at Alègue.

• • • • • • •

A few months ago Yvette was sick and went to her mother's house to live. Her mother and sister are deep into voodoo, so I was quite concerned. Thankfully, she remained faithful to the church and school, but I sensed a little distancing. On Sunday afternoon she came to Pastor Levi and reported that Bruce has asked her to come to Port and work for him. She definitely did not want to go. This experience strengthened her faith and brought her back more fully into the influence of the church. Her heart is once again more free and open.

What is Bruce up to? We don't know. We hear rumors of him starting a clinic at Belamy, and of working against the local schools. Whispers abound. One thing we know, our lives are in God's hands. We must advance on our knees, trusting our Commander-in-Chief.

. . . .

I was able to have a meeting with Bruce. It was a good meeting, even though painful at times. Tears flowed as Bruce confessed some things, but he seemed reticent about others. Although Bruce is no longer with us, he does want to keep open communication with the mission workers. I am thankful the door has slightly opened again. I counseled him to guard his heart lest he be destroyed by a spirit of bitterness, and he seemed to accept my concerns. Now we have to sort out and uncover the truth about the many rumors.

. . . .

Moyiz Family

On Sunday Madame Moyiz's daughter Rhode from Port-au-Prince was at church in Alègue. She stood and gave a lengthy testimony about her life and some difficulties she has faced. It seems she is seeking the Lord, but she needs a complete surrender. She is an educated lady—a policewoman.

We are saddened that Madame Moyiz's heart appears to be hardening. Pastor Levi informed me that she is determined to not allow any more of her neighbors to become converted. The irony is that she sends her daughters to our school and church. Although we believe her interest in being converted was sincere, there is a deep spiritual stronghold in her family that the Gospel needs to conquer. For one, they own the cockfight shack and promote its wickedness. Although Madame Moyiz herself is not openly practicing witchcraft at this time, I hear reports of her anti-Gospel efforts.

Perhaps the greatest hindrance to her becoming a Christian is her fear of curses from other voodoo worshipers. And, indeed, this is no light matter. No one knows the power of the evil one better than those who have been under his control. With man, victory over such an influence is hopeless, but with God all things are possible.

Chapter 58

Mission to Girard

- June 2001

My heart bled as I looked at the huge group of heathen neighbors and friends. The place nauseatingly reeked with strong drink. We were in a place called Girard, a two-hour hike from Alègue, for the funeral of a brother. Very few Christians lived in this area, so our deacons were in charge of the funeral. The Gospel torch was bright, with the arrows of truth piercing into many hearts for probably the first time.

At the close of the service, Deacon Adolph asked Brother Dan, visiting from the States, to share. With a deeply touched shepherd's heart, he shared the precious call of God to each one present with urgency, judgment, and compassion.

■ ■ ■ ■ ■ ■ ■

Olive

A woman from Girard named Olive sent word that she wanted a nurse and also a minister. She wanted to be converted.

A group of us, including Deacon Norès and Nurse Melissa, clambered on board the pickup and bumped the first four miles. Then we hoofed the next thirty-five minutes over the rocky, rugged trails to Olive's home. On the floor of the hut we found Olive— frail, bony, and emaciated—lying on a coconut mat. Sick though she was, a glint in her eyes seemed to emanate expectancy. Faithful Melissa donned her latex gloves, checked her vital signs, and tried to diagnose the frail woman's medical needs.

After some singing and praying came the spiritual diagnosing as Deacon Norès shared the Gospel and diligently probed her needy heart with the sharp knife of the Word. We learned that her husband had been killed by a curse from a *bòkò* and that she had also frequented *bòkò* doors. After a period of counseling and instructing, Olive confessed her sins. She renounced her demonic involvements and put her complete trust in Jesus. Olive had a new heart! What a time of rejoicing we had! Later, out on the trail, we put a match to all her voodoo paraphernalia.

■ ■ ■ ■ ■ ■ ■

Meeting Her Maker

A few weeks later we got word that Olive had died. I was thankful to be able to go to her funeral. As I entered her hut, I was given the only chair available. It was rickety, filthy, and squeaky, but most graciously given. As I sat waiting, I remembered how in this same room Olive had raised her weak, bony arms to heaven and received the gift of salvation. She never did have the privilege of coming to our services. We just praise God that she came to know her Saviour before she drew her last breath.

I was the only *blan* there. Secluded in the same bleak, bare room, concealed by a white bed sheet, was a crude coffin. We waited for over an hour before a few Haitians started dribbling in. The scent of drink filtered through the doorway as a staggering, drunk man pretending to be in charge shouted to others to come. Several other men soon chased him off.

The whole atmosphere surrounding the service was sad and despairing. Brother Adolph repeatedly used the Scriptures to point the hearers to Jesus, but few seemed to be listening. Even grown men acted much like undisciplined children—gawking, laughing, poking, and grinning.

Olive had died, having received an eleventh-hour salvation. Now God was calling others in Girard! How merciful He is!

Chapter 59

Sickle of Death

• July 2001

It was visiting time at Alègue. Some friends from Tennessee and I walked to the houses of several neighbors near the mission to visit, sing, and pray. How the nationals revel in such visits! They are such warm, openhearted, friendly, loving people. Their thanks and blessings flowed freely. Our itinerary, unplanned, took us from hut to hut. The climax of our stops was at the hut of Entès. A past serious infection of his foot had developed into blood poisoning, and finally his right leg had to be amputated. We wondered how he was faring by now.

We were shocked when we entered his small, dilapidated hut. There lay Entès on a smelly mat, covered with a dirty blanket. The room reeked of stale urine. Though he was only about fifty years old, his gaunt face seemed to portray seventy years of wear, pain, and futility. When he spoke, we could hear the futility of his heart.

"I can't walk," he told us hopelessly. "I can't prepare food. I can't feed myself. I can't care for myself. I can't do anything." Our hearts bled for the hopelessness of the situation. For a while, like Job's comforters, we simply were there, silent. Kneeling beside him, I held his hand. As we sang and prayed for him, a faint glimmer of hope seemed to once more rise in his heart. We told him we would be back again on Saturday and bring some food.

The whole episode with the one-legged, despairing Entès cut into each of our hearts. I thought of the goodness of God to me, of my freedom in Jesus, my health, my friends, my house—yes, blessings beyond number.

When we returned on Saturday, we sought to transform his despair into true hope in the Lord Jesus, but his despair seemed even greater than at our first visit. "He can't live long anymore," someone remarked as we left. How true it was.

The radio call came early the next morning. "Entès's son Ti Nonm just came and said his father died last night!"

Once more the sickle of death had reaped a life. Entès had met his Maker. He was in eternity. An avalanche of memories flooded my mind: the times the nurses had worked so diligently with his infected foot; the meeting with him at his house, dealing with both body and soul; the foulness and extreme nauseating stench of his rotten flesh; his strong-willed spirit that needed to surrender to the Lord; and finally, our parting from him just a few hours earlier. Truly life is but a vapor.

That afternoon when we arrived for the funeral, the singing had already started. Some men were still digging the grave just below the hut. Many heathen relatives and neighbors were gathered at the site, some sitting here and there on the hillside on rocks.

The spirit of the service was subdued, with the message being a challenge to the living to prepare for death.

As the Gospel service concluded, a man lifted the coffin lid and quickly tilted a bottle to his mouth. With gusto, using his mouth as a pressurized gun, he repeatedly spewed a vapor-like liquid into the face of Entès. With a cloth he smeared it over Entès's face. My nostrils quickly detected the smell of kerosene. Suddenly a whistle blew and the coffin was hoisted to be taken the short distance to the grave site.

Onlookers seemed to consider the whistle the key to open up the powers of confusion and darkness. With lightning speed, pandemonium broke loose. Ti Nonm, Entès's son, fell to the ground, thrashing and screaming. Neighbors and friends seized his body as he easily tossed them about. The other seven children, from two to twenty, with none converted, started crying, screaming, and thrashing about.

Meanwhile, five or six men overpowered Ti Nonm, sitting on him and holding him to the ground. Many others gathered about using whip-like branches to beat him, particularly his feet and legs. I drew a weeping son, about nine or ten years old, into my arms and sought to comfort and encourage him. Other relatives were working with a shrieking, screaming thirteen-year-old girl. I shared with her a little comfort and told her I would be back the next day. The situation was so sad, so futile. Suddenly an older girl in her mid-twenties plummeted to the ground and took up the screaming, wailing, and thrashing about. I recognized her to be a cousin of Ti Nonm. How sad, how hopeless to be without Jesus! Everyone present clearly saw the need for the delivering power of Jesus.

The next day passed rapidly for me. Tired, I plodded up the steep trail to my lovely little mountain *kay*. It was so good to be home again. I had eaten my evening meal and was ready to unwind and prepare for the night when I remembered what I had promised Entès's daughter. I struggled for a moment, but quickly decided I must go. I gathered some food articles, clambered down the trail, and took off on my four-wheeler.

I then walked up the rocky ascent to the hut of the deceased Entès. There, in the quiet of the evening, I found the children sitting on rocks and a log. How lovely, how special, to be their friend at a time like this.

As I once more plodded up the steep trail to my mountain *kay*, I did not seem quite as tired. I was deeply concerned for Entès's children, especially Ti Nonm. The sadness of the whole situation seemed to be symbolic of Haiti in general. How the captives needed to be freed!

Chapter 60

Struggles

• September 2001

Some things are painful and difficult to share. Our only real enemy, Satan, gains a foothold where he can. To our great sorrow, Bruce continues to cause concern to the church here at Alègue. At the beginning of our work here about four years ago, Valsiyis, an unscrupulous, ungodly man, worked against the church here. He was Bruce's enemy. He even put a curse on Bruce.

Now it seems Bruce is in cahoots with Valsiyis. Working through Valsiyis, Bruce is trying to get Yvette to come to Port and work as a maid for him and his wife. She refuses. Her sister Edline is also making threats. "If you don't come," she told Yvette, "I will disown you as my sister. I will make it hard for you and you will wish you had come!" We are praying that Yvette can stand firm. Bruce is also attempting to get Yvette's sister Itanya to work at a clinic he is starting at Belamy.

We certainly face a time of testing, sifting, and refining. At a pre-service meeting, Pastor Levi requested special prayer for the needs we face. Yes, the devil knows he has but a short time. Oh, to redeem the time! The days are certainly evil.

· · · · · · ·

Spread It Before the Lord

The onslaughts continue to intensify, and the fiery darts continue to fly. Not only do we hear reports coming from various nationals, but Bruce keeps sending letters to Remòn, trying to threaten and discourage the work here. In what seems like an effort to intimidate us, he is working with a number of schools on the mountains surrounding us.

He is seeking to turn our people against Pastor Levi and the church. People here are very needy and hungry and thus vulnerable to any promise of hope. He claims to have a *blan* backing him financially. He promises food, work, and hope for the future. He tells the Haitians that the mission at Alègue will soon be gone. He is using his stance in the areas surrounding us to influence others against the church here.

We are deeply saddened by what is happening and have chosen to band together in prayer for him. Bruce is a very capable, persuasive, and influential man, but God is God, and we have chosen to "spread it before the Lord" as Hezekiah did with Rabshakeh's letter in Isaiah 37.

■ ■ ■ ■ ■ ■ ■

Another Blow

Right now I feel like Jeremiah, "Oh that my head were waters, and mine eyes a fountain of tears, that I might weep day and night for the slain of the daughter of my people!" (Jeremiah 9:1).

The enemy of our souls strikes where he can. Ever since being delivered from deep demonic involvement, Gèline has been a faithful member of the church—until now.

After Deacon Dodo's son Efanyèl expressed an interest in marrying her, the church leaders said he must first show that he is able to support her and her young child. He was reluctant to accept this counsel, and last week it was revealed that he had enticed her to fornication. Public confessions were made by both last Sunday, and the church leaders met and decided on a plan to counsel them. But now they have both disappeared, allegedly to Port. We earnestly desire their spiritual and physical protection and restoration.

Ringing deep in my memory is when Gèline came to me personally on Monday. She said, "Grandpa, you are like my own grandpa. I know I confessed and asked the church for forgiveness yesterday. But I want and need your forgiveness personally as a grandpa."

I freely granted her the same and encouraged her to walk closely with Jesus. The destroyer, Satan, wants this maiden back in his kingdom. A battle, a war, is raging.

■ ■ ■ ■ ■ ■ ■

Mysterious Illness

Bay, Remòn's husband, was an energetic, strong young man until the last few days when he started having some strange attacks, or seizures. Without warning, he becomes somewhat paralyzed on his one side, cannot talk, and gets very weak. He has been checked by doctors and has had a battery of blood tests which failed to give a diagnosis. Remòn is trying to find a doctor in Port to further examine him.

As we prayed and shared, we all seemed to sense a spiritual significance in the whole experience. The forces of God seem to be battling with the forces of evil. Bay uses a small motorcycle to go from job to job, and we are so grateful that the strange incidents have not occurred while motoring. Unfortunately though, the attacks seem to be increasing in frequency and intensity. Is there a brain tumor or some other serious physical problem? Or is it some kind of curse against the work at Alègue?

Truly the Lord is letting us go through trials, but I am encouraged by the words of James 1:2: "My brethren, count it all joy when ye fall into divers temptations." I want to do that!

Chapter 61

Rags to Riches

• October 2001

I have seen and entered many huts in the last years, but this one was the worst I had ever seen. It was not even fit for animals. Much of the plastered mud had fallen from the slats of the exterior walls, and I needed to be careful not to push them over. From the outside I had seen large, dried banana leaves draped on the rusty tin. Once inside, I understood. Much of the aged tin looked more like wire fencing than roofing. The recent four inches of rain must have literally drenched the unprotected occupants. These were the poorest of the poor.

From the dilapidated hut wafted a most offensive odor—an odor of disease. On the floor lay the wasting form of Junior, dying of starvation and disease, his body draped with a tattered blanket. His wife was not in much better shape. Her toes were peppered with dirty, oozing, infected sores, and on the back of one foot was an ugly, egg-sized swelling covered with black, smelly ulcers. Many onlookers were also present. The ghastly face of one poor lady continues to haunt me. Her lips, nose, and chin looked much like a leper—ugly, blackish, ulcerated, and decomposing.

Someone had come to the clinic telling of the desperate need of the sick man and the request of his wife to be converted. Some of us, including the nurses and Deacon Adolph, drove to Girard, and then walked back into the mountains. After Deacon Adolph shared the Gospel with the needy couple, we sang and prayed. All items involving demon worship were brought out for burning or destruction. Growing here and there were tobacco stalks, and even a plant of marijuana.

Rags to Riches

209

Finally everything was gathered together. The tobacco and marijuana plants were hacked to pieces and the other items burned amidst rejoicing. Then this simple, ignorant lady was led to the Lord and turned "from darkness to light, and from the power of Satan unto God" (Acts 26:18). How we rejoiced, prayed, and sang. She went from rags to riches spiritually, but this desperately abject couple is still in rags physically. Oh, for my heart to be continually touched with the things that touch the heart of God.

. . . .

It was several weeks later that the message came—Junior had died. Over twenty of us decided to go to the funeral. We were also eager to see how his wife was coming along in her new-found faith.

When we reached her hut, I did not see her. A few feet away was a garden of stunted, five-foot corn. I followed Deacon Norès a few feet into the garden. There, lying in the only shade available, was the newly widowed woman lying prostrate on a banana mat. She was hardly conscious, suffering from dehydration due to several weeks of diarrhea.

A curious man, I asked to view Junior's corpse. He appeared as if gasping for a last breath, with mouth and eyes open. How cruel life seemed, but it was reality. While Junior "lay in state" in the crude coffin, his wife, "lay in suffering" on the crude mat in the corn garden. How my heart went out to her.

. . . .

Jesus said, "Blessed are the poor in spirit." With great depth of need and poverty of soul, we are told to seek God. The call to my heart is to pray with a burdened heart as a true pauper to find the solutions for the intense, mounting needs here. How deeply do I love? Do I care? Do I feel? Do I pray? Do I give of my time, my things, my money, my feelings, and my real self? Do I really believe that Jesus commands me to not lay up treasures for myself upon earth, and that the Word shouts in 1 John 3:17, "But if anyone has this world's goods (resources for sustaining life) and sees his brother and fellow believer in need, yet closes his heart of compassion against him, how can the love of God live and remain in him?" (Amplified Bible).

Chapter 62

Answered Prayers!

• October 2001

Bruce Melts

With much "fear and trembling," yet with hopeful hearts, we began a meeting with Bruce at CAM. After expressing our earnest desire for peace and a good relationship, we dropped a bombshell.

Just last Sunday God had convicted a sister in the mountains to uncover a past relationship with Bruce. When confronted with this accusation, Bruce broke down, and we sensed the convicting hand of God's Spirit upon him. Finally truly broken, he acknowledged his sin and duplicity in hiding the relationship. In fact, the burden had been so heavy, he shared, that at one point he had despaired of his own life.

In the end, Pastor Eris, a national adviser for CAM, gently but wisely counseled Bruce that if he wants any real clearing and victory, he should go back to Alègue to confess his sins and ask forgiveness. He agreed to come and share after we had time to work out a few matters.

During our closing prayer my heart beat with joy as we all joined hands and hearts. When we arose, big, brawny Bruce and I fell on each other's shoulders for an embrace of acceptance and forgiveness. I was completely exhausted, but so thankful that our God is faithful. He did so much beyond my feeble faith.

• • • • • • •

More Answered Prayers

We're all rejoicing that Gèline and Efanyèl have come back home and repented of their stubbornness. Right now Remòn has taken

Gèline under her wings. She is also giving her some work so that she can make a little money. We're so thankful for this arrangement. Once again we're reminded that prayer does make a difference. God can and does work in people's hearts.

We also praise the Lord that Bay, Remòn's husband, is better. He has had several major medical tests and was given medication. We're so thankful his attacks were not demonic.

Time will not soon erase from my memory the trauma and suffering this man experienced several weeks ago. At one point when he had an attack, his well-meaning older brother kept ramming a bottle of ammonia in front of his nose, supposedly to bring him out of his attack. I tried desperately to ward him off, but to no avail. When he placed it on his finger and rammed it up Bay's nostrils, the pain and torture of the potent, reeking ammonia caused him to writhe in agony, with bulging, glaring eyes. Since he was unable to speak, Bay tried to bite his brother in his desperate attempt to make him stop torturing him. He thrashed in wild protest, and many strong men could hardly restrain him. Even the unconverted onlookers assumed he had a demonic seizure. When the "ammonia cure" was finally over, Bay vomited again and again to clear out the horrible poisoning.

On Sunday Bay and Remòn sang a lovely song of God's goodness and grace. Later Bay shared a grateful testimony of God's grace and power in his illness and trauma. He thanked and blessed the God of heaven. He also thanked the church and all who had prayed for him and stood by him during this time of emotional and physical pain and uncertainty. He confided that at one point he thought he was facing death.

Earlier Remòn had shared with some of us that she believes it was not the medicine that actually healed her husband, but the prayers of all the people praying for him. Not only did God touch Bay's body with his healing hand, He also did a deep work in his heart.

. . . .

Gèline's Wedding

Today was Efanyèl and Gèline's wedding day. It was a touching service. Pastor Levi preached a lovely message, encouraging them to fulfill their God-given duties. After the marriage, Levi called on me to pray for the kneeling couple. What a privilege to cry out to God to bless, protect, and lead this young couple.

When the service ended, I joined the joyous wedding procession down the slippery mountain trails to the couple's house. It was a time of singing, rejoicing, and clapping. There's been lots of rain in the last few days, and the clouds were again dark overhead. As a light drizzle started, the procession accelerated. I picked up a large banana leaf to cover my head and shoulders.

When we reached the couple's house, they served us Haitian cola and bread, and then a huge dish of rice and beans with goat meat and sauce—the best ever! I indeed could "sit where they sit." I felt as Haitian as ever as I shared this delightful time with my friends.

While eating, the heavens broke loose. The rain pounded so hard on the tin roof that we could scarcely hear each other. Late that afternoon when I wanted to head up to my mountain kay, Gèline gave me a black plastic bag. I slit holes for my arms, slid it over my body, and tore out a hole for my eyes and nose. My Haitian friends roared with laughter as I walked out into the pouring rain with my unique raincoat. Such is life at Alègue. How enjoyable!

Chapter 63

Unwelcome Visitor

· January 2002

This morning I once more gazed at the grim evidence from last night: blood-soaked paper towels and washcloths, my blood-stained floor, and my trampled, crushed flower beds. What had happened?

Last evening was a *blan* meeting at Lowell's house, so I was gone for the evening. At the same time, Levi was at Remòn's house for a meeting with our school principal and Dr. Smay, the head doctor at our clinic. After the meeting, Dr. Smay sent Levi to get his cell phone, which was at my house for charging.

We had just finished listening to a tape on the Christian's armor when there was a frenzied knock on the door of Lowell's house. "Brother Levi wants Grandpa Harold to come home immediately," the man blurted out. "There's a robber at his house." After a quick prayer about the situation, I jumped on my four-wheeler, zipped away, and parked at the church, where my trail starts. Haitians were flocking up the trail with me, babbling about the situation.

When Levi had entered my house, he noticed that the top latch was loosened, but thought little about it. But then he thought he heard a little rustling. He froze and listened intently. Yes, somebody was in the house! Stealthily he entered the front room and saw a movement. There he was—Ti Nonm, Entès's son, caught in the act!

Blocking the doorway so Ti Nonm could not flee, Levi tried calling us on my radio, but it didn't work. Ti Nonm had pushed a button that had messed up the channels. As Ti Nonm threatened to kill him, Levi called for help, but no one heard. Suddenly he thought about his cell phone and quickly called Dr. Smay, who was about three hundred yards away. In minutes the place was swarming with people.

Someone sent for newly elected Judge Marcel, while someone else ran to tell me. The news spread like wildfire. When I entered my courtyard, I had to push my way through the crowd to the door of the house. Later, as they unwillingly exited, I counted a total of about sixty people. This was their Friday night excitement!

Levi took me to my crude bench. There was my cash pouch with three $100 Haitian bills lying beside it. How the thief ever found it was a marvel, as nothing was ransacked. The money had been hidden in a cupboard behind some junk. Meanwhile, Judge Marcel asked Levi for a rope to bind Ti Nonm, who was cowering under the control of many men on the porch.

After tying him up, Judge Marcel came into the house to talk to Levi. Suddenly we heard a cry of pain from the porch. Hurrying out, I found the mob beating up on Ti Nonm. "Let him go!" I yelled.

When they backed off, I brought him inside, with blood gushing from his nose. I got a wet washcloth and gently tried to clean his face and his hands, which were tightly bound. During this time, I seized the opportunity to talk to him about the love of Jesus.

The mob finally left the porch but refused to disperse. They wanted a chance at the thief, meaning they wanted to kill him. I begged Levi to help thwart their purposes. Finally he told me he had discovered the two leaders, had given them each ten dollars, and they had agreed to leave.

Judge Marcel locked Ti Nonm in a special cell in his house overnight and planned to send him to jail in Ti Goâve the next morning. I was told when they started out, so I looked out on the road below with my binoculars. There, with a band of curious onlookers, was Ti Nonm, trudging along on the four-hour walk toward prison with his hands bound behind his back.

Following the desire of my heart and the teaching of Jesus, I later went to visit him in prison and to speak to his heart. I also gave him some food and drink.

Some Haitians who learned of my visit chided me. "Once a thief, always a thief," they said. "Better to end his life."

How sad to hear their hardened hearts.

Chapter 64

A Peep Behind the Scenes

• February 2002

Spiritual Wrestling

At the hut of the Banav family, prayers, praises, and singing wafted heavenward each day as the church families gathered there to support and encourage them. We were very concerned for them as they continued to waver between serving the Lord and reverting to voodooism. A few huts below them, where Madame Banav's mother and brother Sove lived, a voodoo ball was in progress. It was Saturday evening, and I was sitting on my porch, watching and hearing these two forces clash below me. As I heard the beautiful Gospel singing and praises rising above the *tom-tom* of the drums, I was reminded of Elijah and the prophets of Baal.

Late on Sunday afternoon I stopped at Sove's hut to share my concern for him and his mother. On the demon altar lay a half loaf of bread and a bottle of drink. Sove and his mother seemed worn and weary from their night of partying. I reminded Sove's mother of the time she had asked me to pray for her son Towo when he was sick. I pointedly reminded them of Towo's death and of their own appointment with God. They asked me to keep praying for them. Oh, the bondage of the devil!

∎ ∎ ∎ ∎ ∎ ∎ ∎

Voodoo Rituals

I enjoy going down to my little prayer perch below my *kay*. This spot overlooks the valley below, the mountains around, and the glorious sunrises. Here I often pray and read. While there one morning, I gazed at a small bald hill below me close to Madame Moyiz's brother Alfred's *kay*. There, near some tombs and a lonely, protruding mango tree, I saw some people dancing.

With my binoculars I discovered it was Madame Moyiz herself and about a dozen other people. Madame Moyiz was definitely in charge. She welcomed each newcomer with a unique handshake. She continued with a slow motion, swaying and dancing, sometimes taking a large bottle to her mouth, then dancing from one to the other, sharing the brew. Sometimes she would raise her hands heavenward. At one point Moyiz, her husband, left and returned with a machete for her. After performing a ceremony, she flung it high into the air. It arched upward higher than the trees before plunging into a cornfield. It was then retrieved, and they appeared to pray over it.

At one point they seemed to be initiating a young man into the group. Then Madame Moyiz started crawling on the ground in an animal-like manner. After that, the ceremony abruptly concluded and the group headed off. I saw them walking toward the mission. I wished I knew what the ceremony represented, so I decided to go to the mission. There I found the group in the middle of the road in front of the cockfight shack. By now others had joined them, and there was much wicked, sensual, diabolic dancing. One older lady tore off her blouse in her demonized frenzy and could not be clothed by those who tried.

Later a demon altar was built on the property across the road. A neighbor lady told Anna Joy about some of their scheming. They were desperately trying to win back the Haitian Christians and drive out the *blans*.

Levi later told me the purpose of the strange ceremony. Behind the cockfight shack is a mango tree dedicated to the devil. There the demons descend and mount the people. The local judges have requested that the cockfight shack be moved, so the voodoo worshipers needed another place for the demons to "do their thing." Apparently Madame Moyiz was dedicating another spot and tree to the devil for his purposes.

Moyiz bragged recently that they will have the grandest, biggest, six-day voodoo ball ever at their house at the end of February. They have tried to do this in the past, but it has always failed. They blame the praying *blans*.

Madame Moyiz wanted to send her children to Remòn's house during the ball. She did not want them involved. She said she cannot get free from the strong ancestral demonic control, but she wants her children to become Christians.

Chapter 65

God Overrules

When we come to the end of our hoarded resources
Our Father's full giving has only begun.
His love has no limit, His grace has no measure.
His power has no boundary known unto men.
For out of His infinite riches in Jesus,
He giveth, and giveth, and giveth again!

—Annie Johnson Flint

How beautiful are God's ways. We had prayed much against the announced voodoo ball and were disappointed when it began to take place on Friday evening. Our prayers were answered Sunday evening, however, when it came to a crashing halt. Two events took place. First, many demonized people at the ball turned on each other and began to fight one another. Also, an untrue report came to them that Moyiz's brother had died. This detracted the Moyiz family and the ball.

It was a brief but very intense voodoo ball. Even with his earplugs and muffs, visiting Brother Jay said it was like sleeping at the gates of hell. But I rejoice that Jesus said, "I will build my church and the gates of hell shall not prevail against it."

From my *kay* on the mountain, the ball was in complete view on a lower knoll. Words are inadequate to paint a picture of the demonized group as they worshiped the devil and gave themselves to evil spirits. Red was the predominant color—red head turbans, red dresses, and one man even wore a red dress-like robe. Possessed women rolled around on the ground, nearly tumbling down the cliff.

At one point the worshipers, chanting and singing, marched to a high hill overlooking the mission houses. One red-turbaned young man, Alfred's son, sat backward on a horse and raced with the group. They then returned and had a service at the recently constructed demon altar directly in front of the mission property.

* * * * * * *

Defeats

Sad to say, Madame Moyiz, who seemed to spearhead the ball and take the main offensive against the Christians, reportedly sent a demon on Madame Banav, who unwillingly participated. She wanted to flee but was physically restrained. "You belong to us now," Madame Moyiz told her. "And we won't let you get away again!" With glee she told the others, "We have Madame Banav back. Now we need to get her daughter Klomàn."

Klomàn has gone through some deep struggles. Many have prayed and sung with her to encourage her in the Lord. She is going on, but faces some heavy trials. Also, Mano, who had been our close neighbor, has given himself once again to demon worship. Indeed, there is clash of forces at the deepest levels. Both Mano and the Banavs seem to be in deep fear. Levi said we should do more praying instead of pressuring. He wants it to be for real if they choose to be free once again.

I continue to marvel at God's ways. Indeed He is God! Brother Jay, like Paul at Athens, had "his spirit stirred within him when he saw the idolatry" (Acts 17:16). At one point Madame Moyiz led the demon worshipers to a high hill overlooking the mission houses. She said she had a debt she owed to Satan. They had a service there and she half buried a sacrifice bottle to pay her debt.

A few days later when I was walking down the trail, I heard several gunshots. *What's up?* I wondered. Soon I learned that Madame Moyiz and her sister had asked to speak with Pastor Levi. I continued downward. There I saw a frenzied, angered Madame Moyiz. She was prancing and dancing back and forth with deliberate short steps, all the while angrily shouting at Levi. Levi, as usual, was "cool as a cucumber," at least outwardly. *Why is she so angry?* I wondered.

We soon learned that Brother Jay had in his zeal climbed the mount to the spot of the buried bottle, seized it, and with a forceful stroke smashed it upon a large rock into a hundred pieces and loudly shouted, "Hallelujah!" It was like a tinderbox ignited. Boisterous, angry voodoo worshipers quickly assembled. Moyiz's son-in-law said he would like to shoot this white man. Brother Levi was able to at least momentarily appease Madame Moyiz. I was stirred deeply in my heart and asked her forgiveness for the visiting *blan's* trespassing on and destroying of private property. Levi shared the Gospel with her at the same time and told her that her problems would be solved if she truly came to Jesus.

Meanwhile, down at the cockfight shack a group of angry dissidents were spewing and venting their feelings. Here again Levi calmed them down and shared the Gospel.

Sometime later I shared my concern with Brother Jay, who humbled himself and apologized to Madame Moyiz. At that time God gave Jay a beautiful opportunity to share Jesus and tell her the debt she thought she owed the devil was paid at Calvary. She listened with tears in her eyes. With hands upon her head, he concluded with an earnest prayer for her deliverance. She even asked us to tell our friends in the States to pray for her.

By Monday all was quiet—like the calm after a storm. "And the fear of God was on all the kingdoms of those countries, when they had heard that the Lord fought against the enemies of Israel. So the realm of Jehoshaphat was quiet: for God gave him rest round about" (2 Chron. 20:29, 30).

This is my desire for Alègue.

Chapter 66

Victories

· May 2002

A Brokenhearted Bruce

As he had promised, Bruce came to Alègue to confess his sins and seek forgiveness. As the day of the meeting approached, we found ourselves wondering what would happen. Would he be sincere and open, or would he try to hide things again? Many times we "spread it before the Lord" and asked for God's blessing.

When I met Bruce at the rear of the churchyard, he gave me a warm but sobered embrace. As we entered the church house, Bruce, along with his wife and daughter, sat down beside the Lamar Nolt family, who had brought them to Alègue.

After Pastor Levi concluded his message, he gave Bruce the opportunity to share. All eyes were riveted on him. All ears were intent. He soon made very clear the purpose of his presence after so long an absence. His heart and head were deeply weighed down. The pain and guilt were too deep to live with any longer. He briefly shared his past—how he had gone to the States and contracted a marriage to do so, and how he later married Colleen, and why that was wrong. He explained that his first wife had died since.

Then he dumped out his heart with his duplicity, adultery, lying, and more. He asked forgiveness from the church. He said he knew he had sinned against Levi and deeply hurt him, and asked his forgiveness. Turning to each other, they embraced in front of the congregation.

Next he went on to specifically name others he had sinned against and hurt. He named Mama Matthew and especially Remòn and the *blans*. There seemed to be no self-justification.

I listened with rapt attention. Then he said that if Levi and the rest could accept his desire for forgiveness, he wanted to kneel before the congregation while they had a special prayer for him. Levi called the deacons, Lowell, me, and some others to come forward. We laid hands on the head of a humbled Bruce and prayed. I could hardly pray for my weeping. Afterward, we gave him a hand of acceptance or an embrace. It was a heart-touching time. There were many tears among everyone involved.

I praise God for this important step of Bruce's clearing and reconciliation with the church and the mission. There are many other details, however, that need to be faced. I am especially concerned that Remòn can find her way in forgiveness and clearing of her own heart. I sense some bitterness and am very concerned.

God has had a glorious victory, but I have learned that in this dark land the enemy will not let this victory go unchallenged, both with Bruce and the church at Alègue. Through Christ, however, we can be victorious in this battle for righteousness.

■ ■ ■ ■ ■ ■ ■

Another Glorious Victory

Long before the voodoo ball, Madame Moyiz had asked that her younger children stay at Remòn's house during the ball so that they would not be touched by the horrible demonic influences. Before the ball when Kathy visited her, Madame Moyiz shared that she was "two people." Indeed she is! Kathy had the privilege of praying with this deeply bound prisoner.

Natasha, Moyiz's daughter, has been coming to church and to school. She has been seeking the Lord for some time. During the ball, Ada Fisher and some others shared their hearts with her, and the reality of God and hell seemed to grip her.

That evening she asked to talk with Pastor Levi. There in the courtyard, in the presence of Kathy and Rhonda, she confessed her sins and her need of a Saviour. She also renounced the hold of Satan and the bondage of her family. Levi helped her to consider the costs—that she might have to leave her home if her parents threw her out.

We know the angels in heaven rejoiced as Levi led her in a prayer of complete consecration. We also know that Satan is angry that his kingdom has been trampled upon.

Chapter 67

Revival

• July 2002

Before the service this morning, I climbed the steeps beyond my *kay*. I found a clump of dried grass for a cushion and sat down on the ground. I always find it inspiring to survey the huge amphitheater of mountains, and this morning I felt a special burden to pray for the deep needs we are facing—the seeming dryness of the church, the lack of recent conversions, and the need for revival. I pondered the many specific needs, especially the struggle of Remòn. Then I entered into prayers for revival in all our hearts. As I gazed at the spectacular view of God's creation, I thought about a prayer of Caleb I often prayed years ago as I thought of coming to Haiti, "Now therefore give me this mountain" (Joshua 14:12).

This is still my prayer.

∙ ∙ ∙ ∙ ∙ ∙ ∙

If We Confess Our Sins

This morning before the service Pastor Levi told me that he and Remòn want to talk with me about her struggles. She had shared with the missionaries some time ago that she'd had a child some years earlier, fathered by Bruce, and they had hidden it by duplicity. We had forgiven her, but Pastor Levi and the mission felt that since it was known by the local community, it should be publicly shared before the church for full clearance. In Haitian culture this would be a most debasing step, so we were afraid she would be unwilling to do

225

what needed to be done.

To our delight, at the close of Pastor Levi's message, he stated that Sister Remòn wanted to share. Without pretense or justification, she confessed her sin, stated that she wanted go on with the Lord, and asked forgiveness from the congregation. This was freely granted. Then there was a time of special prayer for her and other needs.

Mama Matthew had told Anna Joy months ago that the church was tied up because sin had been hidden. How prophetic and true this had proved to be.

· · · · · · ·

Snatched From the Enemy

Pastor Levi preached a powerful message, and then Lowell led the closing prayer. The service was about to be dismissed when God prompted the moderator to give an invitation for anyone who wanted to be saved. I didn't see who went forward, but soon Pastor Levi came and asked me to go forward to pray with the seeker. He told me it was his aunt Eunice, who lived just across the ravine. Furthermore, he said she was Madame Moyiz's right-hand helper and was deeply steeped in voodoo.

As always, the devil does not give up without a fight. By the time I got up front, Eunice was half prostrate and demonized, her body thrashing. Her eyes were glazed, glowering demonically. The whole congregation was asked to rise to their feet and pray—and pray they did! They prayed, sang, and rejoiced. It was a momentous time of drawing the whole group together.

Especially rewarding to me was the presence of Remòn and Mama Matthew. Since Remòn had just cleared her heart, she was able to freely join the others in seeking the deliverance of her demonized aunt.

The battle that ensued is difficult to depict. The mixture of singing, praying, and demonic utterances rose to a high din; the intense struggle of the demons to keep command knew no bounds. Eunice was their slave. But she desired to be free, and she was delivered. She renounced Satan and her ugly sins and gladly committed her entire life to serving Jesus.

She readily agreed to destroy her voodoo paraphernalia. It was a time of rejoicing as most of the church traipsed across the ravine to her ramshackle, crumbling hut. Out came her fetishes, necklace, crockery, voodoo robe, and all. There on the little trail it was heaped, doused with kerosene, and then lit with a match. As the smoke ascended, shouts of praise and exultations of victory and thankfulness also ascended. Hallelujahs resounded. Undoubtedly, the angels in heaven rejoiced. I pondered what might be transpiring in the demon world. This was no light matter. For years Eunice had been an ardent adherent to demonism, and everyone knew about her ungodly ways.

But God, who is not willing that any should perish, worked in her heart. A much-beloved little granddaughter of hers had been very sick recently. The nurses had cared for her at our clinic, but later she died. Eunice shared that one of her own demons had "eaten" her own beloved granddaughter. God used this to bring her to seek the true God.

Immediately after the burning, Pastor Levi was called to the hut of Eunice's daughter and husband just a few feet away. They, too, wanted to find deliverance and seek the way of Jesus. What rejoicing! May this be the beginning of the revival we are seeking.

■ ■ ■ ■ ■ ■ ■

People are talking about what happened. "Next Madame Moyiz will be converted," some say. "Now God can work in other hearts."

But the enemy is angry. Last night the drums were resounding below my *kay*, calling up the demons. I awoke at 2 a.m., but people were still chanting, still calling on their Baal, and still plotting. Oh, that Eunice can truly find cleansing and grow in grace—that she can be a true handmaiden of the Lord Jesus. I often walk the back way down to the mission and pass her shack. Twice yesterday I shook her hand, blessed her, and gazed into her clear, open eyes. What a stark contrast to the demonized eyes of yesterday as the evil spirits fought an intense battle to retain lordship of her soul.

Winds of God's Spirit

They came from the north, south, east, and west; they also came from Alègue—many needy nationals. We all prayed for a working of God, especially in the areas of morality and integrity. Our recent meetings climaxed on Sunday morning when Brother Raymond, a missionary from Grenada, preached a concluding, powerful, penetrating message on brokenness and a contrite heart.

When the invitation was given, an amazing number responded— several dozen. It was an overwhelming answer to prayer.

The number needing counsel was so great that the leaders divided into two groups to hear their hearts. Among the penitent were Bruce's brother Mèjil and Ti Nonm, who just recently got out of jail for his attempted robbery at my house. We were overjoyed to see him.

For over an hour and a half there were confessions, conversions, and further counseling. Wives were sent for to hear their husbands confess unfaithfulness, public confessions were given to the whole congregation, and wrongs were made right with neighbors. It was truly a time of brokenness before the Lord. We rejoice at the miracle God worked, but realize the awesome responsibility we now have to nurture these new converts.

Chapter 68

Perils in the Sea

• August 2002

Lamar Nolt with Life Ministries, his son Duane, and I decided to make another trip to La Gonâve Island, this time to distribute Gospel literature. Before we left, Lamar studied the satellite weather map. Hmm, clouds covered the Caribbean area. Should we go?

After discussing the situation, we decided a short trip like ours shouldn't be a problem. We soon left on a sixteen-foot motorboat. The several-hour trip was a delight! I reveled in the slapping waves and the distant, towering mountains capped with the strangest cloud formations. The flying fish also fascinated me as they emerged from the ocean, scooted several inches above the waves, and sank once more into the ocean depths.

When we arrived at the secluded little village on the island, we anchored our boat, stepped into the water, and walked to the shore. The nationals came hurrying to meet us. Indeed, they remembered Lamar. They even remembered me.

Despite being in Haiti for years, my heart tugged deeply as these dear, simple, needy people gathered around us and asked questions and listened to Lamar. He opened the box of literature and shared with them. Emotions similar to those I had on my original trip to Haiti stirred in my bosom. We walked with them around the village and saw their neat little church/school building that stood empty. Without money to pay teachers, they couldn't operate a school. They also had no pastor and no medical help. Isolated as they were, they seemed like one large family.

We learned that it takes about a half hour by boat to go to the only main town on the island. Both Lamar and I had often wished to see this place. We decided we had plenty of time and could ride over there. We bought some gasoline to make sure we had enough to return. The nationals bid us farewell and we were off.

Unexpectedly, the waves started to mount higher and higher. Soon we crossed through a strait, and our little boat seemed like a bobbing cork. Concerned now, we put on our life belts. In the distance, the dashing waves shot huge white sprays high into the air as they smashed into the rocky coast. The angry waves now became more boisterous, mounting to nine or ten feet high. Up and down we splashed. Fear struck my heart. As I prayed and pondered a watery grave, I thought of the disciples' plea, "Lord, save us, for we perish." I clung tightly to the boat rail. Lamar suggested that I move to the rear seat to make the front end lighter and tip the nose up higher. If too much water entered the front, it would be more dangerous.

Fortunately, the waves were wide and long rather than abrupt. Gradually my spirit began to compose and I started to feel more secure. *My life is in God's hands,* I realized. *What a sweet place to be.* As I relaxed, I actually started to enjoy the long, sweeping ups and downs.

Suddenly, to our consternation, water started deepening in the rear of our puny vessel. The sump pump had quit working! Lamar asked me to steer while he lay on the floor to unclog and fix the system.

The half hour needed to reach the village stretched to over an hour. Gallons of salt water continually drenched my entire body as I tried to steer. I couldn't wear my glasses and had difficulty seeing the reefs, which we had to avoid. I even missed seeing the dock entrance to the village, and we had to turn around. We finally found the little bay and headed in.

We decided to see the town while there. I stayed with the boat at the dock while Lamar and Duane took a little, rickety *taptap* to tour the place. Then it was my turn while Lamar replenished the gasoline containers. We rattled around the village in a junky, smelly diesel pickup. Our gracious Christian driver pointed out the schools, churches, and business places. The roads were only gravel, often with deep washouts—a typical small Haitian town.

By now it was after 2 p.m. Everybody told us there was no boating today; there was a nasty cyclone, and the ocean was much too rough. Not convinced, we left the inlet harbor and headed out to check. They were right—the waves were rougher and more boisterous than earlier. We returned and waited awhile. Several hours later we tried again. We ventured farther out into the ocean this time, but angry, boisterous waves tossed our frail boat like a cat flipping a mouse. We had no oars or spare motor, and wisdom told us we had best return to shore.

Time was slipping away. It would soon be dark. Other schooners and ships were preparing for the night. What should we do? We had no lodging or food. I considered sleeping on our little boat.

We saw a small truck hauling soft drinks. Perhaps the driver could help us find a local mission. "Sir," I asked, going up to him, "would you know of a mission somewhere that could put us up for the night? We are stranded on this island and need a place to sleep."

"Sure!" he replied. "There's a Wesleyan mission not far away. Hop in and I'll take you over there. And if they don't have room for you, you can sleep at my house!"

In a few minutes we arrived at the mission. Yes, they had a small guest house and gladly welcomed us to spend the night there. What a blessing to wash our salted, weary bodies and to have a good place for the night. Indeed, our God is good.

We got up refreshed the next morning and hoped things had calmed down. The wind was still blowing, but we decided to head for the dock and our boat. We loaded our gasoline containers and headed out to investigate the water. Onlookers watched with interest and said, "You'll be back soon."

The water was a little choppy, but we decided to go on. Out in the deep ocean the waves were only moderate. Captain Lamar revved the motor and we took a direct course across the ocean toward land. It was a delightful, speedy half-hour. *We'll soon be back at Lamar's house,* I thought.

But suddenly the winds picked up. We still had several hours of following the coastline toward Lamar's home. As the wind picked up speed, the angry waves became more and more boisterous. These waves were not the long, sweeping type, but were cruelly abrupt. Their height was only five or six feet, but they lunged with ferocious speed toward the frail fiberglass boat. They would flip it suddenly upward, and then just as abruptly, drop it with a crash as the violent wave moved on. Relentlessly, one huge, torturing wave after another tossed us up and down, up and down. I tenaciously clutched the windshield frame and braced my feet, allowing my knees to "knee-action" the flipping, tossing, and crashing pattern.

Hours passed. I kept watching the time. Our speed was tediously slow because of the turbulent water. Would we ever arrive? Suddenly there was a rasping, crunching noise, and our boat slowed abruptly.

"What was that?" I asked.

"We hit a coral reef!" Lamar blurted out.

The boat refused to propel properly, so we hoisted the engine and looked at the propeller. One fin was broken off. Thankfully, Lamar had recently purchased a spare propeller, so while the boat bobbed and flipped with the waves, Captain Lamar stretched out in the stern of the boat and made the repair. Again I was grateful for the goodness of God!

We finally arrived home safely at about 11 a.m. Our normal two-hour trip had stretched to four hours. But God had protected us and brought us safely to shore and solid ground. I thought of the words of the Apostle Paul, "I suffered shipwreck, a night and a day I have been in the deep . . . in perils in the sea" (2 Corinthians 11:25b, 26b).

Indeed our heavenly Father is our sovereign God. Oh, to simply trust Him!

Chapter 69

Stirring the Pot

My experience with the turmoil and danger of an ocean journey was intense, but the journey of my heart recently was even more fearful and threatening than those scary waters. I finally cried out in despair, "Lord, save me from myself!"

I "died a thousand deaths" in the process. Like God did to Abraham of old, He called me to offer up my "Isaac, my son of old age" and leave the work here. It became a deeply traumatic, painful experience.

Being spared from the deep, angry, fearful ocean and the prospect of a watery grave humbled me greatly. How kind God was to spare my life. I earnestly began seeking Him and asking Him to work deeply in my heart in the way He would choose. The following prayer became my earnest desire:

> Lord, make me childlike. Deliver me from the urge to compete with another for place, prestige, or position. I want to be simple and artless as a little child. Deliver me from pose and pretense. Forgive me for thinking of myself. Help me to forget myself and find true peace in beholding thee. That thou mayest answer this prayer, I humble myself before thee. Lay upon me thy easy yoke of self-forgetfulness, that through it I might find rest. Amen.

Yes, I asked God to help me change my many temperamental and personality flaws. I asked Him to give me deeper love, grace, and gentleness; to love the nationals more sincerely; to be able to truly bless and honor my co-workers; to have my tendency to be rash, impulsive, and impatient replaced with godly graces; to root out the ugly pride and self-pity of my flesh; to destroy my overbearing, demanding spirit of expectation toward others. Yes, in short, I wanted to be like my dear Jesus.

A.W. Tozer's prayer in *The Pursuit of God* speaks my heart and desire so powerfully. I could not say it so well myself. I quote:

> O God, be thou exalted over my possessions. Nothing of earth's treasures shall seem dear unto me if only thou art glorified in my life. Be thou exalted over my friendships. I am determined that thou shalt be above all, though I must stand deserted and alone in the midst of the earth. Be thou exalted above my comforts. Though it mean the loss of bodily comforts and the carrying of heavy crosses, I shall keep my vow made before thee. Be thou exalted over my reputation. Make me ambitious to please thee even if as a result I must sink into obscurity and my name be forgotten as a dream. Rise, O Lord, into thy proper place of honor, above my ambitions, above my likes and dislikes, above my family, my health, and even my life itself. Let me decrease that thou mayest increase; let me sink that thou mayest rise above. Ride forth upon me as thou didst ride into Jerusalem mounted upon the humble little beast, a colt, the foal of an ass, and let me hear the children cry to thee, "Hosanna in the highest!"

. . . .

Ways of God; Ways of Men

"All things work together for good" (KJV). "All things . . . are fitting into a plan for good" (Amplified Bible). What powerful words of truth to secure my heart when in deep turmoil.

For well over a year I had asked the mission board, under the supervision of a group of churches in the United States, to find someone to replace me in the lead role here on the field. I was aware that the stress of the work was once again getting the best of me and that I was not coping well with all the demands, decisions, and responsibilities. I knew I would need to make some major adjustments to truly release the reins I had held for so long.

There were a number of things the board was concerned about: the extreme overload of the nurses in the clinic, the lack of time to work with the spiritual needs of nationals who come for medical help, the increasing financial load of the clinic, the continued request for funds for the schools, and the growing dependency of the key national leaders upon foreign support. Therefore they said some drastic changes needed to be made. In their words, "The pot has to be stirred."

In the midst of stirring the pot, some hot contents splashed on me. Although I had resolved to walk within the context of all the decisions the board made, some of them caught me unprepared. Following is a quote from the board's decisions: "In our meetings with the missionaries while in Haiti, we decided it is best to have Brother Harold come home for a break. When Harold asked for a time period, we said perhaps a month or two. Also, we asked Brother Lowell to take responsibility while Harold is gone."

By the grapevine other reports trickled through to me, suggesting that my future here is limited. I confess that I became discouraged. Self-pity is always fleshly and needs to be crucified. The enemy took advantage and I had to deal with wrong thoughts. At one point deep despondency seized my hurting heart.

One morning after some deep soul searching, God made it plain to me. As with Isaac, there would also be a ram caught in the thicket for me. God would provide. I simply needed to trust Him. That same morning at my prayer perch, I read Romans 8 aloud.

There God's Word states so simply, "All things work together for good." Yes, this message was for me. God had a plan for me. I must not choose my own path.

I also remembered a past experience when there were some drastic changes in my service for God. At that point God had spoken to me so plainly: "I don't need you, you need me. The people don't need you, they need me."

Painful and difficult as it was, I humbled myself and took the necessary steps to leave my beloved Alègue. The tears and heart tugs were multiplied in the days before my departure. My friends came to bless me and pray for me. How they cared. But God cared too and gave me grace day by day.

> *O let my trembling soul be still,*
> *And wait thy wise and holy will!*
> *I cannot, Lord, thy purpose see;*
> *Yet all is well since ruled by thee!*
> —John Bowring

Chapter 70

Sabbatical in Pennsylvania

• November 2002 to August 2003

After returning to Pennsylvania, the struggle in my soul continued. I lived in a wooded area with a steep hill nearby, much like the hills and mountains of Haiti. Each morning I would hike the mountains in prayer and meditation, seeking to find rest for my soul. I thought I was finally committing and fully surrendering all to God. *After several months I'll return to Alègue,* I thought. But God was not yet finished using His scalpel upon my heart. He needed to cut more deeply.

After consideration by the board, the month or two became a complete withdrawal from Haiti. I was advised to make a brief visit to Haiti for closure, but then let someone else take my place. A few months later I did return for several weeks, but then I headed back to Pennsylvania.

Intellectually, I submitted to the board's request, but I was heartbroken. Where was the ram caught in the thicket for me? I had asked God to help me change my heart and meet my needs. Was this how He was answering my prayers?

I was not bitter or angry, but I was deeply crushed. In Haiti God had showed me plainly that I was to "take thine only son Isaac, whom thou lovest . . . and offer him . . . upon one of the mountains." But did He mean I was to pull up stakes and leave the place where I had been freely pouring out my time, finances, sweat, and heart?

Daily I faced my ugly, carnal self. I thought I had yielded myself, but over and over I had to fight the battle against uselessness and despondency. All this time, however, God was at work in His own gentle, powerful way. Had I not asked Him to replace my tendency to be rash, impulsive, and impatient? Had I not asked Him to root out the ugly pride and self-pity of my flesh, and to destroy my overbearing, demanding spirit toward others? Yes, I wanted to be like Jesus. Had I not said I was willing to go back to Pennsylvania?

One day I read an account of some missionaries who were caught in the Boxer rebellion in China and found themselves trapped in very difficult circumstances. They chose to submit to the ways of God, but they still struggled. Finally God showed them the need to not only submit, but to do so joyfully and thankfully. Only then was there release and peace of mind for them.

These words spoke to my heart. Was God asking me to thank Him and joyfully receive these circumstances? Yes, He was. I needed to follow the advice of David in Psalm 40:8: "I delight to do thy will, O my God."

Then began a new step in my journey of faith.

. . . .

Back to Teaching

"Would you consider being a teacher again?" the caller asked. "We have a teacher who would like to be released at the end of the first semester, and we thought maybe you would agree to take his place."

I had taught school for many years and enjoyed the involvement, but I wondered if I was emotionally and mentally ready for such an undertaking. As always, God gave me direction, and for nearly five months I poured my heart into teaching, playing with, praying for, and blessing a group of energetic teenage pupils.

Even though teaching at my age was emotionally tiring, it was a time of usefulness, fulfillment, and healing while being of service to others. Slowly but surely I accepted God's plan for my life and allowed God's promised rest to flow into my heart. The future still looked uncertain, however, and I still had not discovered my ram caught in the thicket.

· · · · · · ·

God's Ram

When the school doors closed for the summer and the last goodbyes had been said, I wondered what I should do.

For years I had dreamed of seeing the beauty of the West, especially the Grand Canyon. The more I thought about it, the more I liked the idea. This was my chance! Why not?

After purchasing an older mini motor home, I started out. I visited friends, relatives, and churches from Pennsylvania all the way to California, where my younger brother lived. It was a delightful, educational experience. It also continued the healing of my heart.

One day it happened. While traveling in Colorado, my phone rang.

"Hello. This is Dave King from CAM. How is your trip going?"

"Hello, Dave. How in the world did you know I was on a trip?" I queried.

"Oh, I have ways. I was talking to some friends of yours. Anyway, I was wondering if you would like to work for CAM? We need someone to manage the medicine program in Haiti. We would like for you to consider this."

"Well, this is indeed a surprise, Dave," I replied. "I will ponder and pray about the request and answer you later."

I had a delightful time on the rest of my trip. I traveled over six thousand miles in six weeks. When I got to California, I sold my motor home, and the profit paid all my trip expenses. I then flew back to Pennsylvania.

After a time of consideration, prayer, and counseling with others, I gave my answer. I called Dave, who was CAM's stateside Haiti overseer.

"Yes, Dave," I told him, "I will accept the responsibility with CAM in Haiti. But I have two requests. First, I do not want to be tied full-time to a computer job. Second, I want to have time to occasionally go to Alègue for weekends. After all, I still have my house there."

"No problem," Dave replied. "You will spend a lot of time on the road checking and communicating with the clinics, so you won't be sitting in front of a computer all the time. And as for your second request, your weekends should be mostly free anyway, so you can go to Alègue as frequently as you choose."

I recognized that this was my ram caught in the thicket. Once again I was headed back to the land of my love—Haiti.

Chapter 71

Back in Haiti!

· October 2003

Let Him lead thee blindfold onwards,
Love needs not to know;
Children whom the Father leadeth
Ask not where they go.
Though the path be all unknown,
Over moors and mountains lone.

—Gerhard Tersteegen

I'm back, and I love it! Once more I have returned to the moors and mountains of Haiti and am at CAM in charge of the medicine program and food boxes. I have returned to the mountains of Haiti at God's timing. Like a magnet, they eagerly beckon me—the hills, the mountains, the rocks, the steep trails, the mud, the coursing streams, the majestic palms, the thatched huts, and much more!

But best and most of all, the people—the black Haitians—beckon me. They are so warm and gracious, so hospitable and friendly; but they are also so poor, so hurting, and so needy in many ways. I rejoice that once again I can "sit where they sit" and share their hurts and their needs, now through the CAM medicine and food parcel program.

· · · · · · · ·

Welcomed by CAM

Upon my arrival in Haiti, I was graciously welcomed as a new member of the CAM family. Both *blans* and Haitians immediately made me feel right at home. On one of my first days in Haiti, Jozye, a CAM employee, and I drove to the heart of Port-au-Prince, and I got a quick taste of what I would be doing. We planned to visit a certain widow to ascertain whether she qualified as a recipient for a food box. We entered a maze of little dingy houses seemingly just plopped together, no uniform size, with little walkways between them. Water and sewage squished underfoot as we wended our way past mini house after mini house. Children, parents, and aged were all mingled together in close proximity. After turning right and left and tripping over sticks and steps, we finally came to Madame Jessie's house.

There in a tiny, dark, windowless room lived this destitute widow with seven children. I held an adorable little three-year-old as we learned of her situation. Her only income came from doing washing for others when she could. She was truly a needy widow. I was impressed as my friend Jozye very beautifully shared Jesus with this hurting family.

Later this lady came to CAM to see what we had decided. Without question, she had been accepted for the monthly food box program. Her smile conveyed her thanks as I handed the forty-pound box to her. As she left, I watched her walk down the road with the box on her head. Would she carry it all the way home—seven miles? Or would she get a ride on a *taptap?* I didn't know. But one thing I did know—we surely have it easy in the States.

· · · · · · · ·

Deep Stirrings

Several times recently I passed a small Haitian church a few miles from CAM, so I decided that sometime I would visit this simple, dingy place of worship. Today I did, and how my heart was stirred by the simple yet spirited singing, the unpretentious worship, and the reading of the Word. There were only sixty-five people, and I was the lone visitor, but God was there. I could feel His presence.

This simple service touched my heart! In my spirit I was once again back at Alègue with the common mountain people. I am concerned about the future of the work there. What does God have in mind for Christ to Haiti Ministries? After much consideration, the mission board has chosen to discontinue overseeing the work, as their primary goal was to plant churches rather than focus on schools and clinics. Several other churches, however, have shown interest in the work and are seeking wisdom and direction from the Lord.

· · · · · · · ·

Off to the South

From Monday till Friday last week I roamed the South, visiting clinics, hospitals, and pastors. My first stop was at Alègue. I got there in the evening a little before dark. The welcome by everyone, including the unconverted neighbors, was so heartwarming.

The next day I visited my neighbors and friends. Remòn was so pleased that I stopped by. The staff in the clinic is really doing well, but it seemed so different not to have any *blans* at Alègue.

Yes, God had brought me back once more, not only to Haiti but to my little home at Alègue for a brief visit.

· · · · · · · ·

Unwelcome Surprises
· January 2004

On another trip to visit hospitals and clinics throughout Haiti later in the fall, I had another opportunity to visit Alègue. It was on this visit that I received some unpleasant surprises. No, it was not the people. Their joyous welcome and hospitality were as wonderful as ever.

The first disappointment I had to swallow was when I learned from Pastor Levi that the solar panels had been stolen from my roof the week before. They had been there from my first month in Haiti in 1997. *Okay,* I thought, *the Lord giveth and the Lord taketh away.* I easily, but sadly, accepted the loss.

It was as I walked up the mountain and approached my *kay* that

I received a more serious shock. There, boldly glaring at me was my denuded *kay*, no longer graced and hidden by many lovely trees. In fact, not one tree was left—only five ugly four-foot stumps. Whew! Who would have dared to do this nasty thing? This was hard to accept.

Below me was Klomàn's husband, so I called out, "Who cut down my trees?"

"Pastor Levi," he replied.

Incredulous, I swallowed hard. It was then that God gently probed my heart. I immediately thought of the many Haitians who had recently lost their houses in a flood. Some had even lost their families, literally having nothing left!

Okay, Harold, my heart said, *lighten up and in everything give thanks.*

At that moment I purposely chose to thank God for my manifold blessings. It was good that I did so, as my next discovery was that my bench was missing from my porch. *Oh, well,* I told myself, *God is in charge. All these things are His anyway.*

Later I found out that Bay, not Levi, had asked someone to cut down the trees. Bay claimed he had done it at my request! I wondered how that could be.

Later I found out. The last time I had been there I had noticed that someone had trimmed the lower branches; the locals used them for animal forage. I had inadvertently remarked that I didn't like to see the trees trimmed like that. He thought I wanted them cut down, not just trimmed!

God again taught me the grace of submission. Often our problems are mostly in our heads and our hearts. When we truly submit, we find the burdens much lighter than we had thought.

Chapter 72

War in Haiti?

▪ February 2004

Haiti was in a stew! Rebel groups in the north who wanted to oust President Aristide had overtaken several major cities and now boasted that they would take over Port-au-Prince before long. Many nationals and missionaries decided to flee the country. The Lamar Nolt family decided it best to take their family to a safe place in the States. Glen Zimmerman and I planned to stay and would be the only American staff remaining on CAM's base just north of the capital.

I used my Land Cruiser pickup, and Glen took a large International box truck to load the Nolt household items and transfer them to a warehouse in town. We needed an additional truck, so Glen went for the new Mack box truck. When all was loaded, we headed to town to unload. Since the rebels were expected to arrive soon, all main roads were readied for quick closing. Heavy concrete dividers were placed across the roads, with small openings that could be closed in minutes if the rebels arrived. Police and armed assistants abounded everywhere. The atmosphere was tense and fearful. Port-au-Prince was in a state of chaos and confusion.

After unloading at the warehouse, I left my Land Cruiser pickup for Lamar to use. Glen drove the Mack and I the International. After a right turn at a large Texaco station, Glen strangely made another right turn into the service station. I wondered why he would do that.

It soon became apparent why when several gunmen surrounded his truck. With guns aimed at Glen's head, he was told to back the truck across the one lane of the road. Then it was my turn. More gunmen stood in front of my truck and motioned for me to turn in also. A nervous-looking young gunman positioned his gun toward my head and barked, "Back up." Fearful, I obeyed instantly. Then "Stop the truck." I turned the key, but the engine did not stop. I was nervous and hoped he did not think I was defying him. I suddenly remembered it was a diesel, so I pulled the fuel shutoff and the engine died. "Get down!" he commanded. Quickly I was on my feet with my hands raised high.

The nervous gunman kept that nasty, shining steel barrel aimed at my head while his buddy frisked me. He did not take my cell phone or my wallet, so I immediately knew he was only checking for guns. "Give me the keys!" he barked. I didn't hesitate. Grabbing them, the gunmen quickly ran off, leaving us standing there wondering what to do.

Then I learned Glen's story. The gunmen had first asked Glen to open the rear truck doors to see what he had inside. Had the truck not been empty, they would have stolen it. They also requested his keys. Wodrig, a young Haitian helper who was with Glen, was reluctant to give the keys, but quickly changed his mind when the gunmen threatened to blow off his head. Obviously they were using the trucks for a blockade.

There we were, stranded along the street, a mob of Haitians milling around us. We tried to call Lamar, but did not get a response. We knew there were spare keys at the CAM base, but we wondered if they would do us any good. We contacted Pastor Eris, CAM's national adviser, but he was at the upper end of town. He said Port was in confusion as people prepared for a possible assault by the rebels. About thirty minutes later a man came and, with no explanation, returned the keys.

The nearest road to CAM was blocked, so we headed back toward town to try to skirt the blockades. I was high on adrenalin, so I kept close at Glen's heels. Once again we found a roadblock and had to return to the warehouse. There, Lamar told us he knew a back road to CAM, and we were off again. This time we made it home without any problems.

Lamar's family, Glen, and I ate the evening meal at a neighboring mission base. Lamar's family was planning to fly to Pennsylvania the next day.

The experience with the gunmen so unnerved me that Glen recommended that I fly to the States also. I agreed, so two days later John Robert, a truck driver for CAM, transported me to the airport. Once, we were stopped and told we could not continue because gunmen were ahead. John Robert told me to lie on the floor of the rear seat to avoid being seen, as Americans were especially targeted. I hid myself while he turned around and raced off the other way. We finally got to the airport, which was packed with a wild, jostling, shouting crowd of Haitians seeking to flee the country. Each was vying to get to the ticket counter ahead of the others. The place was also replete with reporters and photographers from around the world.

Not knowing what to do, I finally got a policeman to help me get to the ticket counter. I had never before experienced such pushing, shouting, and milling about.

We finally boarded the plane and were off. I later learned that it was American Airlines' last flight from Haiti for several days due to the security situation. On Sunday morning we learned that President Aristide had been whisked away by an American military jet and the rebels had stopped their advance. Slowly quiet began to reign once more.

In a few weeks the staff began to return and resume the CAM operations.

Chapter 73

Guns Against God

· May 2004

Spring has sprung in Haiti! "The flowers appear on the earth; the time of the singing of birds is come" (Song of Solomon 2:12). The rains are here. Ugly brown grass is becoming green. Plants are growing. What seemed like only ugly bushes and weeds are producing lovely flowers. Indeed, "the desert shall rejoice, and blossom as the rose" (Isaiah 35:1).

Though spring is here, Haiti is still in turmoil. Almost daily there is some disturbance by defenders of former President Aristide. The United Nations and local police seem unable to keep the turmoil in check. CAM has had two trucks stolen at gunpoint. Also, a CAM container of meds, food parcels, meat, and many other items was hijacked shortly after it left the docks. The items were soon on sale in the slums of Port-au-Prince. Thieves offered some of the stolen meds to CAM for $10,000. Of course, CAM did not play into their ploy.

One positive effect of all the unrest and uncertainty is that it forces us to place our trust in God. I am reminded of the words of David in Psalm 20:7: "Some trust in chariots, and some in horses: but we will remember the name of the Lord our God."

My "chariot" was loaded on Thursday afternoon. I planned to head to Alègue to deliver meds and food boxes, check the clinic, and visit for the weekend. At 6:30 on Friday morning, I left CAM and picked up a helper, Wodrig, at the nearby village of Titanyen. Before starting, we had prayer together for safety and security as we traveled.

I was traveling slowly, maybe twenty miles per hour, on Route National One. I had just passed a United Nations checkpoint. Ahead and behind me were some *taptaps*. Abruptly, as from nowhere, two tall young thugs bolted across the left lane, brandishing large automatic guns which they leveled at my head. To my right two more thugs appeared from the sidewalk, each with a similar gun.

This is it, I thought. *They're going to kill us.*

Wodrig started yelling, "Brother Harold, go faster!" At the same time, I was waiting for the crack of the large, menacing, automatic guns.

We pressed on and were relieved when no gunshot rang out. I tried to go faster, but the heavy chariot seemed only to creep. Finally, however, we started picking up speed. Were we spared from the gunmen?

I soon learned that the ordeal was not yet over. In what seemed but a few seconds, another thug appeared ahead of me. Once more that ugly, shining steel was leveled at my head. Near Wodrig, the sixth gunman appeared.

"Stop, or I'll shoot!" he demanded.

They saw the truck, the load of merchandise, and maybe even a possible ransom. Once more I awaited the crack of the gun, but there was only silence—except for the deep pounding of my heart as the truck picked up speed.

As we forged ahead slowly, Wodrig glanced into the side mirror. He saw all six bewildered gunmen with their guns leveled as if they wanted to shoot, but there was only silence. As we left them in the distance, they flung their guns earthward as if in disgust and frustration. Wodrig and I, with heart-felt gratitude, lifted our voices heavenward in praise to our kind heavenly Father.

I called and reported the incident to CAM staff and asked for continued prayer as we proceeded. In my mind I kept seeing the thugs appear, each brandishing his shining steel. I had at least expected some shots to intimidate me if nothing else.

Slowly peace came to my heart, and I saw something else deep in my spirit. I saw something much shinier than any puny gun could ever be. In my inner spirit I saw a shining angel at each gun. God opened my eyes as He did Elisha's servant. I don't know what the gunmen saw or experienced. I will never know what really happened, but I truly believe my guardian angels in their own wise way disabled each gun.

Later we learned how truly God had been in control. The night before our ordeal, Pastor Eris had had an unpleasant dream. When he awoke Friday morning, he told his wife Miriam that he is deeply burdened for the country of Haiti in all its trouble and confusion. He decided to fast and pray that day for the country, the missionaries, the pastors, and the workers at CAM. So while we were experiencing this trauma, Pastor Eris was on his knees praying for us.

"The chariots of God are twenty thousand, even thousands of angels" (Psalm 68:17a). How wonderful!

Chapter 74

Flapping My Wings

▪ March 2006

I am finally preparing to move to Alègue and make it my office to run the medicine program. I feel as free as a bird. I'm out of the computer prison cage. I have greatly enjoyed working for CAM and will continue to do so, but too much office and computer work fries my meager brain and is not my first delight.

The CAM staff who went to the States because of a recent political unrest will return this week. This will then free me to take up the oft-postponed move to Alègue. I plan to travel through southern Haiti for five days; then I will set up my headquarters at Alègue.

Once I get there, I must shake my little house like a rug and fling out the dust, dirt, grime, and rats so that it is fit to live in. I might even break down and get a cat to help ward off rats and mice if I find a decent one.

On the political front, Rene Preval has been given the presidency, but has not yet been inaugurated. He will need to walk a delicate tightrope to try to please those under him. Things have quieted down considerably, and driving through town is once again safer, but we always need to use caution.

▪ ▪ ▪ ▪ ▪ ▪ ▪

Back Again!

The welcome I received from my beloved friends in Alègue was fit for a returning king. It made me anxious to turn the med program over to someone younger and spend more of my time here at the mission.

Someday, I hope, that will happen.

Also there to welcome me was the smell of my rat-infested, termite-destroyed, smelly house I hope to occupy soon.

During the four years I was absent, my poor *kay* suffered many painful misfortunes: a mini fire, part of its roof blown off, and three break-ins.

After giving the *kay* a thorough cleaning, I decided to make the whole thing a bit more secure and also brighten it up by painting the walls. In addition, I needed to add solar panels, batteries, and controls. The whole process was major and expensive.

One thing I am really thankful for is that we once again have some churches supporting the mission here and have several American nurses at the clinic.

▪ ▪ ▪ ▪ ▪ ▪ ▪

Musings in the Morning

As I lift up my eyes this morning, it is not hard to see the needs all around me. From where I sit on the porch of my little *kay*, I can see Madame Moyiz leaving her house. How burdened I am for her soul, how moved with compassion. I have prayed, fasted, and sought the Lord earnestly for her salvation, but she refuses to renounce the hold of Satan on her life.

On Friday night I was weary and critically needed rest and sleep. I had barely fallen asleep, however, when the noises began. And to make matters worse, I had somehow misplaced my very important earplugs. All night long the red-draped *rara* marchers vigorously beat their drums, banged on their plastic pipes, rattled their metal disks, and chanted their demonized songs. They marched, swayed, and drank. They would hike the muddy trails, and then return to Madame Moyiz's house. They continued till Sunday. They were diligently giving of their lives to serve the devil. They sacrificed, sweated, shouted, and surrendered to the spirit of voodoo, the demons of Satan. Yes, as Jesus said, the time is ripe. The time is urgent. "Behold, I say unto you," Jesus said, "lift up your eyes, and look on the fields; for they are white already to harvest" (John 4:35).

Chapter 75

Stirrings in the Mountains

• February 2007

A Peep From My Perch

It's the Lord's Day! From my lofty perch on the porch of my *kay*, I revel in the beauty of the moment. The sun fairly shouts as the green trees shimmer in the light breeze, and the little whitewashed huts on the surrounding hills glisten. Beyond me boldly looms the majesty and grandeur of the awe-inspiring mountains. Roosters lustily engage in a crowing competition. A nearby calf bawls for milk. To my left, below me under a brown tarp, drums resonate with a regular, pulsing beat at a voodoo convention. Red-scarfed women seem to float about. Throughout the night I heard the chanting, moaning, and dancing as they worshiped the evil one and called the demons into their midst. The area below me is like a huge amphitheater. Voices from distant huts are distinct. The people and animals that walk the maze of trails appear like moving toys. The early churchgoers are sliding on the muddy trails.

■　■　■　■　■　■　■

"Pulling Them Out of the Fire"

After our church service, we walked from the church to a native hut. On a banana-leaf mat lay Leon, a man who had served the devil for many years. He was a local root doctor, or mini witch doctor. He had sent curses upon many and robbed many of their meager funds as he prescribed remedies for their healing. There he lay paralyzed, emaciated, helpless—a man my age but ravaged with ill health and the price of sin.

Deacon Dodo had visited Leon lately and witnessed to him, and his tightly bound heart longed to be delivered. The church brothers had already burned the voodoo fetishes he had relinquished, but he still was not completely at rest. They requested him to write out the names of the demons that had him ensnared. Seventeen demons were enumerated and renounced.

When we arrived at his house, Pastor Levi discerned that Leon was not entirely free. Some gentle prodding revealed another demon. After this we prayed, and he publicly renounced all demonic involvement and shared that Jesus is indeed his Lord and Saviour. Weakened as he was, he raised his hand to the Lord and prayed a prayer of faith. What a time of rejoicing it was as Leon was freed.

. . . .

God Is Not Mocked

It is carnival season in Haiti. It is also a time when the voodoo adherents have their special services. A few days ago Madame Moyiz had boldly bragged to the neighbors that she and the rest were going to make it difficult for two Christians who lived close to where the convention would be held. But once again God's mighty hand intervened and Madame Moyiz could not be here. Her daughter-in-law had complications during childbirth, and Madame Moyiz was called to Ti Goâve.

It's evening now. Once more I gaze from my perch. Once more I hear excited babbling and cheering—the voices of drinking, gambling men at the cockfight arena. Here the roosters fight, and the men pay the attending witch doctor, Alfred, to bless their cock or give them the name of the winner.

The place is so dark; the spiritual needs are so great. Oh, for the power of the Gospel to penetrate and truly change men's lives—to snatch them from the enemy.

Chapter 76

A Harrowing Trip

· May 2008

"Turn around. There are problems ahead." The news was disconcerting, but nothing really unusual for Haiti.

Little did I know what lay ahead. I was on my way to Ti Goâve with my Polaris Ranger to have two tires repaired. I wondered what the man meant.

A mile later I had a problem steering and soon discovered my right front tire was nearly flat. *Those mean-spirited rocks again!* Upon inspecting the tire, I found a nasty three-quarter-inch slice. I pumped in some air and drove for another hundred yards or so; then it was flat again. Next I tried my skill at using repair plugs—three side by side. I was skeptical of them holding the side wall, but off I drove.

Soon another warning came from a passing motorcycle rider. "The road ahead is blocked by a big, stranded truck."

I continued my journey and soon learned that he was correct. The previous night a large truck had failed to climb a hill because of recent rains. The driver had started backing down and then slipped off the road at an angle, the rear wheels of the truck plopping into a deep ravine. Now it was blocking most of the road. Only a mule or a motorcycle could squeeze by. Now what?

I measured the space between the corner of the truck cab and the nearby tree. Perhaps I could get through if someone hacked off a large root and dug away the bank with a pick. The landowner agreed with my observation and ran off to get his pick. After working about forty minutes in a drizzling rain, the landowner finished his job and I paid him for his gracious service. Fearfully and slowly, I inched my rig through, only to get it wedged tightly between the tree and the truck cab. The tilt of the machine caused me to get jammed.

I then asked two heavy men to sit on the one side of the open tailgate while four more pushed the top of my rig away from the truck cab. Once again I inched forward, this time even more fearfully and gingerly. A little noise, a little scratching, a little heart-pounding, and then much clapping! I had made it! As usual, the place was now packed with interested onlookers.

It took several hours to get my tires repaired in Ti Goâve, and then I had some shopping to do. Finally, after many delays, I had my rig loaded and was ready to return. Thankfully, Levi had come with his four-wheeler when he heard I was having problems and was now ready to follow me home.

When we came to the stranded truck, a group of men were slowly pulling it forward, inch by inch, using a heavy-duty chain hoist fastened to a large tree. By now motorcycles could pass on the back side. Levi made it with the four-wheeler and everybody encouraged me to try.

"No way," I told them. "I'm afraid I might upset."

So I waited another hour till they finally managed to pull the truck out of the way. On we went uneventfully till we came to a place that was all rock and had about a thirty-degree uphill slant for about eight feet. I shifted to low and started off. Suddenly my critter reared up and I could not steer. It went back a little and plopped down. I tried again and gassed it a little. This time my unwieldy beast reared up nastily and rolled over on its side. Needless to say, I was rattled and shook up. I don't remember, but I must have clambered out the other side.

I quickly reached in and turned off the engine. Gasoline was dripping from the top of the recently filled storage tank.

I eyed the fifteen-hundred pound monster as it arrogantly rested on its side with its ugly bottom protruding. It certainly wasn't going anywhere! How would I ever get it righted again?

As always, a huge crowd gathered, so I asked the group to help slide it to a different position so that the angle would be slightly downhill. Fortunately we could slide it. Meanwhile someone came with a rope and we fastened it to the top of the roll bar, which had protected me from injury.

Several men pulled on the rope and about five lifted on the roll bar. To my delight, in less than a minute my Ranger was on its wheels again. But how was I going to climb over this mean monster of a rock without my naughty machine rearing up again? I decided to ask two men to sit on the front of the machine on the brush guard. Slowly I started out, and this time I easily climbed the rock without incident. I finally arrived at Alègue, late but safe and sound.

Chapter 77

Hurricane Gustav

▪ August 2008

"**J**eriah," I told my fellow CAM worker, "we keep hearing reports that a hurricane might soon strike Haiti. Call the CAM office and find out if they have any current information." Jeriah and I were visiting clinics in the South.

"Yes, Gustav will soon be a category three storm with wind speeds over a hundred miles per hour. It will probably strike the southern parts, near to where you are," we were told.

The sun was shining brightly and prospects of such a storm seemed unlikely. The next morning the sun was shining brightly again, but we wisely headed toward Ti Goâve, where my Polaris Ranger was parked. In a brief time dark clouds encompassed us with strong winds and pelting rain. I quickly donned my rain clothes and fueled my rig. Then with the "pedal to the metal" I sped toward Alègue, while Jeriah headed back to his house near Ti Goâve.

I hoped to reach my house before the storm intensified, but before long severe winds battered and tossed my Ranger. I steered with one hand and shielded my face from the lashing rain with the other. In spite of the difficult driving, I eventually reached Girard, about thirty minutes from my house. It was around 11:30 a.m.

Suddenly I sensed I had a tire problem. What could be wrong? I had just mounted two new rear tires not long ago. To my dismay, the one tire had jumped the rim. I had experience in repairing holes and cuts, but not with mounting tires. I decided I had to take off the tire and perhaps send it to Ti Goâve for mounting. I had a rough time getting the tire high enough to remove the wheel, but after much struggling with rocks and a jack, I finally succeeded. By this time the rain was falling in torrents.

Fortunately this spot had phone service, so I called Jeriah for advice. He suggested using a ratchet strap. I was very grateful when a young man named Watson stopped by and helped me. He pumped the hand tire pump while I manned a ratchet strap to squeeze the tire. After much trying and retrying, we finally succeeded in mounting the culprit tire.

I jumped into my rig and was off. Two minutes later I came to a small creek crossing. To my consternation, I saw an unbelievable torrent of water. Deep, angry, frothy water raced down the stream. The water was much too deep and rapid to attempt a crossing.

Now what? In the midst of the torrential rain and beating winds, I decided to turn back and head toward Ti Goâve again. But I soon met other dashing water too deep to continue. By then I decided it would be best to return to my original location, where I knew I had cell phone service.

■ ■ ■ ■ ■ ■ ■

A Long Night

I parked at the side of the trail and decided to bunker down inside the box on the rear of my Ranger. This box was about three feet deep, five feet wide, and four feet high. It was already piled full of things I was hauling back to my home, but at least I was out of the lashing torrent of rain. Angry winds—predicted to reach over 100 miles per hour—kept rocking and bouncing my "boat." The fierce winds forced water through cracks and crevices of the hinged lid and door which I had not known existed. Hour after hour I moved from one spot to another as water kept dripping on me. Finally I donned my shredded parka to try to stay somewhat dry.

For hours it poured and blew and then poured and blew some more. I heard furious water like a mini Niagara racing and tumbling in a nearby waterway.

By now it was getting dark, so I secured the door with a ratchet strap and prepared to stay the night. I didn't have a morsel of food with me, but fortunately I had water. Since I had cell phone service, I called a few friends to share my plight, asking them to pray and tell my friends about my situation. I could not stretch out because of all my things, so I alternated between sitting and trying to lie down with my knees jutting upward. I was weary, wet, cold, and hungry. I tried covering myself with a smelly, wet canvas tarp, but it didn't do much good. Twice my right leg cramped so painfully that I almost jumped through the roof. What was a seventy-four-year-old man doing in this place anyway? I had lots of time to think, and was able at times to realize that truly I was in God's hands and everything was okay. Even though I was stranded in a furious hurricane, I was not alone.

I would doze off into a brief unconsciousness only to be rudely awakened again as torrents of rain and wind beat madly against the sides. Would the Ranger remain stable or would it capsize with the hurricane winds? It seemed the roaring of the mini Niagara had turned up the volume to an almost shattering din.

It was a long, weary night. Anxiously I waited for morning. As I alternated between sleeping and communing with the Lord, I sensed the angels guarding over me and knew that my Father loved and cared for me.

. . . .

Visions in the Morning

I had hoped the rain would quit and I could drive on at the break of day, but I became increasingly doubtful as the pelting, drenching rain continued all night long. At daybreak the rain was still pouring down when I dismounted my "prison" and sloshed to the bridge nearby.

Wow! Everything was gone! In its place was a huge, twenty-five-foot-wide chasm about five feet deep! There would be no passing for many days—possibly weeks. It was still raining and I was wet and cold and hungry, as well as physically and emotionally worn out. What did God have in mind for me?

God's Angels

Watson, the youth who had helped with my tire mounting soon came on the scene and invited me to his family's nearby house. What a welcome gesture! What a relief to finally be in a dry place and be able to stand upright. They offered me some of Watson's clean, dry clothes. The trousers were much too tight, but I was finally dry! The family was so kind. First they gave me a chair, but when they observed how tired I was, they offered a bed. I gladly accepted, and what a blessing it was to stretch out.

At about 9:00 my new friends came with a cup of hot ginger tea and a piece of bread for my breakfast. I was so thankful—and so hungry. I then gave them some money to buy rice and other things to make a bigger meal. As I lay resting, my eyes burned and itched from the astringent smoke that wafted into the room from the damp wood fire burning in the attached kitchen.

I learned that this family of seven was Catholic. Their house consisted of two main rooms and a center enclosed foyer. The five children, ages eight to twenty-one, were very respectful but also curious, asking me many questions.

At about 1:30 I was honored with a huge bowl of rice and beans—a most welcome meal. I was not able to eat all of it. As we visited, they graciously invited me to spend the night with them, and I readily accepted the kind offer. By then the hard rain had subsided, and Watson said he would carry some of my things to Alègue the next day.

. . . .

Watson's Surprise

Early the next morning I heard Watson stirring around. He had said something about animals, and I thought he had gone to feed the pigs, but he returned with a borrowed mule complete with saddlebags. He wanted to be sure I could take all my things along. What a surprise!

Since we were not able to cross the huge washout in the road, we had to climb a narrow, muddy, slippery trail. We forded small streams, sloshed mud, and slithered and slid, but I was finally homeward bound!

Pastor Levi had asked a young man to bring a mule from Alègue to meet me. When we met him, I exchanged my things, said goodbye to Watson, and continued my trek.

After traveling over some more slippery mountain trails, we finally reached the road that heads back to Alègue. I was curious to see how the Jackrabbit Bridge had fared. I was dumbfounded at what I saw. It was totally washed away—again! The mission was now completely locked in. When I measured the chasm later, it was twelve feet deep and fifty feet long.

When I finally climbed up the mountain to my house that evening, I saw that my porch had been ripped off and lay mangled below my cistern. But at least I was home and could sleep in my own bed. Yes, in Haiti you learn to expect the unexpected—but you also learn that God is good. Yes, He is always good.

Chapter 78

Thirty-Seven Seconds

• January 2010

It was a pleasant afternoon. I was walking up my mountain trail to my little *kay*, visiting with some Haitian neighbors about eighty feet away from my house. CAM had finally found a replacement for me on the med program, and I was now living leisurely with my friends at Alègue. I planned to eat a light snack and then return to the mission compound to greet the incoming team later in the evening.

While I was still speaking, I heard an extremely loud rumbling like an approaching locomotive. The circle of towering mountains surrounding me shuddered violently, tossing me back and forth like a leaf. Unable to stand, I fell to the ground. From nearby mountains, rocks jetted into the air and huge rock slides took place all over the many mountains. The clattering, sliding rocks sent immense clouds of dust spiraling upward like pluming smoke.

My neighbors starting shrieking and praying loudly, some hysterical. Some were crying out "Jesus, save us! Jesus, save us!" while others were shouting, "Down with Satan! Down with Satan!" Some were confessing their sins and pleading to God for mercy. Was it the end of the world?

A short time later all was silent—an eerie silence. It was then I realized we had experienced a severe earthquake. The experience seemed to have affected my equilibrium. Startled deeply, I crawled for several feet and then cautiously got to my feet and continued tremblingly to my house. Upon arrival I saw a gaping four-by six-foot hole. Large rocks from the wall had fallen on the head end of my bed. Inside, items were strewn everywhere—a hodgepodge of broken bottles, dishes, gooey syrup, books, papers, and my wall clock.

Still in an emotional daze, I went out to the porch. Soon everything started shaking violently again. Another tremor! In fear I raced out to the trail and sat on a rock, which too started to pulsate.

I was shook up emotionally and physically, as were many around me. Scores of people gathered on the hillside, jabbering and crying. It was a time of great confusion. Only those who know the Haitian temperament can understand the din and pitch of their excited jabbering.

Night would soon be coming, so people started gathering tarps and plastic to make shelters to sleep in.

Perhaps an hour after the quake, I got a radio call from Nurse Caressa down at the mission. "Would you ask the Haitian nurses to come down and help me? People are coming in with severe cuts, broken limbs, and other injuries, most of them caused by rocks tumbling down the mountainsides."

"Okay, Caressa, I'll walk over and give them your request. But the people are all in such a state of fear that I seriously doubt if they will come down."

I walked over to the nearby house where the Haitian nurses stayed to ask them, but they flatly refused. I understood. I then went back to my house, gathered some needed clothing and other supplies, and prepared to go down to the mission. With many aftershocks continuing, the Haitian nurses begged me not to go, fearing that some stone walls might give way and I might be hurt.

That night I slept in the mission house. It was a difficult time for everyone who was there. Every time new aftershocks shook the house, we rapidly headed for the door. We had not heard from the work team that had been scheduled to arrive, so we were deeply concerned.

. . . .

Where Is the Team?

We finally learned from an e-mail that the work team had been caught in the quake in Port-au-Prince. Then we heard that they would be coming the next day. I was also told by nationals that the road was closed. The Land Cruiser with the team would come to the blocked section, where we could meet them and transfer their luggage.

Michael Martin, a volunteer from the States, and I headed out with my Polaris Ranger to try to find the team. We found rocks and slides everywhere. Less than two miles enroute we came to large rocks that had to be rolled aside and landslides that had to be skirted. This continued for several miles. Meanwhile we did see a few motorcycles. We soon came to an impassible road block. We wondered how the cycles had passed this spot.

Several huge boulders weighing many tons had let loose and completely blocked the road. It would take a bulldozer to move them. The drop-off at the side of the road was scary—it descended several hundred feet. Men stood on either side of the cliff and precariously hand-passed the motorcycles back and forth. Passengers were able to clamber over the monstrous boulders to the other side.

I parked my Polaris and decided to walk ahead to see how things looked. Meanwhile, Michael decided to climb a nearby mountain to radio back to the mission and tell them we needed the other ATV, a John Deere Gator, to help haul the work team if we found them. As I walked on, the road was littered with huge rocks that could only be skirted by motorcycles. There were wide fissures in many places where the earth had cracked and dropped. I measured one that had a fifteen-inch drop.

I continued walking, amazed at the destruction and altering of the terrain. Trying to be helpful, a motorcycle driver stopped and asked me if I wanted a ride. At first I declined; I had never thought it safe to ride a motorcycle on the road. On second thought I decided it could save me much time, so I hopped on and away we went.

We weaved in and out of the many large rocks and bounced over the cracks. All the while I hung on tightly for dear life. At times I had to get off to make a passage between the rocks. At one spot there was a long fissure in the middle of the road at an area that dropped off several hundred feet. I hoped it would not let loose and send half the road down the mountainside.

To my delight, after traveling a few more miles, we found the mission Land Cruiser and the team. How my heart rejoiced. We had a joyous reunion.

We decided the team would take only their backpacks to hike back to the ATVs and then continue on to Alègue. Pastor Levi would drive the Land Cruiser with the other luggage back to Ti Goâve. Later we would have the luggage brought back on mules.

As we hiked, a Haitian friend on a motorcycle stopped. I decided to save my strength and asked him to take me back to the place where the boulders blocked the road. Off we went. He turned out to be a most gentle, gracious driver, and I was not scared in the least. We soon arrived at the spot where my Polaris Ranger was parked, and I sat down to await the team.

As I waited, some people told me that my Ranger had nearly rolled down the mountainside into a deep ravine while I was gone. I laughed, but they insisted it was so and showed me the tracks of the front tires partway over the side. I was shocked. A roll down the mountainside certainly would have been death to my Ranger. "Some children climbed on board," they told me. "While they were playing on it, they released the handbrake." They had run in fear as the Ranger started coasting across the road toward the cliff. There were other older men loitering nearby who had grabbed the machine before it plunged to its death. They pushed it back to its parking spot, placed stones in front of the wheels, and guarded it. Once again, expect the unexpected. I humbly thanked the Lord for my guardian angels and their protection.

I sat in my Ranger to await the team. They arrived several hours later, very tired. The Gator had not come yet, so after a period of waiting, I loaded up the seven team members—a super heavy load. As I attempted to pull out onto the road, we heard the Gator coming and divided the load.

After traveling for some time, it became dark. Next the Gator lost several lugs and the wheel got loose. Unable to repair it, we pushed it to the side of the road. After discussing the situation, the young men decided to walk while I took the girls on to Alègue.

The team did outstanding work during this time of major

catastrophe. With the continuing aftershocks, it was a harrowing time none of them will soon forget.

· · · · · · ·

The Quake in Port-au-Prince

When Haiti's deadly earthquake struck, much of Port-au-Prince was reduced to a pile of rubble—all in thirty-seven seconds. The capital's destruction was shockingly severe but erratic. The devastating earthquake left one building virtually untouched, while the next one was reduced to debris. It was as if a giant had danced a jig over the town, crushing buildings underfoot. For example, a tall five-story children's hospital pancaked to a mere head-high pile of rubble, while nearby a large building was left standing. Although most of the bodies were cleared away as soon as possible, the smell of rotting flesh lingered for many weeks. It is estimated that there were over 230,000 fatalities.

Near CAM's base at Titanyen, on a hillside where goats graze, empty holes awaited the dead. Huge bulldozers dug mass graves twenty feet deep and wide and a hundred feet long. Government dump trucks dropped off bodies day after day. There were no ceremonies, no official count, and no searches for names. Family members were devastated. But there was no other recourse.

Every park and open space in greater Port-au-Prince overflowed with tens of thousands of deeply traumatized quake survivors living in crude tents. With the many aftershocks, Haitians became anxious and jumpy, refusing to spend time indoors. Many with perfectly sound houses still slept outside months later.

An estimated million and a half residents had no homes to return to, and nearly all normal activity ceased. One of the questions that surfaced time and again among Haitians living in huge squatter camps was, "What will we do with the rest of our lives?" Deep down, underneath that question, they realized their lives would be measured by how they responded to this disaster.

· · · · · · ·

The Quake's Effects

Haiti is now a country on its knees. The loss of lives, homes, businesses, government facilities, and infrastructure is beyond one's wildest imagination. The logistics for simply ridding the city of the rubble is stupendous. It will take years and billions of dollars to rebuild.

But Haitians are truly a resilient, thankful people. Situations that would make us throw up our hands in despair are simply more of what they have faced all their lives. Although many lost family members, friends, and most of their material possessions in the quake, they still have not given up hope that better days are ahead.

．．．．．．．

The earthquake blocked the fourteen-mile road from Ti Goâve to Alègue, allowing only motorcycles to travel it. David Ringler from Pennsylvania and I have legal ownership of a bulldozer that is kept near Ti Goâve. David was able to come with a CAM team immediately after the quake, and headed out to Ti Goâve. There were immense boulders and numerous major landslides that needed removal, and David was the man for the job. We were so thankful when the road was once more usable and work teams started coming back to Alègue to help with severely damaged houses. The walls of hundreds of houses had completely toppled but still had posts supporting the frame and roof. Within a few months, work teams wrapped nearly a thousand houses with heavy plastic tarps to keep out the rain and winds.

The earthquake drastically changed the life of the missions and organizations serving in Haiti. All major services were disrupted or destroyed. For example, no planes could land in Haiti because the control tower was disabled. Everyone coming to help in this devastating disaster had to come through the Dominican Republic. After our road to Ti Goâve was opened, I took many trips across the border to pick up and return teams coming to help.

Chapter 79

The Unexpected—Again

Goodbye to Haiti

Five months after the earthquake I once again returned to Pennsylvania. I was uncertain about my stay, not knowing if or when I would return to Haiti.

For many years I had a problem with glaucoma, and with my eyesight worsening, I knew it was time to do something about it.

Over the next few months I had laser surgery, which was unsuccessful, followed by two cataract operations. After several months my surgeon gave me a clean bill of health and saw no problem if I chose to return to Haiti.

■ ■ ■ ■ ■ ■

Hello to Haiti

I had not really planned to return to Haiti at this time, but then the unexpected happened. LIFE Literature, an organization that supplies Creole literature to Haiti, and for which I had served as a committee member for several years, informed me that they needed someone in Haiti to help manage their work there. What a surprise! After thinking and praying about the matter, I returned after Thanksgiving in 2010 to help oversee the LIFE program of distributing Bibles, tracts, and other Christian literature in Haiti.

Amy Martin accompanied me on the way down. She planned to teach and give general help at the nearby New Horizons Orphanage.

We arrived safely at Port. But then our adventures started.

Once again Haiti was in deep turmoil because of the coming election and the cholera epidemic. For hours we traveled in congested traffic and inched along slowly. At one spot we were halted by a serious semi-truck accident. Next we were diverted from the main road to a narrow trail through a wooded area. After several miles, the trail exited into a wide riverbed with lots of stones and little water. Here, scores of vehicles were trying to get through and get out on the main drag again. There were five lanes, and all were impatient to proceed.

I decided to follow some cars up closer to the bank and perhaps get through sooner. Near the bank were tall bushes. Unknown to me, the trail of cars ahead of me belonged to one of the presidential candidates in the election. Suddenly repeated gunshots rang out from the bushes! Simultaneously, rocks began to fly toward our group of cars. *Crack!* A rock narrowly missed my windshield and hit the hood of my truck. Another hit the truck cage. Another broke the rear tail light.

Wow! Amy and I were in a crossfire of bullets and rocks. Desperately I tried to sneak away and hide behind a line of large trucks and buses.

Even though I have had many close calls, this was the first time for bullets and rocks so close. I also felt deeply concerned and responsible for Amy. After many tense moments, we were able to sneak out to the main road and continue to Ti Goâve, where we stayed for the night.

How very thankful we were for God's protection in this unexpected situation, but how typical of Haiti. Indeed, what else could we have expected? Were we not in Haiti, the land where we expect the unexpected? But we had arrived safely, and I thanked God for once again allowing my dream to come true. With joy I had returned to my beloved friends at Alègue—yes, this was "home sweet home."

Afterword

The Ways of God

At the close of this book, as I reflect upon the goals I penned when I first visited Alègue, and now review the hand of God as He worked out His purposes in these remote mountains of Haiti, it causes me to retreat in humility and brokenness. Jesus said in Luke 17:10: "So likewise ye, when ye shall have done all those things which are commanded you, say, We are unprofitable servants: we have done that which was our duty to do."

Indeed, it was in spite of me that God accomplished anything of value here. The struggles have been intense. My failures have been replete. Again and again God has needed to rebuke and chasten me. He has been so merciful, patient, tender, and forgiving.

God has also been very merciful and forgiving to my dear friend Bruce. Currently he is a pastor and school administrator close to Ti Goâve where he lives with his lovely family.

As I ponder the past and the future, my mind is drawn to the words of Acts 1:11: "This same Jesus, which is taken up from you into heaven, shall so come in like manner as ye have seen him go into heaven."

Yes, Jesus is coming again. He is coming soon. Maranatha! "And God shall wipe away all tears from their eyes; and there shall be no more death, neither sorrow, nor crying, neither shall there be any more pain: for the former things are passed away" (Revelation 21:4).

When that day comes, the struggles of life will end and we can be in His care. We will no longer expect the unexpected!

Pronunciation Key

Alègue*	AH lehg
Alsiyis	AHL see yees
Anis	ah NEES
Bainet*	BAY neh
Banav	BAH nahv
Bay	BAHY
Belamy*	BAY lah mee
blan	BLAH...............*white; foreigner*
bòkò	BAW kaw..........*male witch doctor*
Bon Repos*	BOH ray POH
Dejoni	DAY zhoh nee
Dibonno*	dee BOH noh
Dodo	DOH doh
Edline†	AYD leen
Efanyèl	AY fahn yehl
Enèl	ay NEHL
Entès	ayn TEHS
Eris	AY rees
Eristan	AY rees tah
Eslèn	AYS lehn
Filibè	FEE lee beh
Gèline†	GEH leen
Girard*	GEE rah

gwo bab	GWOH bahb	....*big beard*
Itanya	ee TAHN yah	
Jakline†	ZHAHK leen	
Jil	ZHEEL	
Jira	ZHEE rah	
Jiryòn	ZHEER yawn	
Jochèn	ZHOH shehn	
Joslen	ZHOHS leh	
Jozye	ZHOHZ yay	
Kadèt	KAH deht	
kay	KAHY	...............*house*
Klesiyis	KLEH see yees	
Klomàn	KLOH mahn	
Krismàn	KREES mahn	
La Gonâve*	LAH goh nahv	
Lamatinye	lah MAH teen yay	
Larifi	LAH ree fee	
Leda	LAY dah	
Lejitim	lay ZHEE teem	
Léogâne*	LAY oh gahn	
Lewo	LAY woh	
lwa	LWAH	................*voodoo spirit; evil spirit; demon*
Madaline†	MAH dah LEEN	
Malis	MAH lees	
manbo	MAHM boh	......*female witch doctor*
Mano	MAH noh	
Mariklòd	MAH ree KLAWD	
Mèjil	MEH zheel	
Michline†	MEESH leen	
Moyiz	MOH yeez	
Nèli	NEH lee	
Nereyis	NAY ray ees	
Norès	NOH rehs	
Obès	OH behs	

Ogitè	OH gee teh
Onès	oh NEHS
Petit (Ti)Goâve*	PEH tee (TEE) gwahv
rara	RAH rah............*informal musical groups, often dressed in red colors and active especially during Carnival time*
Remòn	RAY mawn
Selès	SAY lehs
Selina	say LEE nah
Sove	SOH vay
taptap	TAHP tahp.......*small pickup truck used for public transportation*
Te	TAY
Ti Klis	TEE klees
Ti Nonm	TEE nohm
Titanyen	TEE tah YEHN
Towo	TOH woh
Valsiyis	VAHL see yees
Wilfrid	WEEL freed
Wodrig	WOHD reeg
Yvette†	ee VEHT

*French spelling
†Modified Creole spelling

Expect the Unexpected

About Christian Aid Ministries

Christian Aid Ministries was founded in 1981 as a nonprofit, tax-exempt 501(c)(3) organization. Its primary purpose is to provide a trustworthy and efficient channel for Amish, Mennonite, and other conservative Anabaptist groups and individuals to minister to physical and spiritual needs around the world. This is in response to the command ". . . do good unto all men, especially unto them who are of the household of faith" (Galatians 6:10).

Each year, CAM supporters provide approximately 15 million pounds of food, clothing, medicines, seeds, Bibles, Bible story books, and other Christian literature for needy people. Most of the aid goes to orphans and Christian families. Supporters' funds also help clean up and rebuild for natural disaster victims, put up Gospel billboards in the U.S., support several church-planting efforts, operate two medical clinics, and provide resources for needy families to make their own living. CAM's main purposes for providing aid are to help and encourage God's people and bring the Gospel to a lost and dying world.

CAM has staff, warehouse, and distribution networks in Romania, Moldova, Ukraine, Haiti, Nicaragua, Liberia, and Israel. Aside from management, supervisory personnel, and bookkeeping operations, volunteers do most of the work at CAM locations. Each year, volunteers at our warehouses, field bases, DRS projects, and other locations donate over 200,000 hours of work.

CAM's ultimate purpose is to glorify God and help enlarge His kingdom. ". . . whatsoever ye do, do all to the glory of God" (I Cor. 10:31).

Expect the Unexpected

Steps to Salvation

The Bible says that we all have "sinned and come short of the glory of God" (Romans 3:23). We sin because we give heed to our sinful nature inherited from Adam's sin in the Garden of Eden, and our sin separates us from God.

God provided the way back to Himself by His only Son, Jesus Christ, who became the spotless Lamb "slain from the foundation of the world" (Revelation 13:8). "For God so loved the world that he gave his only begotten Son, that whosoever believeth in him should not perish, but have everlasting life" (John 3:16).

To be reconciled to God and experience life rather than death, and heaven rather than hell (Deuteronomy 30:19), we must repent and believe in the Son of God, the Lord Jesus Christ (Romans 6:23; 6:16).

When we sincerely repent of our sins (Acts 2:38; 3:19; 17:30) and by faith receive Jesus Christ as our Saviour and Lord, God saves us by His grace and we are born again. "That if thou shalt confess with thy mouth the Lord Jesus, and shalt believe in thine heart that God hath raised him from the dead, thou shalt be saved" (Romans 10:9). "For by grace are ye saved through faith; and that not of yourselves: it is the gift of God" (Ephesians 2:8).

When we become born again in Jesus Christ, we become new creatures (2 Corinthians 5:17). We do not continue in sin (1 John 3:9), but give testimony of our new life in Jesus Christ by baptism and obedience to Him. "He that hath my commandments, and keepeth them, he it is that loveth me: and he that loveth me shall be loved of my Father, and I will love him, and will manifest myself to him" (John 14:21).

To grow spiritually, we need to meditate on God's Word and commune with God in prayer. Fellowship with a faithful group of believers is also important to strengthen and maintain our Christian walk (1 John 1:7).